MARKET STRUCTURE, ORGANIZATION AND PERFORMANCE

MARKET STRUCTURE, ORGANIZATION AND PERFORMANCE

AN ESSAY ON PRICE FIXING AND COMBINATIONS IN RESTRAINT OF TRADE

ALMARIN PHILLIPS

HARVARD UNIVERSITY PRESS
Cambridge, Massachusetts
1962

DISTRIBUTED IN GREAT BRITAIN BY OXFORD UNIVERSITY PRESS, LONDON

PUBLICATION OF THIS BOOK HAS BEEN AIDED BY A
GRANT FROM THE FORD FOUNDATION

LIBRARY OF CONGRESS CATALOG CARD NUMBER: 62–19222

PRINTED IN THE UNITED STATES OF AMERICA

To D. B. P.

A. P. P.

F. P. P.

T. R. P.

D. J. P.

E. L. P.

PREFACE

Conversations and correspondence with colleagues and friends have made me quite aware that neither the policy suggestions nor the theoretical framework presented in this book is likely to win easy acceptance. The theory has foundations in organizational and group behavioral principles and, with these principles and the expected reception of my theses in mind, I have sometimes wanted to abandon my heterodoxy and to adhere more closely to the norms of the profession.

Fate has dictated, however, that this preface be written within a week of the announcement by several steel firms that prices were to be increased. Later, having felt the force of government and public reaction, these decisions were rescinded. The particular event, while it may be unimportant in the sweep of history, has served to strengthen my conviction of the relevancy of both the theory and the suggested policies to the serious economic issues of coming years. It seems clear that the problems of the steel industry are problems of market structure, organization and performance which, unless solved more adequately than in the past, may compound into severe effects on the aggregate economy. The event in steel also suggested that the policy tools now available are inadequate to deal with these fundamental problems.

Present antitrust policy is marked by sharp contrasts. It is most difficult to bring a restraint of trade case where overt conspiracy does not exist. For the Sherman Act to be applicable, it is necessary to infer agreement from parallel behavior or price leadership, and bridging the gap between parallelism and agreement is typically difficult. Under the policy proposed herein — a policy which recognizes that at least implicit agreements always exist in stable, oligopolistic markets — the need to infer agreement would be foregone and the issue of the degree of market rivalry could be analyzed on its merits. If, as is likely, the important pricing cases of the future will involve parallelism and leadership such as that which has existed in steel, the abandonment of the per se illegality doctrine and its emphasis on conspiratorial agreement could result in more effective antitrust enforcement, and not the fostering of cartels as some of my colleagues appear to believe.

At the same time, blanket exemptions exclude some segments of the economy from Sherman Act prosecution. Yet one cannot long contemplate recent history in an industry such as steel without raising questions concerning the economic impact of labor unions. The acuteness of issues growing from relations between productivity gains and wage increases, the spreading of wage patterns from "key" industries to others, and the compatibility of full employment with relatively stable prices may for some years be determined by price-wage behavior in such markets. The companion suggestion that per se *legalities,* including the virtually complete exemption of unions from the antitrust laws, be withdrawn would permit an analysis of union power in selected market contexts without abrogating the basic right of employees to bargain collectively. Paradoxically, I anticipate that many of those who disagree with the conclusions with respect to per se illegalities on the basis that it will tend to create monopolies will disagree with the other conclusion concerning the removal of per se legalities and exemptions.

I recognize that the theory underlying my arguments has several shortcomings. It remains vague and invites one to use subjective judgments for the values for certain variables. A more definitive group equilibrium concept is required to analyze more effectively the factors which induce firms to participate or refuse to participate in express or implied group decisions. In addition, the relationship between investment decisions and the market organization requires detailed investigation. Since one of the most obvious by-products of a stable market organization is the reduction or absorption of uncertainty for the individual firms, plausible hypotheses relating investment to the characteristics of the organization seem possible.

I am indebted to many people — more, in fact, than can possibly be acknowledged. James R. Schlesinger read and criticized the manuscript at several stages. Of more importance, however, was the sustenance he afforded me by continued encouragement and friendship. The perceptive, if skeptical, questioning of George R. Hall has proved invaluable and has resulted in the recasting of several parts of the essay. Charles C. Abbott and Herbert A. Simon provided several very helpful suggestions.

Cyrus V. Anderson and Richard C. Packard, both of the Pittsburgh Plate Glass Company, have offered useful comments on both the theory and the policy conclusions. In addition, they checked Chapter IX for factual accuracy. Louis B. Schwartz, with whom I had most pleasant association at the University of Pennsylvania, has attempted unsuccessfully to persuade me of the error of my ways, and for this, too, I am grateful. Laurens H. Rhinelander, of the University of Virginia Law School, has listened to several of my arguments; the ensuing discussions have been most fruitful. He also succeeded in making available to me the record in the *Pevely Dairy* case which is discussed in Chapter III. T. M. Ragland, Executive Officer of the Virginia State Milk Commission, offered considerable "aid and comfort" as well as excellent instruction in the economics of the milk industry during my tenure as Economist Member of the Commission. I would also like to acknowledge the aid of my late father, Wendell E. Phillips, who characteristically sought out for questioning several retired potters in Trenton, New Jersey, when the lack of a written history had denied me a comprehensive background for the *Trenton Potteries* case.

Basil Blackwell, Ltd., has given permission to use portions of the article, "A Critique of United States Experience with

Price-Fixing Agreements and the Per Se Rule," *Journal of Industrial Economics,* 8:13 (October 1959). Similar permissions have been received from the Harvard University Press to excerpt from "A Theory of Interfirm Organization," *Quarterly Journal of Economics,* 74:602 (November 1960), from the American Economic Association to excerpt from "Policy Implications of the Theory of Interfirm Organization," *American Economic Review,* 51:2:245 (May 1961), and from the Virginia Law Review Association and my co-author, George R. Hall, to use material from "The Salk Vaccine Case: Parallelism, Conspiracy and Other Hypotheses," *Virginia Law Review,* 46:717 (May 1960).

Mrs. Grace Mulhauser, librarian at the Graduate School of Business Administration, University of Virginia, unearthed many obscure references and aided in footnoting. Mrs. Gladys Batson, Mrs. Banner Bruton and Miss Christine Jones typed the manuscript. To all of them go my sincere thanks.

Finally, I wish to thank the Social Science Research Council for a grant which permitted me time to prepare the first draft of this book.

ALMARIN PHILLIPS
Charlottesville, Virginia
April 17, 1962

CONTENTS

PART ONE

SOME BACKGROUND AND SOME THEORY

I INTRODUCTION 3
OF BIASES AND VALUE JUDGMENTS
A PREVIEW OF THE BOOK
OBSERVATIONS ON ADAM SMITH, COMPETITION AND RELATED MATTERS

II A THEORY OF INTERFIRM ORGANIZATION 21
INTRODUCTION
THE ASSUMPTION OF INTERDEPENDENCE
THE DETERMINANTS OF RIVALRY: FIVE STATIC GENERALIZATIONS
INTERRELATIONS AMONG STRUCTURE, BEHAVIOR AND PERFORMANCE
OBSERVATIONS ON PROFIT MAXIMIZATION, SUPPLY AND DEMAND AND GAME THEORY

PART TWO

SOME CASES

III CONSCIOUS PARALLELISM AND THE INFORMAL ORGANIZATION OF OLIGOPOLY 47
INTRODUCTION
CONSCIOUS PARALLELISM AND THE ANTITRUST LAWS
MORE RECENT CASES
CONCLUDING REMARKS

IV EXEMPTED INDUSTRIES: SANCTIONED ORGANIZATIONAL FORMALITY 74
INTRODUCTION
THE SCOPE OF EXEMPTIONS FROM THE ANTITRUST LAWS

RIVALRY IN MILK PRODUCTION AND DISTRIBUTION
RIVALRY AND THE ORGANIZATION OF LABOR

V UNITED STATES v. ADDYSTON PIPE AND STEEL COMPANY 99
INTRODUCTION
THE STRUCTURE OF THE MARKET
MARKET PERFORMANCE AND FIRM BEHAVIOR
THE ADDYSTON AGREEMENTS
THE DECISIONS AND THEIR AFTERMATH
COMMENTS ON THE ADDYSTON CASE

VI ORGANIZATION AND THE BITUMINOUS COAL INDUSTRY 119
INTRODUCTION
THE PERFORMANCE OF THE BITUMINOUS COAL INDUSTRY
PLANS TO ORGANIZE THE COAL INDUSTRY
APPALACHIAN COALS, INC.
EVENTS AFTER THE DECISION
CONCLUDING OBSERVATIONS

VII THE HARDWOOD CASES 138
INTRODUCTION
HISTORICAL BACKGROUND
THE AMERICAN COLUMN AND LUMBER CASE
THE MAPLE FLOORING CASE
COMMENTS ON THE HARDWOOD CASES

VIII THE TRENTON POTTERIES CASE 161
INTRODUCTION
THE POTTERIES CASE
LEGAL ASPECTS OF THE POTTERIES CASE
ECONOMIC COMMENT ON THE POTTERIES CASE

IX THE PLATE GLASS MIRROR CASE 177
INTRODUCTION
BACKGROUND OF THE CASE
THE CONSPIRACY TO RAISE PRICES
COMMENT ON THE MIRROR CASE

PART THREE

SOME COMMENTS ON PUBLIC POLICY

X THE DEVELOPMENT OF THE PER SE RULE 199
INTRODUCTION
THE COMMON LAW
THE SHERMAN ACT

XI POLICY CONCLUSIONS 221
INTRODUCTION
THE FUNCTIONS OF THE PRICE SYSTEM
THE INTERFIRM ORGANIZATION AND THE PRICE SYSTEM
PER SE AND THE INTERFIRM ORGANIZATION
A PROPOSED RULE OF REASON

TABLE OF CASES 245

INDEX 249

PART ONE

SOME BACKGROUND AND SOME THEORY

CHAPTER I

INTRODUCTION

OF BIASES AND VALUE JUDGMENTS

"It seems unfortunate," Professor J. M. Clark has lamented, "if economists who defend realistic forms of competition thereby expose themselves to the charge of defending monopoly." [1] Realistic competition, to Clark, necessarily involves structural and behavioral elements which, when compared with the assumptions of the theory of pure competition, are monopolistic in character.

It is not only the defenders of "realistic" competition who are subjected to criticism, however. Those who defend the more classical forms of competition are chided by others whom they have failed to persuade or who have lost their faith. The basis of the criticism is not the lack of logic in the classical case — here, if anywhere, those wedded to the doctrine of pure competition have the upper hand — but, again, the realism (or lack thereof) of the underlying assumptions. Any economist who writes in the area of public policy toward competition is exposed to some such charge, for what is realistic to one is absurd to another. Thus, despite repeated admonitions that the economist should be neutral rather than normative in his approach to problems of public policy, it is impossible to attain such detachment in practice. Economics — perhaps fortunately — has not progressed to such a point that there is uniformity in even the assumptions, explicit and implicit, which are required for generalization. So long as the

[1] J. M. Clark, "Competition: Static Models and Dynamic Aspects," *American Economic Review,* 45:452 (May 1955).

underlying assumptions are subject to value judgments — as, indeed, they must be — the claim for objectivity in theoretical conclusions must be ill-founded.

To noneconomists it is the disagreement rather than the agreement among their economist brothers that is outstanding in issues of public policy. Economists seem to delight in accusing one another of defending all sorts of subjective ends. To those within the discipline more harmony may be apparent but even here the development of established schools is widely enough recognized and the confusion of political ends with economic analysis frequent enough that the observations of the noneconomists cannot be lightly dismissed. One economist can often predict another's approach and position on many policy issues. In short, economists cannot escape their own preconceptions and biases, not because they are less honest than their fellows, but because they are as human.

A PREVIEW OF THE BOOK

The chapters below treat a dual problem. Its first aspect concerns the theory of competition; the second, problems of public policy. The treatment is admittedly subjective since the basis for both the theoretical underpinnings and the policy conclusions is an assumption about the nature of rivalry among sellers and the consequent market behavior.

Viewed in its entirety, public policy toward competition appears as a maze of inconsistencies. The goals of the Sherman Act are thwarted not only by the "mean rapacity" and "monopolizing spirit of merchants and manufacturers" — to use Adam Smith's famous descriptions — but also by a veritable host of other laws and an amazing complex of government policies which foster monopoly and encourage restraints of trade. In part, the apparent policy inconsistencies are attributable to the triumph of alternative theories of competition. More important, perhaps, are differences in the objectives of the laws. Some are obviously not designed for the purpose of maintaining competition. But even while it must be granted that inconsistencies exist, they may not be quite so pronounced as has been believed. This, at least, will be one of the conclusions drawn from the somewhat new theoretical approach employed here.

In the next chapter, a theory of interfirm organization is presented. This theory — based in part on developments in the behavioral sciences — attempts to overcome two apparently intractable problems which have plagued economists in their attempts to apply the traditional theory of the firm to real world problems. The first of these problems arises from the traditional assumption that the firm is an economic unity which rationally pursues the maximization of profits as its only goal. As they are observed in the real world, firms do not display such internal unity. There is conflict within the firm as well as competition from without. And this alone may be enough to prevent the firm from seeking to maximize profits as an economic unit.[2] In any case, viewed externally, firms appear to conform to the canons of profit maximization only if long-run and dynamic considerations are allowed into the maximization concept, and sometimes perhaps not even then. The records of the 1920 *Steel* and the 1945 *Alcoa* cases illustrate circumstances in which the profit maximization explanation of firm behavior is simply inadequate. Extending the concept of maximization so that it covers the behavior of United States Steel and Alcoa is possible, but then the concept becomes tautological and not very helpful.

The second of the problems which beset economists in using traditional theory concerns oligopoly. Despite the stalwart efforts of Cournot, Edgeworth, Bertrand, von Stackelberg, Chamberlin and many others, realistic generalizations about the determination of price and output — or, more generally,

[2] See R. M. Cyert and J. G. March, "Organizational Structure and Pricing Behavior in an Oligopolistic Market," *American Economic Review* (March 1955), and "Organizational Factors in the Theory of Oligopoly," *Quarterly Journal of Economics* (February 1956).

about the behavior of firms — in markets characterized by interdependence have not been produced. In part this, too, is due to the retention, in one form or another, of the profit maximization assumption.

A few years ago it seemed that the theory of games had finally reduced the oligopoly problem to manageable terms. And it can hardly be denied that game theory has helped in gaining more understanding of interdependence even though it has not yet led to the development of a general theory of value which significantly improves the prediction of market performance. Game theory has demonstrated that under conditions of mutual interdependence among firms neither market strategies of sellers nor market equilibria can be analyzed through the traditional profit maximization approach. The very existence of interdependence — a condition which, it will be argued, is practically universal — transforms the context in which decisions are made. The process of optimizing on the part of the individual concern is a far more complicated process than the equating of appropriate marginal functions because the firm must adjust to a group situation.

These problems in applying theory have led to something of an enigma in public policy toward competition. The structural and behavioral conditions postulated in the theory of pure competition lead logically to market performance which is ideal. The same structures cannot be duplicated in real markets, however, and it appears in some instances that the markets which approximate the competitive structure most closely are characterized by performance which is far from ideal. It is generally true that, absent *every* condition of pure competition, there is no theoretical bridge between market structure and market performance. There has been some tendency, both in policy and in economic analysis, to avoid this drawback either by ignoring the departures from the competitive structure or by the recognition of standards of "good" market performance. Given the latter standards, any market structure is deemed acceptably competitive so long as the performance it has produced is acceptable. This, of course, means that *current* policy is predicated primarily on *past* performance since, without a model connecting structure and performance, inferences about *future* performance cannot be validly drawn.

The purpose, then, of the theory presented in the second chapter is to suggest a nexus between structure and performance. The primary focus of the theory is on the market group, not on the individual firms in the group. In addition, the theory covers a complex of structural-behavioral-performance characteristics which conventional theory has compartmentalized into separate, sometimes competing theories. Chapters III through IX are reasonably comprehensive analyses of alternative structural and behavioral market situations and the resulting market performance. The cases were chosen because of their value in illustrating the application of the theory, not because of their importance as legal precedents or because they demonstrate what is regarded as either the correct or incorrect public policy. Chapter III surveys markets the outstanding characteristic of which is the small number of directly competing firms. Chapter IV concerns the opposite extreme — markets in which large numbers of sellers appear and which in many instances have been granted some sort of exemption or immunity from the antitrust laws. The *Addyston* case is treated in Chapter V. This case illustrates the need for a market organization to rationalize independent competitive behavior and indicates interrelationships between market organization, market structure and market performance.

Each of the following four chapters treats particular market details in greater depth. The bituminous coal industry is surveyed because of the lack of responsiveness its structure has demonstrated in the face of decades of poor performance and because of the illustration it provides of the difficulties involved in privately organizing a market in which there is a large number of sellers. In Chapter VII, the *American Column and Lumber* case is compared with the *Maple Flooring* case to show the effects on market performance of alternative numbers of sellers. These cases also afford an opportunity to examine the degree of homogeneity among the firms and the importance of free entry on a market organization and the performance of the market.

The *Trenton Potteries* case is used in Chapter VIII to illustrate the influence of leadership in the market group and also to indicate some of the difficulties that may be encountered in effecting cohesive, parallel behavior within the market group. The final case, presented in Chapter IX, treats the latter difficulties in still more detail.

Judicial and legislative policy toward competition is noted in each of the chapters which deals with particular markets or cases. These are summarized and other cases and policies are added in Chapter X, in which the chronological development of per se rules is traced. The final chapter presents the policy implications of the theoretical approach used. Though some will doubtlessly fail to be so persuaded, the conclusions do not constitute an apologia for monopoly, or even for a particular school of thought. Careful reading, it is hoped, will convince most that this is so whether or not the conclusions and method of analysis are accepted. It will be maintained on the one hand that a rule of reason approach is preferable to per se illegality in cases involving restraints of trade imposed by private parties. On the other hand, it will be argued as forcefully that many publicly authorized immunities from the antitrust laws might be removed to encourage more competition. Similarly, though the alternative of government intervention in, or regulation of, markets is one reason advanced for abandoning per se in favor of a rule of reason, no fear is expressed concerning government regulation or, for that matter, government ownership in instances in which the amount of private power necessary to make free enterprise operate is so great that social well-being is threatened.

OBSERVATIONS ON ADAM SMITH, COMPETITION, AND RELATED MATTERS

It is clear that this is an essay in dissent and that, as such, it is especially likely to be accorded the type of criticism noted by Professor Clark. Here the dissent is twofold, starting on the question of the relevant theory and concluding on the problem of public policy toward competition. Historical reflection, however, suggests that the thesis of the book is not really unique.

Much of the thinking about monopoly and antitrust problems seems colored by what Mason refers to as "the illusion that at some not too remote period the economy was competitive." [3] This "illusion" was undoubtedly given substantial credence by the mergers and consolidations of the late nineteenth and early twentieth centuries in the United States and by the attendant reactions of public authority. The antitrust legislation, the newsworthy antimonopoly suits and the writing of persons like Moody, the elder Fetter, and John B. Clark did create an atmosphere which made it easy to believe that there was competition in yesteryear but little save monopoly today.

Burn's classic *Decline of Competition,* the famous Berle and Means study, the new theoretical writing emerging with Professor Chamberlin and Mrs. Robinson, the investigations of the T.N.E.C. and the Federal Trade Commission did little to destroy the idea. Indeed, even as late as 1948, the F.T.C. opined publicly that "the giant corporations will ultimately take over the country" unless something is done.

It would be foolhardy to argue that there is no monopoly

[3] Edward S. Mason, *Economic Concentration and the Monopoly Problem* (Cambridge, Mass., 1957), p. 54.

problem in American capitalism. Of course there is. It is equally unrealistic and perhaps more dangerous to look at the former century as essentially more competitive than the present one and to advocate antitrust policies predicated on the ill-founded notion that atomistic competition in fact once prevailed.

Adam Smith did not regard the English economy of 1776 as being competitive in the modern sense. *Wealth of Nations* is replete with passages indicating Smith's awareness of the then existing monopolistic industrial organization. He speaks of sections of the country where "we can scarce find even a smith, a carpenter, or a mason, within twenty miles of another in the same trade." [4] "[L]aws which restrain . . . competition," he argued, ". . . may frequently, for ages together, in whole classes of employments, keep up the market price of particular commodities above the natural price." [5] Smith noted that combinations of masters were rarely heard of but added, "whoever imagines, upon this account, that masters rarely combine, is as ignorant of the world as of the subject. Masters are always and every where in a sort of tacit, but constant and uniform combination . . ." [6] The policy of Europe "no-where leaves things at perfect liberty." [7]

Smith observed that in small towns, because "of the narrowness of the market," persons engaged in wholesale or retail trade may have a high rate of profit on stock.[8] But even where the market is broader and corporations exist, "the corporate spirit, the jealousy of strangers, the aversion to take apprentices, or to communicate the secret of their trade, generally prevail in them, and often teach them, by voluntary associations and agreements, to prevent that free competition

[4] Adam Smith, *The Wealth of Nations* (Mod. Lib. ed.), p. 17.
[5] *Ibid.*, p. 61. See also pp. 119, 123, 124.
[6] *Ibid.*, p. 66. The discussion on p. 126 is in the same vein.
[7] *Ibid.*, p. 99.
[8] *Ibid.*, p. 113.

which they cannot prohibit by bye-laws."[9] "The inhabitants of the country," on the other hand, "dispersed in distant places, cannot easily combine together."[10]

Smith's observations on "people of the same trade" meeting together needs no repetition. The point is that Smith did observe such meetings, did recognize a public danger from them, and more than this, recognized that, "It is impossible indeed to prevent such meetings."[11]

Another source of domestic monopoly studied by Smith was that due to restraints upon importation. "Many . . . sorts of manufacturers have . . . obtained in Great Britain, either all together, or very nearly a monopoly against their countrymen"[12] in this manner. "This monopoly has so greatly increased the number of some particular tribes of them, that, like an overgrown standing army, they have become formidable to the government, and upon many occasions intimidate the legislature." Members of parliament who oppose them were subjected to "the most infamous abuse," "personal insults" and "insolent outrage of furious and disappointed monopolists."[13]

Monopolistic elements existed not only in the sectors of the economy in which the vestiges of mercantilism remained, but as well in the sectors not directly affected by government regulation, franchise or privilege. In the country, people in the same trade were remote enough from one another that effective competition between them was impossible. In the towns and cities, tacit agreements, understandings and overt conspiracies restrained competition. Duties and import prohibitions prevented effective competition from abroad.

Smith, of course, did not favor monopoly. On the other

[9] *Ibid.*, p. 126.
[10] *Ibid.* See also p. 429.
[11] *Wealth of Nations*, p. 128.
[12] *Ibid.*, p. 420.
[13] *Ibid.*, p. 438.

hand, it is probably a mistake to adopt the view that Smith saw an atomistic form of competition as necessary to the proper functioning of a market economy. His phrase, "perfect liberty," has been interpreted as the equivalent of "perfect competition" in the modern terminology.[14] Smith did espouse "perfect liberty" as a means of improving the performance of the price system but he never defined or used the term in a context which permits such an interpretation.

The tendency for Smith's "natural price" to cover the costs of production, including profit, exists "where there is perfect liberty, or where [a dealer] may change his trade as often as he pleases." [15] In this context, perfect liberty has a meaning similar to "free entry" in modern theory. The lack of perfect liberty in the policy of Europe was represented, "First, by restraining the competition in some employments to a smaller number than would otherwise be disposed to enter into them; secondly, by increasing it in others beyond what it would naturally be; and, thirdly, by obstructing the free circulation of labour and stock, both from employment to employment and from place to place." [16] Again, it is freedom of entry (and exit) being discussed.

Smith, then, saw the market working well if free entry and free international trade existed. Large numbers, he recognized, made effective conspiracy difficult[17] but, even without relying on large numbers, Smith was not inclined to view domestic conspiracy with alarm. "In a free trade" (i.e., one without incorporation), he argued, "an effectual combination cannot be established but by the unanimous consent of every single

[14] R. de Roover, "Monopoly Theory Prior to Adam Smith: A Revision," *Quarterly Journal of Economics,* 65:511n(November 1951).

[15] *Wealth of Nations,* pp. 56, 62.

[16] *Ibid.,* p. 118.

[17] In addition to the previous reference relating to this point, see Smith's discussion of the improbability that corn would be monopolized "wherever the law leaves the trade free," *ibid.,* pp. 491–492, and of the comparative chances that 2 and that 20 grocers could combine to raise prices, *ibid.,* p. 342.

trader, and it cannot last longer than every single trader continues of the same mind." A corporation "will limit the competition more effectually and more durably than any voluntary combination whatever." [18] That is, in voluntary combinations every single trader does not stay of the same mind for very long.

Smith, it was noted, found tradesmen too remote from one another in the country and in tacit or open association with one another in the towns. These market characteristics, considered in the light of Smith's discussion of the division of labor and its being limited by the extent of the market, suggest that, in modern terminology, Smith saw markets which were local monopolies and oligopolies; that, to forestall the use of monopoly power, Smith advocated a system which allowed freedom of entry and exit in both factor and goods markets, including the right of entry of foreign goods to be accomplished through removal of foreign trade restrictions. The monopoly against which Smith argued so strongly was the monopoly of license and privilege, not the modern day "monopoly power" associated with a relatively small number of sellers in any market.[19] As Macgregor points out, "at his [Smith's] time competition could hardly mean anything else than the competition of individuals, and it is reading too much into his views to assume that he would have advocated in the nineteenth century the breakup of the various forms of association." [20]

[18] *Ibid.*, p. 129.

[19] See de Roover, "Monopoly Theory," p. 523.

[20] D. H. Macgregor, *The Evolution of Industry*, Home University Library ed. (New York, London, 1912), p. 187. For a different view, see George J. Stigler, "Perfect Competition, Historically Contemplated," *Journal of Political Economy* (February 1957). Though Stigler notes that modern economists tend to read more into Smith's statements than they should, he himself may have fallen into this very trap. Stigler (p. 2) argues that Smith had five conditions of competition including: (1) independent action, (2) a "sufficient" number of rivals to eliminate "extraordinary gains," (3) "tolerable knowledge," (4) freedom from social restraints and, (5) time for the resources to flow as directed by their owners. Despite the fact that

It is impossible to assess with precision the course of competition after the time of Adam Smith. This is only partly because of the lack of relevant data. Even more important are qualitative aspects of the competitive process which defy the use of quantitative data. That laissez faire became increasingly the principal rationale of public economic policy in both England and the United States requires no elaboration. It is by no means so clear, however, that the period of economic liberalism was also a period of intensive competition. Free trade became the fact in England, and monopoly power originating from special privileges, franchise and the guilds largely disappeared. But at the same time, the factory system was being introduced, joint-stock companies were being formed in manufacturing, the scale of productive units was increasing and, especially after the repeal of the Combination Acts in 1824, labor organizations were being formed. In England, the nineteenth century was one in which economic market units were increasing in size and, probably, reducing in number.[21]

In the United States, but for the facts that protective tariffs were employed throughout the period and that the general combination movements followed those of England by a few decades, the same pattern was emerging. In neither country does it appear that competition was necessarily becoming less intense. Competition among groups of people — large firms,

---

Smith was decrying the then existing monopoly conditions, Stigler (pp. 2–3) suggests that "every informed person knew, at least in a general way, what competition was" and that "the conditions of numerous rivals . . . were matters of direct observation." In the one passage used by Stigler to support this view — which he contends is "all that Smith has to say of the number of rivals" — Smith was writing in the conditional tense. Moreover, while Smith did hold that the chance of twenty grocers combining to raise the price is less than of two combining, he adds in the very next sentence, which Stigler does not quote, that the competition of the twenty "might perhaps ruin some of themselves; but to take care of this is the business of the parties concerned, and it may safely be trusted to their discretion." It is to be doubted that Smith or anyone else observed as many as twenty grocers (or even alehouses) in multilateral competition in 1776.

[21] See Macgregor, *Evolution of Industry,* pp. 41–47.

associations of firms, and associations of people — tended to replace competition among individuals, but the precise effects of this on the intensity of competition varied with time and among the several component markets which comprised the economic system.

Compared with those of England, data on industrial concentration in the United States are relatively abundant. Using these to evaluate the strength of competitive forces is greatly complicated, however, by other equally important phenomena. Primary among these are the developments in transportation and communication, the growth in population and its movement into what were previously frontier areas, technological changes and the development of "new" industries, the ascendency to political power of the manufacturing-transportation-financial interests at the expense of the agrarian interests, the rise of an organized capital market, and the emergence of a system for uniform currency and bank credit.

The period following the Civil War in the United States is frequently thought of as one in which competition declined, for it was in this period that the "trusts" made apparent the tendency toward combination. But with improved transportation and communication, with new centers of population spread over increasingly large geographic areas, with commerce facilitated by a better capital market and a uniform banking system, and with the stimulus to business afforded by a stable and sympathetic government, it appears likely that markets were expanding more rapidly than the size of the business unit despite the tendency toward combination. The vast aggregations of capital into single enterprises in the 1880's and through the turn of the century must be considered in this light.[22] The oil, beef, whiskey and steel trusts resulted in a lessening of competition vis à vis conditions immediately preceding their formation. When compared with conditions of

[22] See B. F. Shields, *The Evolution of Industrial Organization* (London, 1928), pp. 53–54.

fifty years earlier, however, their formation may have given rise to hardly more monopoly power than that possessed by the local distiller, butcher, blacksmith or merchant. Surely competition never closely approached "purity" at any time in the century. Capitalism and laissez faire, even during the late nineteenth century when they reached their apex, were not characterized by markets in which each firm competed directly with large numbers of other firms. Trades in which large numbers of firms existed tended to have localized market areas and, when these disappeared because of improved technology, transportation, or other factors, the firms usually combined — first in loose combination, perhaps, and later through consolidation.[23]

The argument that competition is today perhaps as intense as at any time in the past is less unorthodox than the view that it is not only impossible but sometimes actually detrimental to market performance to prevent "people of the same trade" from meeting together. By and large, economists and lawyers have adopted Smith's view which strongly implies that practically all meetings among businessmen result in harm to the public. Among economists, the position of Professor Corwin Edwards is typical. Collusive price fixing, he writes, is "usually the least defensive kind of anti-competitive policy."[24] The same opinion extends to economists who are less oriented toward "maintaining competition" than he. Even J. M. Clark, who tends to defend "realistic competition" and who orig-

[23] I intend here only a limited acceptance of the so-called "transportation growth-merger hypothesis." On a *ceteris paribus* basis, I will argue below that as the number of firms in direct competition increases, the tendency toward association among them increases also. There are, however, many factors other than transportation cost which influence the number of firms in direct competition and many ways other than mergers by which firms can associate. Because of these, I do not regard empirical tests of the transportation cost-merger hypothesis as conclusive. See the discussion of Ralph L. Nelson, *Merger Movements in American Industry, 1895–1956* (Princeton, 1959), pp. 71–105.

[24] Corwin D. Edwards, "Can the Antitrust Laws Preserve Competition?", *American Economic Review,* 30:1:175, pt. 2, Supplement (March 1940).

inated the concept of workable competition, has argued that "a workably competitive result requires that there be no outright collusion." [25]

The harmony is not complete, however, and one need not search far to find dissenters. Theodore Roosevelt, the first of the "trustbusters," took a more reserved position. In his Annual Message for 1905 he remarked:

> It has been a misfortune that the national laws on this subject . . . have in part sought to prohibit what could not be effectively prohibited, and have in part in their prohibitions confounded what should be allowed and what should not be allowed. It is generally useless to try to prohibit all restraints on competition, whether this restraint be reasonable or unreasonable; and where it is not useless it is generally hurtful.[26]

Eddy, writing about a decade later, went still further with a general denunciation of price competition in his *The New Competition.*[27] It is difficult to find precisely the extent to which Eddy would have had co-operation supercede competition, but the chapter "Competition is War — And War is Hell" indicates the flavor. Even less moderate views can be found, including some which regard price competition as "a violation of human conduct" and "not competition at all, but . . . the most criminal restraint of trade." [28]

There are, nonetheless, a number of reputable economists among the dissenters. The late F. W. Taussig noted an analogy between the labor market and many product markets. He was willing to allow certain types of combinations and agreements among producers on the same grounds as collective bargaining among workers. "In both cases there is a chance for the purchaser to play off one seller against the

[25] J. M. Clark, "Competition: Static Models," p. 461.

[26] As quoted by Oswald W. Knauth, *The Policy of the United States Towards Industrial Monopoly* (New York, 1913), p. 201.

[27] Arthur Jerome Eddy, *The New Competition,* 4th ed. (Chicago, 1917).

[28] Alexander Levine (in collaboration with George J. Feldman), *Does Trade Need Anti-Trust Laws* (New York, 1931), pp. 62–66.

other, and in both there are causes which justify permanent organization for combined action." But Taussig added the caveat, "This is far from saying that a tight and exclusive combination is necessary to protect sellers, whether capitalists or laborers. An organization for standardizing competition is a very different thing from one for eliminating competition." [29]

Others have from time to time taken the view that excessive competition might occur in the absence of some organization among competitors. Sumner Slichter criticized the antitrust laws for their failure "to distinguish between combination for the purpose of preventing cutthroat competition and combinations to oppress the community." In his opinion there was a "need for combination to prevent cutthroat competition." [30] Similarly, Lewis Haney argued at one time that public policy should be changed so that, "business men would not fear to form any socially beneficial agreement organization . . . in which business practices could be reasonably standardized, and cutthroat competition eliminated wherever desirable." [31] Much of J. M. Clark's famous piece on workable competition deals with open price reporting systems — certainly a form of limited cooperation among firms — and the systems were defended as "something intermediate between pure oligopoly and the ruinously low prices likely to result from unlimited market chaos: more strongly competitive than the first, and more workable than the second." [32]

Schumpeter's views on price competition are well known. He could find "no general case for indiscriminate 'trust-bust-

[29] F. W. Taussig, *Principles of Economics,* 3rd ed. rev., II (New York, 1923), 457.

[30] Sumner H. Slichter, "Preliminary Announcement by the Committee on Study of Antitrust Legislation of the Committee on Industrial Inquiry," as quoted by Roy E. Curtis, *The Trusts and Economic Control* (New York, 1931), p. 493.

[31] Lewis H. Haney, *Business Organizations and Combinations,* 3rd ed. (New York, 1934), pp. 189–190.

[32] J. M. Clark, "Toward a Concept of Workable Competition," *American Economic Review,* 30:253, pt. 1 (June 1940).

ing' or for the prosecution of everything that qualifies as a restraint of trade." [33] Some monopolistic price practices were to Schumpeter "unavoidable incidents . . . of a long-run process of expansion which they protect rather than impede." [34] Short-run price rigidities in industry make "fortresses out of what otherwise might be centers of devastation" [35] and prevent depressions from causing even greater unemployment and general havoc. Whatever the short-run rigidities, "we practically always find that in the long run prices do not fail to adapt themselves to technological progress . . ." [36]

A few lawyers have joined in the view that some combinations among competitors ought to be allowed. Jaffe and Tobriner, after reviewing the law through the *Trenton Potteries* case and noting "provocative anomalies in the law" due to the "hard line drawn under the Sherman Act between loose and integrated combinations," proposed that the Act be amended so that "no contract, combination, or agreement shall be adjudged unreasonable for the sole reason that it tends or is designed to fix as between the parties the price at which goods . . . are to be bought or sold. . . ." [37]

After the *Socony-Vacuum* and *Apex*[38] cases, Peppin decided that:

It is to be hoped . . . that the Court will not condemn agreements which eliminate price competition between parties who have no monopoly power or control of the market and whose purpose is not to raise, depress or affect general market prices, i.e., agreements such as the one involved in the *Appalachian Coals* case. It would seem that such agreements are desirable and necessary in many situations . . . Sooner or later . . . the Court will have to recognize . . . that there are good and bad price-fixing agree-

[33] Joseph A. Schumpeter, *Capitalism, Socialism and Democracy,* 3rd. ed. (New York, 1950), p. 91.

[34] *Ibid.,* p. 88.

[35] *Ibid.,* p. 95.

[36] *Ibid.,* p. 93.

[37] Louis L. Jaffe and Mathew O. Tobriner, "The Legality of Price Fixing Agreements," *Harvard Law Review,* 45:1192 (1932).

[38] Apex Hosiery Co. v. Leader, 310 U.S. 469 (1940).

ments or other loose combinations — just as there are good and bad trusts, and that cases under the Sherman Act should be determined by examination of the actual nature, extent and effect of the restraint in each case, rather than by categorical assumptions or mechanical rules.[39]

Still more recently, Oppenheim has taken the view that the per se rule is too harsh. He concludes that:

For the areas of antitrust law where the *per se* violation has been most pronounced — in price fixing and other restrictive agreements among competitors . . . a prima facie case of illegality should be substituted for the rigidity of the *per se* doctrine.

It is not a convincing refutation of the views just stated to contend that the antitrust enforcement agencies . . . are not equipped to cope with the burdens that will be imposed upon them by opening the Pandora's box of perplexities incident to a thoroughgoing application of the elastic Rule of Reason. American antitrust policy will never come to grips with the inescapable task inherent in the administration and enforcement of the federal antitrust laws so long as either government or business hides its head in the sand to shut out the constantly changing and varied conditions in American industries and markets as they actually exist in structure, behavior, and accomplishments.[40]

These views, however, are not only minority views. In addition, they are neither uniform nor based on a single and consistent theory of the market process. Attention will now turn to an effort to fill the virtual void in theoretical explanations of why, under certain circumstances and for some reasons, people of the same trade must meet together.

[39] John C. Peppin, "Price-Fixing Agreements Under the Sherman Anti-Trust Law," *California Law Review*, 28:731 (1939–40). It seems doubtful that Peppin intended the phrase "no monopoly power" in the sense of sellers with perfectly elastic demand functions.

[40] S. Chesterfield Oppenheim, "Federal Antitrust Legislation: Guideposts to a Revised National Antitrust Policy," *Michigan Law Review*, 50:1158, 1161 (1951–52). Milton Handler suggested a doctrine of presumptive illegality for price leadership cases in *A Study of the Construction and Enforcement of the Federal Antitrust Laws*, T.N.E.C. Monograph no. 38 (Washington, 1941), pp. 43–45.

CHAPTER II

A THEORY OF INTERFIRM ORGANIZATION

INTRODUCTION

Recent years have witnessed several significant criticisms of conventional value theory. Each goes beyond the Chamberlin and Robinson contributions of the 1930's, especially since factors other than profit maximization are included in the explanations provided for firm behavior and market performance. Mention was made above of the theory of games. In addition, there have been Fellner's notion of limited joint profit maximization,[1] Boulding's concept of homeostatic behavior,[2] the work of Sylos[3] and Bain[4] in the area of entry preventative pricing, and the Cyert-March-Simon[5] research on the importance of organizational influences and, particularly, of "satisficing" in the attainment of economic objectives. Still more recently, Baumol has suggested a theory of limited sales maximization to replace the usual profit maximization theory.[6]

While all of these have had some influence on the theory to

[1] William Fellner, *Competition Among the Few* (New York, 1949).

[2] Kenneth Boulding, *A Reconstruction of Economics* (New York, 1950).

[3] Paolo Sylos Labini, *Oligopolio e progresso tecnic* (Milan, 1957), reviewed by Franco Modigliani, "New Developments on the Oligopoly Front," *Journal of Political Economy* (June 1958).

[4] Joe S. Bain, *Barriers to New Competition* (Cambridge, Mass., 1956).

[5] In addition to the Cyert and March articles cited above, see Herbert A. Simon, *Models of Man* (New York, 1957), chs. 14 and 15.

[6] William Baumol, "On the Theory of Oligopoly," *Economica,* new series (August 1958), and *Business Behavior, Value and Growth* (New York, 1959).

be presented, none is a direct predecessor. Fellner's initial assumption that groups of firms attempt to maximize joint profits and his studies of the limitations imposed on the attainment of this objective by economic and institutional factors are clearly related. The emphasis on "quasi-agreements" gives explicit recognition to a sort of group decision-making in oligopolistic markets. Similarly, Fellner's treatment of limiting factors indicates possible areas in which the objectives of individual members may be in conflict with the group objective. Still, Fellner gives no consideration to the possibility that the group, qua group, may have objectives at variance with and in addition to the objectives of its individual members. The theory of "mutual restraint" posited by Alexander Henderson in a provocative, posthumously published article, though obviously not completed, is even more suggestive of the approach to be developed.[7]

It appears that a new and more realistic theory of oligopoly is emerging. It is based partially on a willingness to drop the assumption of profit maximizing behavior. More important, it is based too on a growing recognition that firms in oligopolistic markets are members of a group (or interfirm organization) which has an identity apart from the individuals of which it is comprised. That is, there are *some* decisions which must be group decisions for market stability to result. Paradoxically, until recently the theory underlying work in industrial organization has been lacking in organizational content; market behavior has been treated as an amalgamation of individual motives and actions. To understand oligopolistic behavior and performance, the interfirm organization as well as the firms in the group must be studied. As with people, firms may behave differently in a group than they do in isolation.

The study of group behavior has been a field of the be-

[7] Alexander Henderson, "The Theory of Duopoly," *Quarterly Journal of Economics* (November 1954).

havioral sciences — of sociologists, social psychologists and social anthropologists. Recent developments in the theory of group behavior and in organization theory make significant contributions when applied to the theory of value. Combining economics with the behavioral sciences suggests generalizations concerning relationships between market structure, market performance and firm behavior which are pertinent to issues of public policy.

THE ASSUMPTION OF INTERDEPENDENCE

The theory of interfirm organization is based on the assumption that competition, as it appears in the real world, takes the form of interdependent rivalry. Clair Wilcox has argued forcefully that this is an inappropriate assumption — that oligopoly is not so ubiquitous as many economists believe.[8] His argument, based on concentration ratios which show the presence of numerous firms in many lines of production, is not conclusive. It may be true that high concentration ratios are good indicia of the absence of pure competition, but the converse is not true. That is, it may be incorrect to assume that as the number of firms increases interdependence tends to disappear and that rivalry approaches the structural — and the performance — characteristics of pure competition or the large-number case of monopolistic competition. Low concentration ratios give little assurance that a more complex form of oligopoly does not prevail among the firms.

Henderson described the more complex form of oligopoly as follows:

> There may be thousands of grocers, yet each grocer will be intimately affected by a *very small number* of neighboring grocers — who may be close geographically, or similar in type of customer to whom they cater. Among dozens of makers of electrical machinery,

[8] Clair Wilcox, "On the Alleged Ubiquity of Oligopoly," *American Economic Review* (May 1950).

each will have his own *small group* of particular rivals. An industry is like a forest; each tree is far from almost all the rest, but each has some close neighbors. What looks, at first sight, like an imperfectly competitive industry turns out to be a series of linked oligopolies.[9]

This appears, in fact, to be but one of two types of complex, large-number interdependence. In it — and grocers or filling stations do provide a good illustration — each firm can identify a few close rivals. Among the close rivals, oligopolistic relations exist since their interdependence is recognized by the rivals themselves. The other firms — those which do not intimately affect the first, those from whom the small group is far away — comprise an amorphous group whose individual members seem to have little direct competitive effects because of locational, service and product differences. But, of course, these more distant rivals really do have some effects on the first. If even one of them, for example, lowers its offering price, a chain reaction may begin which ultimately affects the demand for all firms, even those far away. The fact that the relationship cannot properly be called oligopolistic because of the inability of firms to recognize the effects of tactics of firms outside its own small group should not obscure the fact that interdependence still remains.

The second type of large-number, complex interdependence differs from the first in that in the second individual sellers tend to be unaware of their interdependence with even a few close rivals. Continuing Henderson's analogy with trees in the forest, the individual trees, while close enough to constitute a forest when viewed from some distance away, are not very close together when viewed from within. Rivalry is not subjectively oligopolistic since individual firms do not recognize the effects of their own behavior on any of the others. But again, objectively if not subjectively, interdependence exists. Here, the lumber industry, absent trade associations, and per-

[9] Henderson, "Theory of Duopoly," p. 565. Italics added.

haps the unorganized soft coal industry of the 1920's provide examples.[10]

Reflection suggests, then, that even though simple oligopoly may not be ubiquitous, some form of linked interdependence may be. That, in any case, is an underlying assumption of the theory of interfirm organization and, to the extent that the assumption is incorrect, the theory loses validity.

Finally, to avoid confusion with the traditional meaning of competition — which has fairly specific structural and performance connotations — the term "rivalry" will be used to denote behavior on the part of one firm which, because of cross-demand conditions, reduces the demand or profits of other firms. In simple oligopoly, rivalry is fully conscious, in the sense that each firm recognizes all of its rivals. Rivalry is only partially conscious in the case of complex, large-number oligopoly since each seller identifies only a few close rivals and conceives of the rest as an amorphous group. In the second type of large-number interdependence, rivalry still exists — the behavior of one firm still influences others — but none of the sellers is aware of even a small group of other firms as its particular rivals. And, of course, rivalry need not be restricted to price rivalry, though that is undoubtedly the most important, or most potent, form.

THE DETERMINANTS OF RIVALRY: FIVE STATIC GENERALIZATIONS

Rivalry and the Interfirm Organization — It has long been recognized that firms in a simple oligopolistic market are likely to behave as though an agreement restricting the rivalry

[10] To help visualize this sort of market structure, consider what the market for corporate securities would be like if the organized exchanges were suddenly abolished. Individual sellers, bargaining bilaterally with whatever buyer could be found, would be unaware of the effect of their transactions on others, yet each would have an impact on market price. The lack of good communication of market knowledge and the absence of a central exchange for all transactions — both of which are usually provided by the market organization — would prevent anything like the competitive results from

among them had been reached. Moreover, while no one has shown how such firms can achieve the degree of market stability necessary to keep them in business without this pattern of behavior, it is generally agreed that the restraint imposed on rivalry by their parallel behavior may produce market performance which is less than "workably competitive."

The parallel action of oligopolists is evidence that they recognize themselves as members of a group. Their behavior, not surprisingly, is similar to that observed in other small groups. Many of Thrasher's conclusions with respect to group behavior, derived from a study of juvenile gangs, have equal validity for oligopoly.[11] A leader arises in the group, often by apparently spontaneous recognition and without the need for showdown fights. An unwritten code develops, partly from emulation of the leader and partly because the leader enforces certain rules of conduct. The code distinguishes between relations internal to the group and the group's relations with other groups and the community at large. Fighting *within* the group is closely regulated by the code.

The analogues in oligopoly are obvious — price leadership, the frequent lack of price competition, the vigor of some forms of nonprice competition, and so on. As in other groups, the behavioral code of the oligopolists may be the result of conscious decisions and express communications. But with so few members, the parallelism of simple oligopoly may easily arise as "unconscious sensitivity to certain stimuli," or as a "learned response" based on past experience.[12] The birth and mortality rates in oligopoly are much lower than in a group of juveniles and, even if express communication and the use of the leader's power were necessary as the group was form-

---

occurring. Note, too, some of the obvious favorable effects which an extremely formal, privately inaugurated and regulated market organization may have, especially on the breadth of the market.

[11] Frederic M. Thrasher, *The Gang* (Chicago, 1927).

[12] See Michael S. Olmstead, *The Small Group* (New York, 1959), pp. 82–88.

ing, it is likely that no verbal communication or demonstration of power is necessary to its continued operation.

The behavioral sciences place emphasis on one point which has not been stressed in the economic treatment of oligopoly. In the behavioral science approach, it is recognized that the firms have established an interfirm organization, however informal it may be. This carries connotations which go beyond Fellner's "quasi-agreements" and Henderson's "mutual restraint" since both of these focus attention on the individual firms.

To this point it has been satisfactory to leave the concept of the organization vague. There are perhaps as many definitions of organization as there are of economics, none of them satisfactory for all purposes but all having to do with much the same thing. The definition supplied by Clark and Ackoff is particularly appropriate here:

1. An organization is a social group, a collection of individuals all of whose members can (potentially or actually) communicate with each other.
2. The group has at least one objective (or goal). Some of the individual members of the group may not be interested in this objective, but collectively (as opposed to distributively) they are.
3. The group has a functional division of labor relative to pursuit of the group goal.

This division of labor implies the existence of subgoals for the organizational components. The attempts to achieve these subgoals can result in conflict situations among the functionally defined subgroups, and necessitate compromise between these subgroups in order to attain the group goal.[13]

The similarity between this definition of an organization, even though it was conceived for intrafirm groups, and the

[13] Donald F. Clark and Russell L. Ackoff, "A Report on Some Organizational Experiments," *Operations Research,* 7:281 (May–June 1959). For a more general but equally appropriate concept within which market analysis might be conducted, see P. G. Herbst, "A Theory of Simple Behavior Systems," *Human Relations,* 14:71,193 (1961).

identifying characteristics of mutually interdependent firms is striking. The firms do comprise a group and they are able to communicate, either expressly or through mutual understanding. The group, as opposed to its individual members, does have a general objective — the objective of providing and enforcing such standards of conduct as will eliminate the indeterminacy which accompanies markets in which firms are mutually interdependent. Without some such group action, each firm will be worse off in terms of its own subgoals. Thus, while the group goal may be closely related to the firms' subgoals, being a member of the market group involves the surrender of *some* amount of the firm's sovereignty and of its freedom to seek its own subgoal to the detriment of other firms.

There is a division of labor among firms, though it may not be functional in the sense in which Clark and Ackoff use the term. The division of labor among horizontally related firms is one of duplication, with each firm performing somewhat the same functions as the others. In addition, some or all of the firms may have vertical as well as horizontal relationships. Looked at in another way, there is a clearer division of labor because the individual members retain their identities for the purpose of measuring their own performances. Each has subgoals concerning its own profits, output, prices, etc. These are the subgoals which tend to result in conflict situations (rivalry) among the firms. The group, qua group, must act to contain and to direct the extent of this conflict since it is unlikely that there is such an identity in the demand and cost functions and in the subgoals of the members that a unique price-output combination can be found which is optimal for all the firms simultaneously. The group, that is, acts in a way to encourage individual firms to be satisfied with a group equilibrium which, in terms of the usual marginal conditions, is a disequilibrium for most or all of its members. If, for example, each firm has maximum profits as its individual subgoal, firms with higher costs and/or less elastic demand would prefer higher prices;

those with lower costs and/or more elastic demand, lower prices. But these subgoals are themselves in conflict. Unilaterally pursued, more profit to one frequently means less to another; a larger market share for one, a smaller share for another. Retaliatory action — rivalry — may mean that the subgoals of none are achieved. The interfirm organization — tacit and informal in the case of simple oligopoly — acts to resolve these conflicts to the mutual advantage of all if to the unique advantage of none. And in the process, total market behavior seems to reflect the pursuit of the group goal more than it does the striving of the individual units for their own subgoals. The firms, that is, appear not to be — and in a real sense they are not — profit maximizing even though within each firm more profits may be regarded as preferable to less.

The interfirm organization need not be as informal as that of simple oligopoly, however, and as will be developed below, there may be tendencies for its formality to vary with certain other characteristics of the market. But, in general, as the formality of the interfirm organization increases — that is, as more rules of market behavior are promulgated, accepted and enforced — the more the firms approach integrated, group-controlled management. *Given the values for other things which contribute in the determination of the degree of rivalry, rivalry tends to decrease as the formality of the interfirm organization increases.*

Rivalry and the Number of Firms in the Market — Interdependence may involve but a few firms or it may include thousands. As the number increases, however, the probability that mutual understandings and implicit agreements will be effective in restraining rivalry decreases. This is the result of several factors. Two-way communication is sometimes difficult, especially if the individuals communicating have conflicting interests and if the language used must be nonverbal. Communications difficulties tend to compound as the dimensions of the required communications multiply. One channel, for example, is adequate for two-way communication between two people. But with four, and no central exchange among them, six channels are needed if each is to be able to communicate directly with each of the others.

Communication among rival firms is in many instances nonverbal. A firm "sends" a message to others by altering its behavior. Whether the receivers of the message properly interpret the intentions of the sender depends on whether their perception is acute enough to notice the altered behavior and on their analysis of that behavior. The need for relatively simple and unambiguous signals is apparent — a function which many formal interfirm organizations perform — and just this requirement may cause firms to modify the extent to which they seek true optimization of their own subgoals. If misinterpretation of the message implied by a particular action is apt to occur — resulting in the breakdown of an acceptable mode of group behavior — a firm may choose to "satisfice" rather than optimize with respect to its own objectives.

Misinterpretation and the resulting independent rivalry is more likely to occur with large numbers of firms than with small. As numbers increase, the group situation and the group objective have to be understood by more individuals. More individuals have to recognize that their own objectives must be compromised for the sake of the group and, ultimately, for the sake of each. In addition, with a larger number of firms it becomes more probable that one will intentionally stray from the group, moving prices downwards, for example, and forcing the others to follow. *Thus, again given the other factors, independent rivalry tends to increase as the number of firms in the market group increases.*[14]

[14] The organizational problem created by a large number of firms is hardly different from that within an office, firm or government agency. Hierarchical authority and red tape, that is, more formality, are required to prevent independent behavior from obstructing group objectives when the

Rivalry and Leadership Power — The third generalization pertains to leadership within the group and the equality with which market power is distributed among the firms. The definition and the measurement of leadership power have eluded both economists and behavioral scientists, yet its influence on group behavior is not denied. Populations of economic units, like populations of insects, animals, people, and even college professors, do not typically have equalitarian distributions of power. Differences in power positions may cause gross inequities, but they also encourage a stable social order. The fact, then, that some firms lead while others follow is not an unmixed blessing but, so far as rivalry is concerned, the effect of leadership is quite clear. The powerful unit has the capability of assuring coordinated efforts toward the group goal and the requisite subordination of subgroup goals without elaborate plans and lines of authority. Leadership, that is, is in some measure a substitute for a formal organization. *Hence, the more asymmetrical the distribution of power in the market group, given the other factors, the less intense will independent rivalry tend to be.*[15]

The power to make others follow can be traced to a number of sources. One firm (or a coalition of firms) may have a large sales volume relative to each of the others and, because of

number of members is large. On this general point, Thrasher, *The Gang*, p. 318, concludes that the informal organization "does not usually grow to such proportions as to be unwieldy in collective enterprises or to make intimate contacts and controls difficult." See also A. Paul Hare, "Interaction and Consensus in Different Sized Groups," *Group Dynamics* (eds. Dorwin Cartwright and Alvin Zander, White Plains, 1953). The point is related to the "span of control" principle and to the complexity of communications systems in large, hierarchical organizations. See Herbert A. Simon, *Administrative Behavior* (New York, 1957), 2nd ed., pp. 26–28; Chester I. Barnard, *The Functions of the Executive* (Cambridge, Mass., 1938), pp. 104–110; and William H. Newman, *Business Policies and Management* (Cincinnati, 1953), 3rd ed., pp. 406–407. For relationships between communications and the choice between optimizing and "satisficing," see James G. March and Herbert A. Simon, *Organizations* (New York, 1958), pp. 161–171.

[15] See Ronald Lippett, Norman Polansky, Fritz Redl and Sidney Rosen, "The Dynamics of Power," *Human Relations* (1952).

this, have an advantage in cross-demand elasticities. In the event of open conflict the larger firm is apt to have the bigger guns and the greater staying power. Fearing the strength of size, smaller firms may be willing to follow when from their individual points of view the market decisions made by the leaders are not optimal. Some vertically integrated firms acquire power through their joint role as suppliers and customers as well as competitors of the other firms. A number of other factors might be mentioned, going to such vague influences as historical prominence and a reputation for wisdom and fairness.[16] But whatever the source of power, it tends to diminish the degree of rivalry.

Rivalry and Value Systems — The fourth generalization concerns the similarity of the value systems among the firms in the market group. If the firms are substantially similar with respect to the products being produced, types of customers and marketing channels, production and cost functions and if their managers have substantially coinciding views on the extent to which various prices and profit levels are thought to attract new rivals, the "equitable" division of the market, the "fair" price, etc., the interfirm organization is presented with few conflicts and, hence, need not be equipped to use either force or persuasion to resolve them. As the value systems of the firms in the group become more alike, both the advantage of and the desire for rival behavior tend to lessen. *Generally, as value systems tend to become more homogeneous, independent rivalry tends to become less pronounced.*

The specific factors to be included within the notion of value systems are difficult to enumerate. It is clear, however,

[16] See William F. Whyte, *Street Corner Society* (New York, 1943), pp. 258–261. The role of history and experience in market stability should not be neglected. For a suggestive treatment quite in harmony with the thesis of an interfirm organization, see Richard B. Heflebower, "Stability in Oligopoly," *The Manchester School of Economic and Social Studies,* 29:79 (January 1961).

that they extend well beyond the factors of traditional economic analysis and must include at least the primary forces determining behavior. Whatever these factors are — and they probably vary considerably from group to group — the greater the uniformity or homogeneity in the values or opinions of the individual firms, the more effective will be the interfirm organization. Stated alternatively, a more formal organization and better communication are required to achieve a given amount of suppression of independent behavior if the group is heterogeneous than if the group is homogeneous.[17]

Communication, of course, affects the homogeneity of value systems. It is generally to be expected that communication leads to conflict resolution and, hence, the more effective the interfirm communication, the more homogeneous will values tend to be and the less intensive will be independent rivalry. Moreover, frequent and effective communication — whether verbal or nonverbal — is a constant reminder to the firm of its membership in a group, causing the firm to identify more often with the group and to adopt values consistent with that identification.

Finally, the effect of entry and exit on rivalry and market performance is related to the value system variable. The ignoring of possible new entrants by an existing group of firms may, especially through the group's price policies, encourage new firms to join the group. And the new firms may have value systems quite different from those of the firms in the market. Thus entry, both because it increases the number of rivals and because it may add heterogeneity to the set of values, tends to increase rivalry. On the other hand, entry preventative pricing by existing firms, even while it may not

[17] Leon Festinger, "Informal Social Communication," *Psychological Review,* 57:271,274 (1950), advances the hypothesis that "The pressure on members to communicate to others in the group . . . increases monotonically with increase in the perceived discrepancy in opinion . . . among members of the group." See also March and Simon, *Organizations,* pp. 58–65.

result in either predatory behavior or exorbitant prices, denies the market whatever favorable or unfavorable influences increased rivalry might have on other aspects of market performance. Exit from the group tends to occur if an individual firm does not share the values of others and if alternatives exist which, in terms of its own subgoals, promise greater rewards.

Rivalry and Factors External to the Group — Interfirm organizations, like intrafirm groups, have to cope with problems which arise from without the group and over which they exercise no direct control. Suppliers exert an influence, as do customers. Sometimes firms which are horizontally related form into two or more smaller groups rather than one large one. Potential entrants are often existing (rather than new) firms and, if this is the case, they may be associated with organizations in other markets only remotely related to the one being entered.

There are, then, several types of outside groups the interests of which may be in conflict with any particular interfirm organization. Such conflict is seen clearly in the relations of a union with a group of employers — one organization, the union, whose interests in the matter of, say, wages, are in opposition to the other, usually informal, organization of hiring firms. It is seen less clearly, but is not less important, when a group of selling firms organizes (either expressly or through tacit understandings) to combat the pressure placed on prices by an organization of buying firms. Large buyers or suppliers — or effective coalitions of smaller ones — may force individual rather than group behavior on the part of the firms with which they deal. The increase in rivalry incident to such behavior may, through time, increase efforts to organize more formally, but until this occurs the static effect is toward more competition.

This suggests the final generalization: *the better organized and more efficient are the other groups with which an interfirm organization has conflict relations, the greater the tendency for rivalry within the interfirm organization.* The groups to whom sales and from which purchases are made, including labor organizations in the latter, are probably the most important external factors. But horizontally related groups and groups which pose a threat of entry are not unimportant. In addition, there are the vague mores and customs of the society in which the organization functions and the host of laws and regulations imposed on the organization and its members by the several governments under whose jurisdictions it operates. In a world of organized activity, the pressure to be a "good citizen" — both within one's own group and in the relations of one group to another — as well as the fear of retaliation by others and of the policeman may have significant effects on behavior.[18]

[18] It may be helpful to summarize this section symbolically. Adopting as nomenclature;

r = the degree of independent rivalry
f = the formality of the interfirm organization
n = the number of firms in the market group
s = the degree of skewness in the distribution of power
v = the degree of homogeneity in value systems
o = the power of other groups to force independent behavior,

the theory to this point indicates that;

$$r = r(f, n, s, v, o),$$

with first order partial derivatives as follows;

$$\frac{\partial r}{\partial f} < 0$$

$$\frac{\partial r}{\partial n} > 0$$

$$\frac{\partial r}{\partial s} < 0$$

$$\frac{\partial r}{\partial v} < 0$$

$$\frac{\partial r}{\partial o} > 0.$$

In the next section, possible relationships among what appear above as

INTERRELATIONS AMONG STRUCTURE, BEHAVIOR AND PERFORMANCE

The actual analysis of the influences of the several variables on rivalry and market performance is more complicated than the preceding pages indicate, especially when changes through time are considered. For the sake of clarity, each of the five generalizations was advanced with the assumption that other variables were constant. The generalizations were then stated in terms of the effect at a given time of each variable on rivalry. The connection between rivalry and performance, on the one hand, and possible temporal interrelations among the variables, on the other hand, were not treated.

Simple oligopoly, it has been noted, may produce market performance which is less than "workably competitive." That is, the interfirm organization, despite its informality, may be too efficient in achieving group goals. This tends to be especially true if, in addition to a small number of firms, there is some skewness in the distribution of power among the oligopolists, if the firms have similar value systems, and if neither suppliers nor buyers exert powerful influences. At the opposite end of the structural-organizational spectrum is the industry with many firms scattered geographically in complex, interdependent fashion, with no formal interfirm organization and with heterogeneous values because of, say, differences in costs. Large numbers of firms, no aggregations of market power and an absence of agreements restraining trade are commonly thought to produce desirable market performance. But, contrary to common thought, the theory of interfirm organization implies that performance will not be very good at this extreme either.

Performance does depend on the degree of rivalry among

independent variables will be investigated. In addition, certain tendencies for the independent variables to change through calendar time depending on the amount of rivalry at a given time will be noted.

firms. Performance is not, however, monotonically related to rivalry. No rivalry is the equivalent of monopoly and the performance it tends to generate is well described by conventional theory. To a point, increases in rivalry generated by changes in, say, the number of firms, distribution of power and formality of the interfirm organization tend to improve performance. But because of the interdependent nature of rivalry, continuously increasing it does not produce continuous improvements in performance. An equilibrium similar to that of pure competition does not emerge; instead, beyond some point performance tends to deteriorate from excessive rivalry and market chaos.[19] Equilibrium among interdependent firms — whether or not their rivalry is subjectively oligopolistic — requires an organization of sufficient formality to prevent independent behavior from destabilizing the market. That is, markets with large numbers of equipowerful firms and very informal organizations tend to have excessive rivalry and poor performance.[20]

It is difficult, though obviously necessary, to be more specific about the meaning of excess rivalry. Its meaning, of course, is bound up in particular performance characteristics. Looked at negatively, rivalry is not excessive nor even adequate in markets in which the interfirm organization is so formal that smaller than optimum scale firms are perpetuated in the long run with positive profits. Similarly, even with

[19] Continuing the nomenclature of footnote 18, and adding *p* as a composite variable measuring performance, the argument of this section is that;

$$p = p(r) = P(f, n, s, v, o).$$

In addition,

$$\frac{dp}{dr} \gtrless 0,$$

and,

$$\frac{d^2p}{dr^2} < 0.$$

[20] For a concurring view, see Walton Hamilton and Irene Till, *Antitrust in Action,* T.N.E.C. Monograph no. 16 (Washington, 1941), pp. 19–20.

optimum firms, rivalry is not adequate if prices fail in the long run to respond to changes in costs or demand. That is, while in the capitalistic market system both the social interest and the private interest require rewards to enterprise, the private interest in rewards to enterprise should not be satisfied at the expense of the social interest in efficiency. The performance indicia of excess rivalry, to the contrary, suggest that neither the social interest nor the private interest is being adequately served. These indicia include such things as prices which are highly responsive to short-run changes in demand and, because of this responsiveness coupled with unrestricted entry into the market, the failure of even optimum scale firms. Excess rivalry is often associated with chronic excess capacity, with new firms replacing those that fail, secularly low — even negative — profits, and a lack of technological change in either products or processes. That such performance is not in the private interest of those whose resources are engaged in the industry is clear. Less clear is it that the performance is not in the social interest.

Historically, industries with the performance characteristics of excess rivalry do not exhibit self-correcting tendencies until conditions arise which portend less, not more, rivalry. And historically, if not in terms of static theories of welfare economics, the social interest in increased output — total and per unit of resources employed — can be judged to have been better served by the growth and innovation which has occurred within the less competitive, more concentrated industries than by the intense rivalry of the so-called "chronically sick" sectors of the economy. It is even questionable that there is historic evidence of the social interest in the elimination of excess capacity being served effectively through the mechanism of virtually unrestrained rivalry. Again, this should not be interpreted to mean that the less the rivalry the better the public interest is served. Rather this should be interpreted to mean that at one extreme of rivalry neither the public nor the private interest is rewarded, while at the other extreme the private interest is so rewarded that society suffers through inefficiency.[21]

The changes in the industrial organization of the United States offers some clues concerning relationships among structure, behavior and performance. Rivalry increased sharply in many markets during the last half of the nineteenth century. The effective number of firms in and the geographic size of market groups were increasing because of improvements in transportation and communication and the increase in population density. Also, as firms which previously had been isolated from one another were brought into market contact, value systems which were locally quite homogeneous tended to become heterogeneous in the larger markets. In most markets excess rivalry was prevented or overcome by increasing the formality of interfirm organizations — through agreements, pools, trade associations, etc. — or by forced or voluntary reductions in the number of firms and a concomitant rise of leadership — through failures, mergers and other types of consolidations. But in some markets, such changes did not occur to thwart the increase in rivalry. Labor markets, for example, which had a great deal of rivalry on the supply side even prior to this time, were denied either of these ways of reducing rivalry. Mergers were impossible because of the

[21] These are, of course, value judgments or, at best, plausible conjectures in an area about which economists know very little. They are in general agreement with the Schumpeterian theory of the capitalist process but do not lend themselves to empirical testing which might increase their credibility. See, however, P. Hennipman, "Monopoly: Impediment or Stimulus to Economic Progress?", *Monopoly, Competition and Their Regulation,* ed. E. H. Chamberlin (London, 1954); Almarin Phillips, "Concentration, Scale and Technological Change in Selected Manufacturing Industries," *Journal of Industrial Economics* (June 1956); Henry H. Villard, "Competition, Oligopoly, and Research," *Journal of Political Economy* (December 1958); Jacob Schmookler, "Bigness, Fewness and Research," the same *Journal* (December 1959); J. K. Galbraith, *American Capitalism: The Concept of Countervailing Power* (Boston, 1952); David Lilienthal, *Big Business: A New Era* (New York, 1952) and A. D. H. Kaplan, *Big Enterprise in a Competitive System* (Washington, 1954).

nature of the service being sold. Interfirm organizations — labor unions in this case — could attempt formality but could not achieve the requisite group cohesiveness because of the power of buyers (employers) and the prohibitions of conspiracies of the common law and, later, of the Sherman Act.

It appears, then, that a high degree of rivalry at one point in time tends to cause subsequent changes in the variables which determine rivalry. Excess rivalry *tends* to be self-correcting through time, the adjustment mechanism being either the formality of the interfirm organization or characteristics of market structure — the number of firms, the development of leadership power and the homogeneity of values. And these may, of course, be interrelated. Given the values for all variables save, say, the number of firms, one can conceive of some maximum number of firms which would be sustainable in the market in the long run. In a fashion quite analogous to that of the "iron law of wages," if that number were exceeded at some point in time, rivalry would be so intense that market performance, through failures and bankruptcies, would cause the number to decrease again. Similarly, if the number of firms cannot be reduced — an assumption not far from true in the production of certain primary goods from scattered natural resources and even more true of labor markets — tendencies develop toward more formal organizations which, because of the poor market performance, are difficult to deny.

These dynamic tendencies include J. K. Galbraith's concept of countervailing power, since one possible source of a high degree of rivalry is market pressure applied by factors external to the market group.[22] While Galbraith's concept seems to imply that power is a sufficient check on power, no such equilibrating mechanism is suggested by the present theory. Excessive rivalry does tend to be self-correcting when the market structure and organization are mutable; too little rivalry, on the other hand, seems more likely to spread like

[22] Galbraith, *American Capitalism.*

contagion than to be self-remedying through market forces alone.

It should be noted, too, that the organizational problem of rationalizing excessive rivalry in complex, large-number interdependency is far different from that of simple oligopoly. Extreme formality with means of punishing recalcitrants may be required because of the large numbers and the temptation on the part of each to chisel. This is especially true in the second type, in which firms do not recognize their interdependence with even a small group of rivals. In such cases, if the numbers cannot be reduced, the power necessary for the organization to be effective may be so great that few would wish to lodge it in private hands. Or, at least, many would want the exercise of that power to fall within the contemplation of public authority.

A final paradox should be mentioned. The lacking or denial of an effective interfirm organization may, through its effects on performance, cause structural change. But the final outcome of the process is not a market without an efficient organization restraining rivalry. Instead, as the structural change continues, approaching more and more the simple oligopolistic market, implicit organization becomes effective in solving the problem of mutual interdependence.

OBSERVATIONS ON PROFIT MAXIMIZATION, SUPPLY AND DEMAND AND GAME THEORY

Little attention has been given to the subgoals of individual firms. Actually, nothing in the theory of interfirm organization is inconsistent with the assumption that the principal subgoal of each is to have profits as large as possible. The phrase, "as large as possible," is devoid of much content, though, and this is true even if things such as the complexity of the firm, problems of communication and internal control, the existence of noneconomic constraints and intertemporal relationships are not involved. The theory views each firm as a member of a group and, as a consequence, suggests that it is illogical to conceive of the firm, so long as it is aware of the group relationship, as pursuing the maximization of its own profits without considering the impact of this behavior on others in the group. This does not constitute an attack on *profit* maximization, per se, for similar qualifications would apply to any other assumed subgoal so long as conflict situations with other firms result when one firm behaves unilaterally.[23] So long as interdependence exists, it is inappropriate to assume that individual firms attempt unilaterally to maximize anything, whether it be profits, sales, or even a "general-preference function" if all the dimensions of the function are variables internal to the firm. For that matter, the theory points with equal validity to the inadequacies of attempts to explain firm behavior on the basis of "satisficing" objectives or organizational factors if only intrafirm factors are considered. The latter may, indeed, constitute valid objections to assumptions of maximizing behavior within the firm, but external factors must be included in the explanation of group behavior. In its simplest form, the theory of interfirm organization posits that firms are members of groups and that the explanation of group behavior requires assumptions beyond those relating to the motivation of the individuals in the group. Assumptions with respect to individual motives are necessary but not sufficient to explain group behavior.

While these remarks indicate weaknesses in marginal analysis, it does not follow that the more general and older forms of supply and demand analysis are similarly to be criticized. An interfirm organization does mitigate rivalry and, in the group equilibrium, does require that individual firms often forego the equilibrium depicted by the marginal equalities. It need not — and usually does not — eliminate the *tendency*

[23] This is not a mere semantic squabble. The concept of maximization as embodied in the calculus is simply not applicable to game strategic situations.

for prices to increase if demand rises or costs increase, or for prices to fall under the reverse circumstances. The hypotheses that supply is aggregated from the marginal cost curves of individual firms and that demand is aggregated from independent and transitive individual preference functions are not the only conceivable hypotheses on which the general "law" of supply and demand could be based. In particular, the hypothesis that an interfirm organization exists and that it may, depending on structural characteristics of the market, significantly affect the quantities supplied at various prices is not at all inconsistent with the general "law." In fact, what appear as disequilibrium market conditions with conventional analysis may, when organizational supply factors are considered, prove to be equilibria.[24] The forces generating the equilibria, however, would be organizational and would override whatever tendencies exist within firms to equate the margins appropriate for profit maximization. Thus, with alternative hypotheses about the detail underlying supply and demand, it may be easier to analyze influences not included in the normal notions and which may, in some circumstances, be more important in determining market performance. In this sense — and as subsequent chapters are intended to illustrate — the theory of interfirm organization should add to, not be a substitute for, traditional market analysis.

In the same way, the theory suggested here is complementary to the theory of games. A game is not an unorganized coming together of several individuals for "no-holds-barred" combat. It is instead a well-defined set of rules which limits the freedom of the players in their selections of strategies and moves. Different results occur if different games are played,

[24] On this point, see Romney Robinson, "The Economics of Disequilibrium Price," *Quarterly Journal of Economics* (May 1961). While Robinson discusses observed market performance which suggests an extremely stable equilibrium, he chooses to label the phenomena "disequilibrium" because the marginal equalities are violated. Perhaps economists have been looking at the wrong equilibrating forces, not disequilibrium at all.

not because the players are motivated by different objectives but rather because varying constraints are imposed on their behavior. Nothing in the mathematics of game theory, however, goes to the problem of how the game is chosen, who establishes the rules and how they are enforced. The game is apparently set by an anonymous outside authority. From an organizational point of view, this outside authority is in the real world the vast, complex institutional-organizational framework of society, including near the apex of its hierarchical structure the several layers of formal government. Individuals, however, are part of this structure and are thus involved in the selection of the rules of the games they play. Their involvement is not limited to the casting of political votes any more than the organizations of which they are a part are limited to the bodies politic. It does not appear unreasonable to suppose that when individuals are engaged in a game which would be a negative sum game with no rules and a positive sum game with established rules, they will make a concerted or co-ordinated effort themselves to establish some rules. Similarly, so long as individual identities remain and the game retains conflicting individual objectives, it is no less unreasonable to conclude that the rules established will not eliminate independent rivalry completely. At least conceptually, then, the theory of interfirm organization could be put in a game theory context, with the rules of the game being established co-operatively (either explicitly or implicitly) but played non-co-operatively.[25]

[25] Thomas C. Schelling's "theory of interdependent decisions," presented in *The Strategy of Conflict* (Cambridge, Mass., 1960), is closely related to this train of thought. Schelling's main interest in this book is international affairs, but his theory need not be so restricted. While put in a game theory framework, it is not the mathematics of interdependent decision-making which is unique, but rather the roles played by tacit communication, perception, customs, value systems, etc., in the mixed-motive game. The explanations of things such as the tacit agreement among the participants not to use poison gas during World War II is quite adaptable as an explanation of why oligopolists may choose not to engage in price competition.

PART TWO

SOME CASES

CHAPTER III

CONSCIOUS PARALLELISM AND THE INFORMAL ORGANIZATION OF OLIGOPOLY

INTRODUCTION

In the present chapter attention will be focused on the subtle and perplexing organizational problems of simple oligopoly. Firms operating in such markets frequently seem aware of what one another will do in particular market circumstances. In fact, their conduct and the resulting market performance sometimes give evidence that they have achieved a set of group goals more effectively than firms in other markets in which formal interfirm organizations are found. The problem will be treated by reviewing quickly the general development of the doctrine of conscious parallelism in the law and by pausing a bit longer on several recent cases. The purpose is to assess the relationships between rivalry and other variables — the distribution of power, the homogeneity of value systems, and power external to the primary market group — in markets dominated by a few sellers and to note the legal difficulties posed by their parallel behavior.

CONSCIOUS PARALLELISM AND THE ANTITRUST LAWS

A specific doctrine of conscious parallelism has arisen in the law only recently. Conscious parallelism, as a legal problem, is related, however, to the more general law of implied — or inferred — conspiracy and here the roots of the newer doctrine are old. Conscious parallelism itself was very nearly recognized by Justice Peckham in the old *Joint-Traffic Association* case. In the decision it was noted that:

> . . . Railroad companies may, and often do, continue in existence and engage in their lawful traffic at some profit, although they are competing railroads, and are not acting under any agreement or combination with their competitors upon the subject of rates . . . It cannot be said that destructive competition, or, in other words, war to the death, is bound to result unless an agreement or combination to avoid it is entered into between otherwise competing roads.
>
> It is not only possible but probable that good sense and integrity of purpose would prevail among the managers, and while making no agreement and entering into no combination . . . the managers of each road might yet make such reasonable charges for the business done by it as the facts might justify.[1]

Further reflection might have led the Justice to modify his statement that such results were probable. If they had been, it is unlikely that the traffic association would ever have been formed. The formal agreement seemed necessary to the roads because they were so many in number, had such a complex rate and traffic structure and were so lacking in "good sense and integrity" (i.e., had such heterogeneous value systems) that the suggested parallel behavior was impossible. All of this was, of course, quite incidental to the case.

The first instance under the Sherman Act in which a conspiracy was inferred from the circumstances was apparently in *Eastern States Retail Lumber Dealers' Association v. U.S.*[2] The number of firms was large and, again, their organization formal. When no express horizontal agreement among the retailers not to trade with "blacklisted" wholesalers could be found, the Supreme Court, through Justice Day, stated:

> . . . [I]t is said that in order to show a combination or conspiracy within the Sherman act some agreement must be shown under

[1] U.S. v. Joint-Traffic Association, 171 U.S. 505, 577 (1898).
[2] 234 U.S. 600 (1914).

which the concerted action is taken. It is elementary, however, that conspiracies are seldom capable of proof by direct testimony, and may be inferred from the things actually done; and when, in this case, by concerted action the names of wholesalers who were reported as having made sales to consumers were periodically reported to the other members of the association, the conspiracy to accomplish that which was the natural consequence of such action may be readily inferred.[3]

The court was presented with the facts of parallelism in 1920 in the *Steel* case.[4] From the 1901 merger until the panic of 1907, the market had been stable. Then came the Gary Dinners, which a lower court had described as "pools without penalties." [5] There followed the period during which the corporation "resorted to none of the brutalities or tyrannies that the cases illustrate of other combinations . . . [I]t did not oppress or coerce its competitors . . . ; it did not undersell its competitors . . . ; it did not obtain customers by secret rebates or departures from its published prices . . . It combined its power with that of its competitors. It did not have power in and of itself, and the control it exerted was only in and by association with its competitors . . ." [6] In short, though there was no charge or proof of agreements among the companies, their behavior suggested agreement.

A "teacher of economics" testified in the *Steel* case that "when prices are stable through a definite period, an artificial influence is indicated; if they vary during such a period, it is a consequence of competitive conditions." To this the court replied:

. . . It has become an aphorism that there is danger of deception in generalities, and in a case of this importance we should have something surer for judgment than speculation, something more than a deduction, equivocal of itself, even though the facts it rests

[3] *Ibid.*, p. 612.
[4] U.S. v. U.S. Steel, 251 U.S. 417 (1920).
[5] *Ibid.*, p. 440.
[6] *Ibid.*, p. 441.

on or asserts were not contradicted. If the phenomena of production and prices were as easily resolved as the witness implied, much discussion and much literature have been wasted, and some of the problems that are now distracting the world would be given composing solution. Of course, competition effects prices; but it is only one among other influences, and it does not, more than they, register itself in definite and legible effect.[7]

This was the same Court which a year and a half later found guilt in *American Column and Lumber* even though a definite agreement was lacking. In the *Steel* case, the Court was not asked to find and did not take note of an interfirm organization; in *American Column and Lumber* the organization was obvious. Yet the facts would indicate that in *Steel* there was little or no price rivalry while, as will be shown below, in *American Column and Lumber* rivalry was vigorous. No doctrine of conscious parallelism could arise until the Court paid some attention to market performance as well as to the formality of the interfirm organization.

Parallelism was an important fact in the 1927 *International Harvester* case.[8] Virtually the sole question at issue was whether competition had been restored to the industry following a court decree of 1914. The Supreme Court found that the company:

. . . has not . . . attempted to dominate or in fact controlled or dominated the harvesting machinery industry by compulsory regulation of prices. The most that can be said as to this, is that many of its competitors have been accustomed, independently and as a matter of business expediency, to follow approximately the prices at which it has sold its harvesting machines; but one of its competitors has habitually sold its machines at somewhat higher prices. The law, however, does not make the mere size of a corporation, however impressive, or the existence of unexerted power on its part an offense, when unaccompanied by unlawful conduct in the exercise of its power . . . And the fact that competitors may see

[7] *Ibid.*, pp. 448–449.
[8] U.S. v. International Harvester Co., 274 U.S. 693 (1927).

proper, in the exercise of their own judgment, to follow the prices of another manufacturer, does not establish any suppression of competition or show any sinister domination . . .[9]

The outcome of this case is not inconsistent with "workable competition." But the argument of the Court refused to face the actuality of an implicit interfirm organization. In *American Column and Lumber,* an implicit agreement had been read into the facts by "the disposition of men 'to follow their most intelligent competitors,' especially when powerful; by the inherent disposition to make all the money possible, joined with the steady cultivation of the value of 'harmony' of action." [10] The men in the harvesting machinery business were, perhaps, similarly disposed. Certainly the power of International Harvester, with nearly two thirds of the national market,[11] should have cultivated such a disposition and encouraged the spirit of harmony. The group of harvesting machinery producers was small and Harvester was its accepted leader. The harmony was complete enough that there was no need for coercion and the abuse of power. The market was, in fact, well organized and, contrary to the opinion of the Court, competition was effectively, if not unreasonably, suppressed.

Conscious parallelism was more obvious in the later *Interstate Circuit* case.[12] Here the manager of the two largest exhibitors of motion pictures in Texas wrote identical letters to eight distributors, each letter naming all eight, asking that the distributors not release their "A," or first-run, movies for subsequent runs to exhibitors who charged an evening admission of less than $.25 and that the same movies not be released to exhibitors for use in "double features." The distributors complied with these demands and as a result there was "a radical departure from the previous business practices

[9] *Ibid.,* pp. 708–709.
[10] 257 U.S. 377, 399 (1921).
[11] 274 U.S. 709.
[12] Interstate Circuit, Inc., v. U.S., 306 U.S. 208 (1939).

of the industry and a drastic increase in admission prices of most of the subsequent run theatres." [13]

The Court drew an inference of agreement among the distributors. In support of this it maintained that:

The . . . letter named on its face as addressees the eight local representatives of the distributors, and so from the beginning each of the distributors knew that the proposals were under consideration by the others. Each was aware that all were in active competition and that without substantially unanimous action . . . there was risk of a substantial loss of the business and good will of the subsequent-run and independent exhibitors, but that with it there was a prospect of increased profits. There was, therefore, strong motive for concerted action . . .

. . . [W]e are unable to find in the record any persuasive explanation, other than agreed concert of action, of the singular unanimity of action on the part of the distributors by which the proposals were carried into effect as written in four Texas cities but not in a fifth or in the Rio Grande Valley. Numerous variations in the form of the provisions in the distributors' license agreements and the fact that in later years two of them extended the restrictions into all six cities, do not weaken the significance or force of the nature of the response . . . It taxes credulity to believe that the several distributors would, in the circumstances, have accepted and put into operation with such substantial unanimity such far-reaching changes in their business methods without some understanding that all were to join, and we reject as beyond the range of probability that it was the result of mere chance.[14]

Rather interestingly, Justice Stone's opinion, written some dozen years after his *Trenton Potteries* decision and a year before Justice Douglas' opinion in *Socony-Vacuum,* did not go directly from the conclusion of an agreement to an announcement of per se illegality. It instead treated the reasonableness of the restraint and concluded against it. Thus it was pointed out that:

[13] *Ibid.,* p. 222.
[14] Interstate Circuit, pp. 222–223.

The restrictions imposed on the subsequent-run exhibitors were harsh and arbitrary. . . . [T]hey were forced upon the distributors and upon their customers as a result of the agreements entered into by Interstate with the distributors . . . There were wide differences in the location and character of subsequent-run houses . . . which afforded basis for the corresponding differences in admission prices charged before the restrictions were adopted. Due to the practice of the distributors of establishing clearance periods between the first and each successive run, later runs are progressively less attractive. The poorer class of theatres, exhibiting the later runs, sometimes offered a double bill as an offsetting inducement for patronage. Despite these differences which normally affect the admission price that could be charged by subsequent-run theatres, the 25 cents admission price was to be required of all alike, forcing increases in admission price ranging from 25 per cent to 150 per cent.

. . . [T]he result was to increase the income of the distributors and Interstate and diminish that of the exhibitors who accepted the restrictions, by deflecting attendance from subsequent-run theatres to Interstate's first-run theatres . . . The effect was a drastic suppression of competition and an oppressive price maintenance, of benefit to Interstate and the distributors but injurious alike to Interstate's subsequent-run competitors and to the public.[15]

It was, then, the unreasonableness of the parallel behavior of the distributors, not the fact of parallelism, which led to the decision. Perhaps without realizing it, Justice Stone noted in the part of the opinion excerpted above that the distributors had at least one other parallel practice — the "establishing of clearance periods between first and each successive run." This perhaps was not an unreasonable restraint on trade though it and many other policies may have been as much "agreed" upon as was the behavior charged in the instant case. Each of the three market organizations involved — the "first-run" exhibitors, the "second-run and double feature" exhibitors and the distributors — had standard, accepted market practices. Group decision-making and the importance of

[15] Interstate Circuit, pp. 230–231.

rivalry among groups of firms are clearly illustrated by the case.

The *Socony-Vacuum* case is only partially one of conscious parallelism. It is true that the conspiracy had to be "pieced together" and inferred from the conduct of defendants but, at least so far as the Mid-Continent and East Texas Buying Programs are concerned, there were formal interfirm organizations in the form of the General Stabilization Committee, the Mechanical Sub-Committee, the Tank Car Stabilization Committee, and the East Texas Refiners' Marketing Association.[16] These organizations, however, were restricted to the functions relating to the purchase of surplus or "distress" gasoline from the smaller, nonintegrated, independent refiners in the spot markets. There were so many of the latter that effective organization would have required great formality — something of the order of the Texas Railroad Commission.

The indictment charged in addition that the purpose of the defendants and the effect of the conspiracy was to raise the wholesale and retail price structure for gasoline in the Mid-Western area. In this, parallelism was involved because there was no formal organization. Standard of Indiana was the price leader in this market; others customarily followed Standard's posted retail prices. Standard was not in the group of defendants whose case reached the Supreme Court, however, having been granted a new trial by the District Court. Thus, even with its sweeping nature, the opinion of the Supreme Court is primarily related to the buying program and its effects on the retail price structure, given the price leadership. While the decision does not go to the legality of the retail pricing parallelism as a problem in itself, it is clear that the effect of the buying program was to increase the homogeneity of value systems among those selling gasoline since that program eliminated the most important source of

[16] 310 U.S. 178–190 (1940).

differences in costs. Parallelism, that is, in wholesale and retail pricing would have been difficult to achieve without formal agreement and powerful group leadership so long as input prices were not substantially uniform.

The 1946 *American Tobacco* decision[17] led some persons to believe that conscious parallelism, with nothing more, had been found illegal. In his opinion, Justice Burton said:

> . . . No formal agreement is necessary to constitute an unlawful conspiracy. Often crimes are a matter of inference deduced from the acts of the person accused and done in pursuance of a criminal purpose. Where the conspiracy is proved, as here, from the evidence of the action taken in concert by the parties to it, it is all the more convincing proof of an intent to exercise the power of exclusion acquired through that conspiracy. The essential combination or conspiracy in violation of the Sherman Act may be found in a course of dealings or other circumstances as well as in any exchange of words . . . Where the circumstances are such as to warrant a jury in finding that the conspirators had a unity of purpose or a common design or understanding, or a meeting of the minds in an unlawful arrangement, the conclusion that a conspiracy is established is justified. Neither proof of exertion of the power to exclude nor proof of actual exclusion of existing or potential competitors is essential to sustain a charge of monopolization under the Sherman Act.[18]

Read in vacuo, or in the context of theoretical oligopolistic behavior, this may appear to outlaw parallelism per se. But in the context of the case, this is far from true. In the first place, the petitions for certiorari granted the companies by the Court were "limited to the question whether actual exclusion of competitors is necessary to the crime of monopolization under Section 2 of the Sherman Act." [19] Many of the references in the decision which suggest that the defendants' conduct was not extreme are related to this, not to questions of agreements in restraint of trade.

[17] American Tobacco Co. v. U.S., 328 U.S. 781 (1946).
[18] *Ibid.*, pp. 809–810.
[19] American Tobacco, p. 784.

In the second place, in the instances in which parallelism is treated in the decision it is included as justification for the finding of a conspiracy in the absence of "a formal written agreement." [20] The facts of this case are not the simple facts of price leadership or of administered prices apparently unresponsive to variations in supply and demand. The facts show remarkable parallelism in the tobacco auction and wholesale and retail cigarette markets. The parallelism was complex and much of it explainable only as a joint endeavor to injure, if not destroy, smaller competitors. "[P]ractices of an informal and flexible nature were adopted and . . . the results were so uniformally beneficial . . . in protecting their common interests as against those of competitors that, entirely from circumstantial evidence, the jury found that a combination or conspiracy existed . . . , with power and intent to exclude competitors to such a substantial extent as to violate the Sherman Act . . ." [21]

This is far from condemning the informal, tacit organization of oligopoly because of its influence on prices and the price structure. Indeed, as Justice Burton indirectly pointed out, interfirm relationships are to be expected in such an industry. "A friendly relationship within such a long established industry is, in itself, not only natural but commendable and beneficial, as long as it does not breed illegal activities." [22] Here, however, the friendly relationship included such effective nonverbal communication and such an identity in value systems — especially regarding the appropriate share of the market for the "big three" group — that rivalry among the defendants was limited to relatively harmless maneuvers and rivalry from without the group was carefully stifled.

U.S. v. Paramount Pictures, Inc.[23] involved several aspects

[20] *Ibid.*, p. 789.
[21] *Ibid.*, p. 793.
[22] American Tobacco, p. 793.
[23] 334 U.S. 131 (1948).

of parallel behavior. The major defendants — Paramount, Loews, Radio-Keith-Orpheum, Warner Bros., and Twentieth-Century-Fox — produced, distributed and exhibited motion pictures. Because of their integrated character, they were interested in prices and rentals at all stages. Some other defendants produced and distributed, but did not exhibit; another was engaged only in distribution. There were, of course, many exhibitors independent of any of the defendants.

The trial court found that there was substantial uniformity, (1) in the minimum admission prices contained in the licenses granted exhibitors to show copyrighted pictures, (2) in the clearances established for subsequent runs of pictures, (3) in agreements with independent exhibitors concerning the acquisition of theatres and pooling arrangements, (4) in certain formulas, agreements and franchises with circuit exhibitors, (5) in "block-bookings" for a series of features and, (6) in a host of relatively minor practices which the court concluded were discriminatory with respect to small independent exhibitors.

The substantial identity in minimum admission prices led to the inference of a horizontal price-fixing conspiracy. Justice Douglas' opinion held that:

> . . . We think there was adequate foundation for it too. It is not necessary to find an express agreement in order to find a conspiracy. It is enough that a concert of action is contemplated and that the defendants conformed to the arrangement . . . That was shown here.
>
> . . . [S]o far as the Sherman Act is concerned, a price-fixing combination is illegal *per se* . . . We recently held in United States v. United States Gypsum Co., 333 U.S. 364, 68 S. Ct. 525, that even patentees could not regiment an entire industry by licenses containing price-fixing agreements. What was said there is adequate to bar defendants, through their horizontal conspiracy, from fixing prices . . . in the movie industry.[24]

[24] Paramount Pictures, pp. 142–143.

The *Paramount* case provides a good illustration of how far an informal organization can go in codifying group behavior. Apparently without express agreements — written or oral — eight firms behaved virtually identically in several rather complicated facets of their businesses, and none seemed disposed to independent behavior. The value systems of the five principal defendants were much alike, mainly because of a combined competitor-customer relationship which existed among them. Each had to use the films of the others in the exhibition phase of the business. And the other defendants had little recourse other than to follow the practices of the integrated companies since the former — lacking full integration into all phases of operations — depended on the latter as suppliers or customers or both.

The *Cement Institute* case[25] was brought under the Federal Trade Commission and Clayton Acts but involved the Sherman Act charges of conspiracy. There was no express agreement among the manufacturers to use the same multiple basing point pricing system. Economists testified for the industry that active competition "was bound to produce uniform cement prices," and that parallel behavior and identical prices would occur "without agreement express or implied and without understanding explicit or implicit." The Commission did not accept this explanation and the Court held that:

> . . . The Commission was authorized to find understanding, express or implied, from evidence that the industry's Institute actively worked, in cooperation with various of its members, to maintain the multiple basing point delivered price system; that this pricing system is calculated to produce, and has produced, uniform prices and terms of sale throughout the country . . .[26]

In view of the formality of the interfirm organization and the power of that organization to punish recalcitrants, the

[25] Federal Trade Commission v. Cement Institute, 333 U.S. 683 (1948).

[26] *Ibid.*, p. 716. A footnote at this point in the case cited *Interstate Circuit* with approval.

case hardly falls in the conscious parallelism category even while an understanding or conspiracy had to be inferred.

The use of the doctrine of conscious parallelism to find conspiracy was extended in *U.S. v. Griffith.*[27] The case was brought against four affiliated corporations and three members of the family which owned and operated them. The corporations owned theatres in Oklahoma, Texas and New Mexico and there was virtually no competition internal to their composite operations. Their theatres were in separate towns, eighty-five in number in April 1939. In thirty-two of the eighty-five towns there were competing theatres owned and operated by other interests.

Until the 1938–1939 season, all four corporations used the same agent in negotiating with distributors. Beginning that year, two agents were used. The agreements, probably because of the size of the Griffith chain, contained "exclusive privileges which . . . unreasonably restrained competition by preventing their competitors from obtaining enough first- or second-run films from the distributors to operate successfully." [28] Original charges that the eight distributors had conspired with each other in granting these privileges were dropped by stipulation or on motion of the government.[29]

The District Court found no conspiracy, no unreasonable restraint of trade and no monopolization or attempt at monopolization.[30] In an opinion by Justice Douglas, the Supreme Court reversed without knowledge or inquiry concerning "the effects these practices actually had on the competitors of appellee exhibitors or on the growth of the Griffith circuit . . ." [31] "The appellees, having combined with each other and with the distributors to obtain those monopoly

[27] 334 U.S. 100 (1948).
[28] *Ibid.*, p. 103.
[29] *Ibid.*, footnote 6.
[30] Griffith, p. 104.
[31] *Ibid.*, p. 109.

rights, formed a conspiracy in violation of . . . the Act." [32] Thus parallelism even within a commonly owned group of businesses was material in finding guilt.[33]

By mid-1948 it appeared that conscious parallelism might constitute an offense with no showing of restraints on competition. The success of the Federal Trade Commission in the *Cement* and *Rigid Steel Conduit* [34] cases was followed by a statement of the Commission to its staff:

> [W]hen a number of enterprises follow a parallel course of action in the knowledge and contemplation of the fact that all are acting alike, they have, in effect, formed an agreement . . . The obvious fact [is] that the economic effect of identical prices achieved through conscious parallel action is the same as that of similar prices achieved through overt collusion and, for this reason, the Commission treated the conscious parallelism of action as a violation of the Federal Trade Commission Act.[35]

The doctrine of conscious parallelism — that is, the legal notion that similar behavior, by itself, reflected a violation of the antitrust laws — seems to have reached its apogee at this point. And in a sense, the Commission's view was correct. Conscious parallel action does, in effect, reflect an agreement among rival sellers. Such agreements, however, need not fix prices nor unreasonably restrain rivalry. Indeed, if it is recognized that rivalry may, even in simple oligopolistic markets, exceed the degree which produces the best performance, it must also be acknowledged that the parallel behavior created by the informal organization of oligopolists is, to some degree,

[32] *Ibid.*

[33] A companion case, *Schine Chain Theatres, Inc. v. U.S.*, 334 U.S. 110 (1948), is quite different. In *Schine* there was a large amount of evidence that the preferences were used to injure competitors in various ways, including price cutting and entry-preventative behavior. See 334 U.S. 114–124.

[34] Triangle Conduit and Cable Co. v. Federal Trade Commission, 168 F. 2d 175 (7th Cir. 1948).

[35] Federal Trade Commission, Notice to the Staff: In Re: Commission Policy Toward Geographic Pricing Practices (October 12, 1948) (as cited in *Report of the Attorney General's Committee to Study the Antitrust Laws.* May 31, 1955, p. 38).

necessary to a proper functioning of the market. The Courts, if not the Commission, appear to have become at least implicitly aware of this shortly after the *Cement* and *Rigid Conduit* cases.

MORE RECENT CASES

Pevely Dairy Co. v. U.S.[36] probably has the least complicated economic facts of any case of conscious parallelism to reach the courts. Two dairy companies in St. Louis, Pevely and the St. Louis Dairy Co., had nearly two thirds of the market and charged identical prices. When one changed its prices the other followed within forty-eight hours. No direct evidence of agreement could be adduced though it was discovered that prior to a Grand Jury investigation in 1942 officials of the two companies had informed one another of decisions to change prices. The price paid by each for fluid milk was the same and was controlled by federal government regulations. Each bargained with the same union and paid identical wage scales. The trial court found a conspiracy to fix prices in violation of the Sherman Act. Accepting the same facts, the Circuit Court was satisfied that there was a reasonable hypothesis consistent with innocence and, since this was a criminal case, reversed the lower court. The Circuit Court concluded:

> The milk as handled by appellants was a standardized product. Its cost items being substantially identical for both appellants, uniformity in price would result from economic forces . . . We are clear that mere uniformity of prices in the sale of a standardized commodity is not in itself evidence of a violation of the Sherman Act.[37]

This illustrates the legal dilemma — not unrelated to the economic problem, competition vs. monopoly — of deciding in such cases whether there is or is not an agreement. The parallelism in the *Pevely* case was nearly complete. It un-

[36] 178 F. 2d 363 (8th Cir. 1949), certiorari denied 339 U.S. 942.
[37] *Ibid.*, pp. 368–369.

doubtedly extended far beyond pricing matters to such things as frequency of delivery, credit terms, the provision of cooling equipment to wholesale accounts, etc. But it did not extend, apparently, to tactics which affected significantly the ability of smaller dairies to keep their one third of the market. That is, there was nothing predatory about the parallel behavior. Still, the Federal Trade Commission's view is undeniable — there was surely an implicit agreement between Pevely and the St. Louis Dairy Co., and the agreement could easily have included some of the smaller firms as well.

It is interesting to note that the Circuit Court turned to an alternative hypothesis — economic forces — to explain the uniformity in prices. The Court, aided by the expert testimony of economists, reasoned that since costs were similar, prices were uniform because of "natural" factors, not because of agreement. The theory of interfirm organization would view the cost factors as important in establishing homogeneous value systems and suggest not that the price uniformity was the result of competition but the result of the little rivalry that tends to occur in such situations. The difference is important for, given the homogeneity of the product, price differences could not exist long without the firm with the higher price loosing its market share. Differences in costs would not negate this market fact but, because cost differences would produce heterogeneity in the values of the firms, they would make it more difficult to suppress rivalry. One firm would always want a higher price than the other — and if the cost differences were great enough, one or the other would be constantly tempted to stray from whatever implicit agreement had been reached.

The *Pevely* case illustrates that oligopolistic market behavior is a blend of group motivated and individually motivated behavior. Questioning whether the parallelism is the result of agreement or "other hypotheses" is tantamount to asking whether tepid water is hot or cold. It really is a little of both. Whether it is *too* hot or *too* cold depends entirely on what one expects to use the water for.

The case also illustrates the importance to good market performance of the fringe of smaller firms with which the market leaders must contend. Their presence tends to make the continuous suppression of rivalry more difficult for firms such as Pevely and the St. Louis Dairy. This is partly because their presence means simply a larger number of firms. But of perhaps greater importance is the fact that the smaller firms are not likely to have the same values as the larger ones. If, for example, the latter tacitly agreed to increase prices, some smaller firm, dissatisfied with its market share, might be tempted to use the occasion to keep its prices down and thus increase its sales relative to the others. The Circuit Court gave no hint that it was the absence of predatory or other unreasonable behavior that led to its decision. Yet implicitly this seems to have been important.

The Supreme Court denied certiorari in *Pevely* and in a subsequent case, *Milgram v. Loews, Inc.*[38] In the latter, eight motion picture distributors had refused to supply first-run films to an independent drive-in theatre even though the theatre offered higher than prevailing rentals. The court stated:

> . . . It is clear that the reasons advanced by the distributors were not reasons peculiarly applicable to the Boulevard Drive-In or to Allentown, but were, with a few exceptions, applicable to all drive-in theatres. The district court properly concluded that the district managers were putting into effect in Allentown a general program adopted and adhered to by the directing heads of each distributor to relegate drive-ins to second run status. This uniformity in policy forms the basis of an inference of joint action. This does not mean, however, that in every case mere consciously parallel business practices are sufficient evidence, in themselves, from which a court may infer concerted action. Here we add that each distributor refuses to license features on first run to a drive-in even if a higher rental is offered. Each distributor has thus acted

[38] 192 F. 2d 579 (3rd Cir. 1951), certiorari denied 343 U.S. 929.

in apparent contradiction to its own self-interest. This strengthens considerably the inference of conspiracy, for the conduct of the distributors is, in the absence of a valid explanation, inconsistent with decisions independently arrived at.[39]

Judicially, then, the "economic forces" in the *Pevely* case constituted a reasonable alternative hypothesis to agreement while in the *Milgram* case, since it appeared that decisions were not "independently arrived at," there was no reasonable alternative explanation. Actually, in both cases, it is clear that the firms were members of small groups and that to an appreciable degree the notion of unilateral, independent action is meaningless. In a group context it was not a contradiction of self-interest for the distributors of films to deny first-run status to drive-ins, even at higher than normal rentals, for the distributors themselves had interests in the existing downtown, first-run theatres which would be adversely affected should the popularity of drive-ins increase. Again, implicitly at least, it appears that it was the unreasonableness of the systematic stifling of the competition from drive-ins, not really the lack of independent decision-making, that led the court to its decision.

The *C-O-Two* case[40] continues this trend. Four manufacturers of fire extinguishers had uniform prices, identical extinguishers except for their labels, licensing agreements with distributors which contained minimum price provisions, a history of policing dealers to assure that these provisions were adhered to, and a record of submitting identical bids to public agencies.[41] The Circuit Court distinguished the case from *Pevely*, where economic forces were said to have resulted in the uniformity, by saying:

[The] question is not whether identical prices throughout the industry *in and of itself* establishes a conspiracy. We would be de-

[39] *Ibid.*, p. 583.

[40] C-O-Two Fire Equipment Co. v. U.S., 197 F. 2d 489 (9th Cir. 1952), certiorari denied 344 U.S. 892.

[41] *Ibid.*, p. 497.

ciding the unnecessary to answer that question. Here, however, we have in addition to price uniformity, the other so-called plus factors . . . They include a background of illegal licensing agreements containing minimum price maintenance provisions, an artificial standardization of product, a raising of prices at a time when a surplus existed in the industry, and a policing of dealers to effectuate the maintenance of minimum price provisions in accordance with price lists published and distributed by corporate defendants, including C-O-Two. Other facts which convinced the trial court, beyond a reasonable doubt, that the conspiracy did in fact exist . . . were the use of a delivered price system . . . and the submitting of identical bids to public agencies. We think that the facts are not only consistent with the guilt of appellants, but also inconsistent with any other reasonable hypothesis.[42]

The real thing which distinguished *Pevely* and *C-O-Two* was not that there was no agreement in the one and agreement in the other. There was tacit agreement, at least, to charge identical prices in both markets. The fact is that in *Pevely* the agreement had not resulted in abuse and injury to the public and that there was no apparent way to increase competition without causing a destructive price war. On the other hand, the agreement in *C-O-Two* went beyond the bounds of reasonableness. It extended to practices unnecessary to prevent market chaos. More competition would have inured to the public benefit. The agreement and the market organization were too strong and too comprehensive to allow for adequate competition.

The Supreme Court adopted the same approach of searching for agreement rather than testing for reasonableness in *Theatre Enterprises, Inc. v. Paramount Film Distributing Corp.*[43] A new theatre in a suburban shopping center charged that nine film distributing corporations had uniformly refused to grant it first-run status in preference for eight established downtown theatres, three of which were owned by the distributors. The trial court, the Circuit Court and the Supreme

[42] *Ibid.*
[43] 346 U.S. 537 (1954).

Court concluded that the distributors had adequate business reasons for their conduct — first-run status was "economically unfeasible" because of the competition of the new theatre with others, the inadequate drawing area of the new theatre etc. Then the Supreme Court held:

The crucial question is whether respondents' conduct toward petitioner stemmed from independent decision or from an agreement, tacit or express. To be sure, business behavior is admissible circumstantial evidence from which the fact finder may infer agreement . . . But this Court has never held that proof of parallel business behavior conclusively establishes agreement or, phrased differently, that such behavior itself constitutes a Sherman Act offense. Circumstantial evidence of consciously parallel behavior may have made heavy inroads into the traditional judicial attitude toward conspiracy; but 'conscious parallelism' has not yet read conspiracy out of the Sherman Act entirely.[44]

This marked a turn in the Courts' attitude since the *Cement Institute* case. It is probable that each distributor was quite confident of the action the others would take on the request. In this sense, "concerted action was contemplated" and the distributors "adhered and participated in the scheme" — enough to warrant a finding of combination in 1948.

The *Morton Salt* case[45] recognized the inevitability of mutual interdependence. Three companies — Morton, Royal Crystal Salt Co., a wholly owned subsidiary of Morton, and a relatively new firm, Deseret Salt Co. — supplied almost all the salt for feeding livestock in the intermountain sale market bounded by Colorado, Nevada, Oregon and Washington. Their prices were the same and "there was a completely free exchange of pricing information" among the firms. "Any changes which were of interest to the other salt producers were communicated immediately." [46] Even with these "plus

[44] *Ibid.*, pp. 540–541.

[45] Morton Salt Company v. U.S., 235 F. 2d 573 (10th Cir. 1956).

[46] *Ibid.*, p. 575. There was also a record of "discussion regarding prices," uniform handling of cash discounts and several other matters.

factors," however, there was no direct evidence of an express agreement. In affirming the conviction, the Circuit Court said:

> . . . The intermountain market in salt is served by only a few suppliers, an oligopoly in economic terms, and the product is a standardized one for which there is a relatively stable, inelastic demand. In such a situation it is almost inevitable that the pricing policies of one company will be influenced and to some extent dictated by knowledge of probable countervailing action by its competitors. And this perhaps detracts from the weight we should give to parallel pricing. But the presence of only a few friendly sellers and the stable demand for the product present a great opportunity and temptation to combine to maintain prices at an artificially high level profitable to all.[47]

It appears that the practice of directly and immediately communicating with one another was an important factor in holding for a violation in the *Morton* case. It must be noted, however, that less direct communication would not likely have changed the competitiveness of the market so long as it is assumed that the communication was solely to *inform* the other firms and was not a broad forum for the joint resolution of prices.[48] That is, the notification by any one of the firms to its customers that it was changing its prices would have been practically as rapid and effective communication to the others as a telephone call. What customer notification lacks and the telephone call affords is the opportunity for the receiver of the message to give his reactions and to suggest a different course of action. If this occurred it was not in evidence, for this type of two-way communication would have taken the case out of the area of conscious parallelism and placed it squarely into the overt price-fixing category.

Whether the behavior amounted to direct price fixing or only conscious parallelism, the Court was correct in pointing out that the market presented temptations for high profits.

[47] *Ibid.*, p. 577.

[48] See the discussion of this point in the decision for *Morton Salt* case, pp. 576–577.

So long as the virtual duopoly remained, however, there was little to be done about it. It is both unrealistic and futile to expect that the managers of firms in markets such as this will ignore one another and initiate aggressive price competition. This would not constitute free and independent competition; it would constitute stupidity and irresponsible management. If the structure of the market cannot or will not be altered, conscious parallelism will be a fact of life.

The difficulties involved in inferring guilt from parallel behavior have seldom been more apparent than in the more recent *Lilly* case.[49] When the experiments of Dr. Jonas Salk appeared successful, the National Foundation for Infantile Paralysis invited eleven manufacturers of biologicals to a meeting. Six of the companies[50] entered into contracts with the Foundation in July and August, 1954, and about a year later — after tests had demonstrated the effectiveness and safety of the vaccine — the Department of Health, Education and Welfare called further meetings to establish a system of voluntary allocation. Later in 1955 the Poliomyelitis Vaccination Assistance Act was passed and voluntary allocation through the Foundation was terminated. Under the Act, licensed companies submitted bids to governmental authorities and distributed vaccine through their own sales and distribution systems.

Eli Lilly & Co. announced a price, after discounts, of $7.13 per 9 cc. vial on March 3, 1955. This was prior to the test report by the Foundation and before HEW had become involved through the Polio Assistance Act. It is clear that among the several companies there had been many rumors,

[49] U.S. v. Eli Lilly & Co., Crim. no. 173–58, D.N.J. (1959). For a more detailed analysis of the case, see Almarin Phillips and George R. Hall, "The Salk Vaccine Case: Parallelism, Conspiracy and Other Hypotheses," *Virginia Law Review* (May 1960). This section draws heavily on this source.

[50] Eli Lilly & Co., Allied Laboratories, Inc., American Home Products Corporation, Merck & Co., Parke, Davis & Co. and Cutter Laboratories. The latter withdrew from production and was not indicted.

much speculation and various conflicting reports on what prices would be. Other companies followed with virtually identical prices, though their announcements spread over a period of some nine months. Also, though the net prices of the companies were the same, the discount systems used in arriving at the net prices were not at this time alike.

Lilly initiated a reduction in price in February, 1956. Within three weeks, the others had announced a similar reduction. Four months later Parke, Davis dropped its price and all the rest followed within one week. This price held for more than a year and then in April, 1957, Merck Sharp and Dohme cut its price to $5.13 per 9 cc. vial. Again, the others reduced to the same level in less than three weeks. By the end of 1957, several of the companies were submitting isolated bids to various state agencies at even lower prices and the practice of announced and generally adhered to prices seems to have disappeared.

The indictment charged that beginning "about the first six months of 1955 . . . and continuing thereafter up to and including December 31, 1957, the defendants . . . engaged in an unlawful combination and conspiracy in restraint of trade." [51] The offense "consisted of a continuing agreement, understanding, plan and concert of action" to "submit uniform price quotations," "adopt uniform and noncompetitive terms and conditions for sales" and "adopt uniform and noncompetitive methods" for pricing on sales to public authorities.[52]

The Government charged that the uniform prices "were not inevitable," did not result from individual decisions and could only have resulted from agreement. In addition, the government presented evidence to show that the defendants sometimes knew of one another's price changes before they were announced; that their discount systems became uniform for the vaccine during the period covered by the indictment;

[51] Indictment, *U.S. v. Eli Lilly & Co.*, p. 5.
[52] *Ibid.*, pp. 5–6.

that there was ample opportunity and a "proclivity" for the defendants to discuss prices at various meetings within the Foundation and HEW; that the pricing procedures within the companies did not follow standard company practices; that the price changes were not in accord with changes in supply and demand and several other similar points.

Following the presentation of the Government's case, the defendants moved for acquittal. The court, dealing individually with each of the charges and each of the companies, decided that there was a reasonable alternative hypothesis for each defendant which was consistent with innocence. The price uniformity, it held, was primarily due to "most favored nation" clauses in the contracts — clauses which were "the invention . . . of the Government." Lilly's pricing was "based on many factors, including manufacturing costs, business risks, and a consideration of the price which the traffic would bear"; the change in its customary distribution setup was because "the sale of polio vaccine did not necessitate the use of the retail outlet" as other Lilly products did; the change in its discount structure resulted from a "survey of the trade," etc. Pitman-Moore, the division handling the vaccine for Allied Laboratories, followed the distribution practices of the others "consciously, but independently." Merck Sharp and Dohme found out about the "customs and policies then prevailing among the other producers" through meetings with officials of HEW. And so the alternative hypotheses go. Thus, contrary to the *C-O-Two* and *Morton* cases, the court determined that there was "no bridge over the gap from fact to inference." [53]

The facts of the *Lilly* case are interesting when viewed in terms of the theory of interfirm organization. The number of sellers was small and this alone, of course, would tend to keep rivalry at a minimum. In addition, Lilly's production was

[53] The quotations are from the opinion of Judge Forman, *U.S. v. Eli Lilly & Co.*

nearly four times that of the next largest firm, suggesting that Lilly may have had some power influence. Similarly, the product itself was homogeneous. But, juxtaposed with these factors which tend to reduce rivalry are several others which work in the opposite direction. First, aside from the product homogeneity, the firms were quite different. They had histories of producing differing types of biologicals and selling them through different marketing channels to different end users. The novelty of the product, the persistence of production difficulties and the inability of anyone, including Mrs. Oveta C. Hobby, the Secretary of Health, Education and Welfare, to forecast the demand created great uncertainty. Widely fluctuating inventories attest to these difficulties and add credence to the idea that the group of firms was not nearly as well organized as the groups encountered in many other conscious parallelism cases. In fact, the behavior of prices — falling rather erratically over the period and at the end losing even their equality with one another — is consistent with the hypothesis that this was a new and very inefficiently organized group. Each firm may have desired more concerted action, but that any could act with reasonable confidence concerning the behavior of the others seems improbable.

CONCLUDING REMARKS

The Comparison of the *Lilly, C-O-Two* and *Morton* cases provides a basis for final observations on conscious parallelism and the relevant public policy. Viewed in one way, it was quite correct to distinguish the *Lilly* case from *C-O-Two* and *Morton.* The licensing agreements, artificial product standardization and policing of dealers in the *C-O-Two* case and the free exchange of pricing information in the *Morton* case go beyond anything found in *Lilly*. Such plus factors do help "bridge the gap" from the fact of parallelism to an inference that the firms had jointly acted to reduce rivalry beyond reasonable limits.

Viewed in another way — the way the Government would have had it — the distinction between the *Lilly* case and *C-O-Two* and *Morton* is not great. There were in the former ample opportunities for the discussion of prices and, although no overt agreement could be proved, such opportunities when coupled with announcements prior to any price change are not radically different in economic effects from the free exchange of information in *Morton*. It can be as easily argued that the pricing decisions were made independently as it can be contended that they were made conspiratorially in any of these cases. But the arguments are almost purely semantic since in each the pricing decisions were undoubtedly a blend of group and individual decision-making.

Similarly, the defendant firms in all three cases could cite reasons for their actions in terms of internal business policy or, at least, nonconspiratorial factors. In *Morton*, for example, one of the defendants was a new firm which had but recently entered the market. It knew that one of the larger, older firms would match any price cuts and must have been aware that it could not sell salt if it attempted to charge a higher price than its rivals. Its decision against having a price policy different from the other firms because it "would cause a major shift in business" is as understandable as an internally reached decision as it is as a part of a conspiracy. In *C-O-Two*, the effects of expired patents and the need to receive the approval of the Underwriters' Laboratories could be cited as nonconspiratorial reasons for the "artificial" product homogeneity. Thus it can be argued that in these cases, as in the *Lilly* case, there were hypotheses other than conspiracy to explain the behavior of the companies.

The comparison of these three cases is not unique. Similar points could be made about others. There are almost always hypotheses other than that of conspiracy in parallelism cases. Even worse, neither the hypothesis of conspiracy nor its alternatives are capable of being proved. Suppose, to take an extreme example, a businessman is informed after the fact that a group of his competitors have formally agreed to change their prices. After receiving the information, the prices of his firm are changed at his direction to coincide with the admittedly conspiratorial prices of the others. He contends that this was an independent, internal decision to parallel consciously their behavior. The government claims he joined the conspiracy.[54] It is literally impossible to prove or disprove either hypothesis and, in addition, so far as economic consequences are concerned, both are immaterial!

The important questions in conscious parallelism cases do not concern whether the firms involved have reached an "agreement" or whether they have "communicated" with respect to price and other matters of rivalry. Because of the smallness of the group of firms in simple oligopolistic markets, the conclusion is certain (if an obvious price war is not in existence) that the firms have — in a behavioral sense — communicated and, to a degree, agreed on certain aspects of conduct. Rivalry is bound to be limited within the group and behavior is directed and tempered by their informal interfirm organization. Their agreement, while varying in subject matter, duration and effectiveness, may be as complete as that reached through the use of explicit and overt communication and a formal organization in markets in which firms are many. The important questions, then, relate to the effectiveness of the organization in restraining rivalry and to the probable impact such restraint has on market performance.

[54] This illustration was adapted from an argument in the Brief for Appellant, *Pittsburgh Plate Glass Co. v. U.S.,* (4th Cir. 1958), 360 U.S. 395 (1959).

CHAPTER IV

EXEMPTED INDUSTRIES: SANCTIONED ORGANIZATIONAL FORMALITY

INTRODUCTION

The theory presented in Chapter II indicates that in the absence of a formal interfirm organization a high degree of rivalry tends to develop in markets characterized by large numbers of sellers with heterogeneous value systems, especially if these sellers are confronted with powerful buyers or suppliers. The present chapter notes the frequency with which such markets have been accorded some sort of exemption from the antitrust laws. Competitive policy in this area, it appears, often consists of government action establishing or encouraging the establishment of organizations which are prohibited in other markets. The thesis is that the nature of rivalry in large-number, complexly interdependent markets is a primary — if not *the* primary — reason for this policy. The subject will be treated by surveying exemptions generally and then looking in more detail at two particular industries — milk production and distribution and labor.

THE SCOPE OF EXEMPTIONS FROM THE ANTITRUST LAWS

The extent of exemptions from the antitrust laws or, more generally, of policies which in one way or another tend to discourage rather than to encourage rivalry among sellers is seldom overstated. The laws which create such policies appear in many forms and at all levels of government. Their inclusiveness is at first rather shocking. Public utility regulation of the so-called "natural monopolies," it is easy to conclude, is but a small part of the total market economy in which, judging by wisdom of the legislators, rivalry requires tempering.

At the federal level, labor unions, agricultural, horticultural and fishing co-operatives have been exempted from the Sherman Act. Co-operative agricultural marketing associations may legally perform certain information services which are denied other trade associations and marketing agreements made with the Secretary of Agriculture effect for some agricultural commodities regulated minimum prices. Rivalry among retail establishments — especially drug and jewelry stores and appliance dealers — is curtailed because of state fair-trade laws and the sanctioning of them by the Miller-Tydings and the McGuire Acts. Export trade associations derive exemption through the Webb Export Trade Act. In addition, firms under the regulations of the Federal Maritime Board, the Interstate Commerce Commission, Civil Aeronautics Board and Federal Communications Commission may under certain conditions receive immunities from the usual application of the antitrust laws.

It was federal policy which in the Great Depression virtually suspended antitrust action through the National Industrial Recovery Act. After the latter was declared unconstitutional, the suspensions were effectively continued by special legislation for some industries, notably coal and oil.

Policies at the state and local level which tend to reduce rivalry probably have more influence when viewed in the aggregate than all the federal policies combined. Fair-trade laws, minimum mark-up laws and prohibitions against selling below cost are well-known illustrations. Often state agencies fix actual or minimum prices, not only for milk, but also for many other trades and usually in the guise of somehow protecting consumers from deleterious, harmful or fraudulantly vended merchandise and services. On similar grounds — and not always without justification other than the economic interests of those in the fields — occupational licensing by states extends in many directions. In 1952, for example, barbers required licenses in forty-six states; beauticians, forty-five states; and chiropractors, forty-four states. Real estate brokers and salesmen, funeral directors, practical nurses, surveyors and insurance brokers, agents and solicitors were licensed in more than half of the states. Seven states licensed watchmakers. Some occupations — attorneys, architects, accountants, dentists, engineers, embalmers, pharmacists, physicians, teachers, veterinarians and others — were licensed by all states. In California, the Department of Professional and Vocational Standards had twenty-one boards attached to it and there were, in addition, five licensing agencies elsewhere in the government.[1]

With but few exceptions, there are marked similarities in the structural characteristics of the industries and occupations which, in one form or another and in varying degrees, have been encouraged to develop more formal interfirm organizations. The number of producers in practically every case — labor, agricultural products, retail establishments, coal, crude petroleum, attorneys, beauticians, pharmacists, etc. — is large. This tends to be true even when the relevant markets are viewed as the immediate locale of particular groups of sellers. The large number of sellers and the fact that these markets are often of the second type of large-number, complex interdependence — in which most sellers are unaware of the impact of their behavior on others in the market and vice versa — make private and informal organization of the market difficult. The accumulation of adequate power to govern the behavior of large numbers of individuals may be impossible without some aid or sanctioning from public authority.

[1] These data are from a report by the Council of State Governments to the Governors' Conference of 1952 and are reported in *State Government*, LII (1952), 275–280.

The export trades and some of the industries regulated by federal agencies may be exceptions to the general tendency for exemptions to be granted in markets with large numbers of sellers. The rationale for the export exemption, however, was from its inception the power of competing organizations abroad so that, assuming without investigation the accuracy of this rationale, there is no exception to the general theory of interfirm organization. In the regulated industries, the complexity of interdependence may arise as much from other market characteristics as from the sheer number of sellers.

The fair-trade law exemptions are a particularly interesting illustration of the impact of large numbers of sellers on rivalry and of the difficulties of privately reducing the degree of rivalry. The effect of the laws is to remove pricing decisions from the many retailers of trade-marked products, leaving such decisions to the relatively few manufacturers. At the manufacturing level, sellers may be small enough in number that consciously parallel behavior restrains rivalry as adequately as overt conspiracy among dealers. The frequent difficulty encountered by manufacturers in enforcing fair-trade prices and the recent rise of discount houses are testimony to the tendencies for collusion to breakdown when the number of sellers is large and when price control is not coupled with entry preventative measures.

The exempted industries are similar in other respects, too. Without the central selling organization which the exemptions frequently permit, labor, agricultural products and the rest are typically sold in markets in which no single seller has adequate power to lead the group. Even if in a local market — in, say, the sale of milk to a local dairy — a particular producer is large enough or persuasive enough to lead his close rivals, his power is inadequate to affect for long total market behavior because of the interdependence between his locale and others. Moreover, without government sanctioning, the probability is small that large numbers of individual sellers can effectively combine to create a position for leadership. Again, these generalizations may be less true of the markets under federal regulatory agencies than of the others.

Both the large numbers of sellers and the lack of power leadership reflect another basic condition of these industries. In labor markets, mergers and consolidations of sellers are physically impossible. Because of the nature of the source of the service being sold, only "loose combinations" of sellers can be formed. To a lesser degree, the same is true of other industries. Farms cannot easily be combined to create an agricultural market structure similar to that in, say, the steel industry. The location and productivity of soil resources, on the one hand, and the location and demands of purchasers, on the other, are not conducive to the degree of consolidation found elsewhere in the economy. These, in addition to probable internal diseconomies connected with substantial increases in the size of plant and firm, preclude the growth of heavily concentrated markets even if market performance is such that many sellers are poorly rewarded for long periods of time. Fishing, coal mining, retailing and most of the service occupations have similar, though perhaps less severe, limitations on the extent to which the scale of individual sellers' operations can be increased. The large number and the lack of skewed power distribution, that is, are largely immutable in any short period of time regardless of the performance results of the markets.

It is not universally true that those who buy from or sell to the exempted industries are powerful enough to disorganize sellers. But there is some tendency for the formality of the organization sanctioned by the exempting legislation to be greater in instances in which such external pressures do exist. The immunities given labor unions and agricultural co-operatives, for example, are so complete that the legislative intent can hardly be regarded as anything other than completely to eliminate price rivalry within the organizations so long as the activities of the organizations are restricted to the primary markets in which the organizations sell. Again, federal milk marketing orders and regulations by state milk commissions fix minimum prices. In these and in several other industries in which similar conditions apply, those who buy from or sell to the affected industries would have substantial power to increase rivalry in the absence of the sanctioned formality.

In markets such as those faced by physicians, lawyers, accountants, etc., buyers have little organized power. The only tendency toward rivalry is that coming from within the group. And in these markets, state licensing is hardly more than minimal control over entry — frequently exercised by those to whom licenses have been granted — and a rather open invitation to those in the occupation to regulate themselves in other respects, including pricing. Considering the lack of organized and even informed buyers and the likelihood that the education and examinations given prior to licensing tend to create rather identical value systems among those in the occupation, however, it is not difficult to see that rivalry may be more restricted in these trades than in others in which the organization is more obviously formal.

Differences in value systems also tend to be great in some of the exempted industries. Crude petroleum production, farming and many branches of retailing, for example, have some large corporate firms in rivalry with small, one-man enterprises. The same condition exists in some nonexempted industries, though rivalry in them is often severe. The differences in values among the firms are pronounced, especially if the size differences imply differing technologies and costs and if the larger firms are aware of interdependence while the smaller firms are not. One obvious illustration of such differences is found in the application of the Robinson-Patman Act. The latter — which many regard as virtually an exemption statute — is a means of assuring through public administration that the differences in values between large, chain retailers and smaller independents does not erupt in rivalry to the detriment of the latter. The law, in fact, seems at times to force the value systems of the smaller firms on the larger.

In the next two sections, the hypothesis that the nature of the rivalry developing from particular structural characteristics is the primary reason for exemptions will be examined further. It is not premature to note, however, that whatever the degree of rivalry tending to exist without the sanctioning of formal interfirm organizations, it is quite possible that the exemptions given by public authority may create quite the reverse situation. Rivalry, that is, may be too restricted if the exemption given is unqualified. This is undoubtedly true of many surveyed so briefly in the past few pages.

RIVALRY IN MILK PRODUCTION AND DISTRIBUTION

The milk industry seems to have been faced with no peculiar problems of rivalry until the second half of the nineteenth century. Until then, milk production — like other agricultural activities — was in most instances carried on either by the consumer himself or, in large towns, by farmers who both produced and distributed milk directly to consumers. The growth of cities changed this however. Metropolitan areas discouraged producer-distributors and farmers sold more and more milk in bulk to distributors who, in turn, peddled door-to-door and to stores. Containers were usually those of the customers and were dipped into tank wagons on the street.

Rail transportation encouraged the milk industry and made it possible for a single distributor to obtain milk from what seemed at the time very distant locations. The expense of transportation and poor refrigeration caused "milksheds" around the major population centers and these, by present day comparisons, were really quite small. As late as 1916, the Chicago market obtained nearly all of its 265,000 gallons of milk per day from points less than one-hundred miles from the city.[2]

Milk producers supplying the larger cities discovered early that the distributors were in an advantageous bargaining position. And producers were quick in attempting to rectify their weakness through associated efforts. The 1883 "milk strike" by farmers in Orange County, New York, against New York City distributors is fairly well-known. But, despite the fact that the association which brought about the strike comprised eight hundred farmers and was successful in gaining an immediate increase in price, it was soon recognized that in the New York milkshed a larger, more inclusive and more powerful producers' group was necessary if the distributors' powers were effectively to be offset. Ten thousand producers were selling to one hundred dealers and the buying policies of the latter were themselves organized. Gradually, local producers associations became affiliated with one another and the Five States Milk Producers' Association was formed in 1898.

It is interesting that parallel events were occurring around other large cities. Boston, Philadelphia, Baltimore, Cleveland, Pittsburgh and Chicago were all supplied by large, formal producers' associations before the turn of the century. But, while the larger cities tended to have these incorporated associations, smaller cities and towns had informal, voluntary associations of producers. In the latter, of course, the milk needs were smaller and the number of producers involved relatively small.

This was the organizational character of the milk industry until the 1920's. Several events of that decade caused significant structural changes in the market and these in turn led to an increase in rivalry which the older associations were incapable of effectively restraining. During the 1920's, technological changes had a large impact. Improved breeding, feed-

[2] Henry E. Erdman, *The Marketing of Whole Milk* (New York, 1921), p. 45. This source provides a detailed account of the industry to 1920.

ing and milking practices increased the milk output per cow, tended to increase the optimal size of milking herds and, hence, to reduce the number of cows and of farms necessary to supply fluid demand. Improved transportation and refrigeration made it possible to ship milk over distances far greater than the traditional milksheds. Increased health and sanitation requirements presented many producer-distributors and smaller distributors with the alternatives of heavy re-equipment expenditures and larger operations or of selling the distributing end of the business to larger firms. The advent of economical motor trucks expanded the most profitable size of delivery routes and the smaller distributors found that the larger companies were progressively assuming larger shares of the market. And all of these happened in the market for a product which had low price and income elasticities of demand. The total market, that is, was growing rather slowly.[3]

Distributors had organized to deal with producers and large local companies had emerged in the city markets before 1920. None, however, was a regional or national concern. The National Dairy Products Corporation was formed in 1923. It acquired what were already large distributors in several of the nation's larger cities and increased its sales from less than $14 million in 1923 to over $300 million in 1930.[4] The Borden Company, which suffered sales losses in the early 1920's, adopted somewhat the same acquisition policy later and tripled its sales between 1920 and 1930. The Beatrice Creamery Company — now Beatrice Foods Company — and Fairmont Creamery Company had somewhat less dramatic and more regionally restricted patterns of growth.

That the national and regional distributors had the effect

[3] For statistical details and an excellent discussion, see "Changes in the Dairy Industry, 1920–50," a statement prepared by the Bureau of Agricultural Economics, U.S. Department of Agriculture, Appendix A, *Utilization of Farm Crops, Milk and Dairy Products,* Hearings before a Subcommittee of the Committee on Agriculture and Forestry, U.S. Senate, 81st Congress (1950).

[4] *Ibid.,* p. 1992.

of reducing rivalry at the distributor level is less obvious than at first appears. Concentration in the large city markets was pronounced prior to their formation and the new national concerns often did little more than change the name and improve the operations of a major distributor in each city. Moreover, the interests of the larger companies in expanding sales led them to begin distribution in some cities which, prior to their entrance into the markets, were dominated by local concerns and in which rivalry among distributors was largely nil. The larger firms often forced the established distributors in these cities to adopt more modern and efficient plant and marketing practices and it appears as reasonable to argue that rivalry increased and market performance improved as it is to maintain the contrary.

At the producer level, however, the effects were even greater. The national concerns could purchase milk from outside the historic milksheds. They had both selling and buying offices throughout wide geographic areas. They had both the knowledge and the facilities to purchase fluid milk wherever its price was lowest and to bargain simultaneously with several producers' organizations. The market posture of the large producers' co-operatives was not unlike that of the small, informal producers' associations of several decades previous.

Actually, the position of the co-operatives was not obvious until after 1929. Until then, despite the rapid growth in the buying power of distributors after 1923 or 1924, milk producers — almost alone among American farmers — were not adversely affected. Milk prices varied little between 1921 and 1929. Gross income of dairy farmers was rising as production rose with fewer cows but increasing output per cow. The percentage of total production used as fluid milk and cream was steady and both the retail price and the percentage of the retail price received by farmers remained unchanged.

The change after 1929 was abrupt. The average price per hundred-weight for all U.S. milk sold by farmers fell from

$2.53 in 1929 to $1.28 in 1932. Milk sold by farmers in the North Atlantic states declined from $2.87 to $1.45 in the same period and that from the East North Central area, from $2.20 to $1.06. The relative decline in the South Atlantic states was less — from $3.35 to only $2.12 per hundredweight.[5] Despite the decline in per capita disposable income, per capita milk consumption remained at levels slightly above the level of the 1920's but, because of the price decline, gross income from dairy farming in 1932 was only a little more than half the 1929 value.[6] Farmers responded by reversing the trend toward a smaller number of cows on farms and total milk production continued to rise — and to rise more rapidly than sales of fluid milk and cream. The decline in retail milk prices was less pronounced than that of milk from the farm, reducing the share of the retail price received by farmers from 60 per cent in 1929 to 53 per cent in 1932.

It is impossible to discover the precise extent to which distributors and dealers bargained price concessions from associations by shifting or threatening to shift purchases from one group to another. Neither can it be discovered how actively the producers' associations encouraged this by actively soliciting business from new distributors. But that both occurred is indisputable. The associations, faced with growing surpluses of a perishable commodity, must have been anxious to dispose of it. Moreover, the "classified" price schemes worked out by the co-operatives during the previous decade increased the incentives of distributors to purchase from other than their usual sources of supply. Intuitively grasping Marshall's principles of derived demand, the co-ops had developed discriminatory prices — a high price for milk used for fluid consumption, where demand was relatively inelastic, and lower prices for milk used for manufactured products, where demand was relatively elastic. During the 1920's, the system operated to cur-

[5] "Changes in the Dairy Industry, 1920–50," p. 2027.
[6] *Ibid.*, pp. 1975, 2034.

tail overproduction. After 1929, however, dealers and distributors increasingly purchased the lower priced "surplus" milk from new sources of supply and used it to fill fluid demand. And the co-operatives, faced with larger, geographically integrated purchasers were not only powerless to prevent it, but probably stimulated it by competing with one another. Their ability to control supply was so weak that neither the production of their members nor, indeed, entry into and exit from membership could be controlled with the view of stabilizing the market.

It was at this point that public policy dictated further reductions in rivalry. The Clayton and Capper-Volstead Acts had been primarily permissive. By their terms, privately organized co-operatives were largely immune from prosecution under the antitrust laws. But permitting private restraints on rivalry and actively restraining rivalry through direct public actions are quite different. The Agricultural Adjustment Acts of 1933 and 1935 and the Agricultural Marketing Agreement Act of 1937 provided for federal milk price supports. These supports depend to a limited extent on purchases of surpluses by the government, but the principal feature is control over the minimum prices paid by dealers and distributors in the regions affected by the regulations. At present, Federal Milk Orders promulgated under the amended legislation of the 1930's set minimum producer prices in about seventy market areas, most of them large metropolitan areas.

Procedures under Federal Orders utilize but are not bound by parity ratios in establishing prices. Too, prices in regions distant from that being regulated are considered through comparisons of alternative combinations of production, transportation and handling costs. The Federal Orders are, nonetheless, protective devices and it is not uncommon for them to be requested by producers when the producers' association which has historically been the major supplier of an area is threatened by a supply of outside milk. Neither is it unusual for the producers to be joined in the request by distributors, for the new supply of milk often finds its way to the market through a new distributor seeking entry to the market or through an older distributor who is attempting a market innovation — the gallon jug, for example. Often the lower retail prices offered by such distributors reflect little other than the lower fluid milk prices paid by them as they purchase surplus milk from other markets. As in the thirties, requests to the Department of Agriculture for Federal Orders are more frequent during depressed periods when proclivities for price cutting among distributors appear. Thus, a combination of circumstances — better refrigeration, more rapid transportation, rising production costs for farms in the immediate environs of large cities and declining agricultural incomes — has been indirectly responsible for the number of Federal Orders more than doubling in the past ten years.

Federal Milk Orders, as contrasted with state milk regulations, tend to facilitate rather than impede the interstate flow of milk so essential to efficient resource usage, especially in supplying large cities. It can be argued, in fact, that Federal Orders, by preventing seasonal sales of distress milk and the concomitant price chaos, have allowed interstate shipments which would otherwise have been prevented by state regulations. But local and state health ordinances may operate to prevent long-distance sources of supply from entering any market and may be by far the most serious impediment to efficient geographic distribution of milk production.[7]

Federally regulated prices are often but not universally lower than prices in adjacent areas protected by state authorities and it is not infrequent that producers' associations can succeed in bargaining for premiums over the Federal price

[7] See *Regulations Affecting the Movement and Merchandising of Milk,* Marketing Research Report No. 98, Agricultural Marketing Service, Department of Agriculture (June, 1955) and J. S. Hillman, J. D. Rowell and V. L. Israelson, *Barriers to the Interstate Movement of Milk and Dairy Products,* Arizona Agricultural Experiment Station Bulletin No. 255.

minimums. While Federal Orders make uniform the prices paid by distributors, they involve no resale price controls. Some minimal restrictions on the freedom of distributors to enter the market area are involved, however, in the provisions necessary to enforce and regulate payments to producers.

It is not difficult to be more critical of the state programs for milk control. Only about a third of the states currently impose such controls and these are located along the Atlantic Coast and in the Far West. The details of state regulations are extremely varied but in general the effects are similar. The outstanding characteristic is the restrictions on the flow of milk into the states from outside. Since the states are unable to control producer prices beyond their boundaries, maintaining producer prices within must be accomplished with something analogous to a tariff wall. In the case of milk, the most frequent means of attaining this end is by assigning specific producers to each distributor and requiring the distributors to pay the assigned producers amounts based on the distributors' sales. This, in effect, prevents even less costly foreign milk from entering except when local milk is available in inadequate quantities to meet fluid consumption demand.

State regulations have also tended to prevent efficient intrastate milk flows by defining production areas for the affected marketing areas as the territories surrounding the markets. This practice allows only those producers in the production area access to the market and prevents less expensive milk in the same state from entering. The obvious lack of economy entailed and the rapidly changing milk supply and demand conditions are forcing the abandonment of such restrictions just as they are encouraging more use of Federal Orders. In Virginia, for example, the entire state was defined as the production area for all Virginia markets in regulations promulgated in 1959. And the northern Virginia market — inextricably intertwined with the District of Columbia — was decontrolled by the state after a Federal Order became effective.

In return for insisting that distributors pay assigned producers stipulated prices, something more than half of the states with milk controls regulate wholesale and retail milk prices. Generalizations about the level of these prices as compared with unregulated prices are difficult to make, but some aspects of the pattern of regulated prices do illustrate a tendency to protect existing distributors and distribution methods. Price differences between glass and paper containers, for example, were used in some states to retard the introduction of the latter and to postpone the time when plants had to be reequipped. Similarly, the introduction of glass gallon jugs has been discouraged by the practice of pricing gallons at the equivalent of four quarts and the shift from home delivery to store purchases of milk has been slowed by maintaining narrow margins between wholesale and retail prices. Some states — notably New York and Virginia — practice restrictive distributor licensing which makes it difficult for new distributors to enter markets. The latter, especially when coupled with requirements that each distributor licensed in a market receive milk from producers assigned to that market, have limited the extent to which national distributing chains and food chains with private-brand milk could erode the market shares of local concerns.

At the producer level, state regulations have allowed smaller than optimum, inefficient farms to continue in operation. While most state statutes require the regulatory agencies to set prices on the basis of production costs, any agency which has attempted to follow such directions has found the task impossible. Dairy production costs are too illusive and varying to offer much of a guide. In practice, prices are adjusted when complaints from producer organizations become numerous and, in fact if not by statutory command, the level of producer prices in the regulated states tend to correspond to prices from alternative sources of supply plus transportation and handling costs.[8] The states, that is, seem to recognize that substantial differences between actual prices and alternative supply prices would topple the politically weak protective wall erected about them.

In all, probably more than three fourths of all fluid milk is subject to either federal or state control. Virtually all of it is subject to health restrictions. And, while it is easy to point out specific harmful effects of particular types of regulations, it does not follow that the general performance of the industry has been extremely poor from either the point of view of the public or of the industry. Over the whole country — even though the price supports are accompanied by only indirect controls over production — the chronic tendency toward milk surpluses has been curbed. The number of cows being milked has increased little while output per cow and cows per farm have increased substantially. Dairy farms are tending to get smaller in number and larger in size. Milk is tending more and more to be shipped greater distances and to follow geographic patterns consistent with improved resource allocation. Dairy practices are constantly improving. Parallel changes are occurring in distribution. Store delivery is becoming relatively more important, home delivery routes are gradually increasing in size and, while there is room for much greater gain, the decreasing number of distributors has caused the elimination of many duplicate routes.[9]

It is possible to argue, of course, that performance would be better with less regulation. To a degree, the argument has much validity. Resale price controls and restrictive distributor licensing, for example, appear to insert public regulations into an area in which they are not needed. But carried to the extreme that no regulation is necessary, the argument that less

[8] See *Regulations Affecting the Movement and Merchandising of Milk*, pp. 87–107.

[9] On this point, see R. G. Bressler, Jr., *City Milk Distribution* (Cambridge, Mass., 1952).

regulation would improve performance is both fallacious and deceptive. The milk *producing* industry is an example par excellence of market situations which require quite formal interfirm organization if rivalry is to be restrained. The number of sellers, the lack of leadership potential by any individual firm, the variety of value systems and the power of buyers all tend to produce so much rivalry that the restraining influence of producer associations and, to a point, government regulations may improve market performance. In addition, the question of regulation cannot be couched in terms of whether there should be regulation, but rather in terms of how much regulation is necessary and who should do the regulating. The removal of state regulations would not mean an end of controls. It would mean instead the encouragement of other kinds of controls. It would impel many small, informal producers' associations to ally themselves with larger, more formal cooperatives or to disband as their members joined the latter. Thus, absent the state controls, private control would tend to increase. It is equally true that the elimination of state controls would speed the use of Federal Milk Orders. But in either case, the result is not an end of control but only the substitution of one kind for the other and, in this illustration, probably a substitution that would be beneficial so long as the power of the private associations is subject to basic antitrust laws.

RIVALRY AND THE ORGANIZATION OF LABOR

It is tempting but probably unnecessary to dwell at length on the application of the theory of interfirm organization to labor markets.[10] The temptation arises from the ease with which labor market practices and public policy toward unions can be discussed in the context of the theory. The lack of necessity is in large measure because it is nearly universally

[10] Since this was written, an article applying the theory of interfirm organization has appeared. See James R. Schlesinger, "Market Realism versus Logical Absolutes in Labor Reform," *Virginia Law Review,* 48:58 (1962).

recognized — among specialists in labor economics, general economists, politicians and the public — that organization among sellers of labor is required for good market performance. The day is long past, it seems, when prevailing economic and legal doctrines concluded that combinations of workers were necessarily conspiracies in restraint of trade and contrary to the common good. Still, there is a growing view that under some circumstances union power may be coupled with labor market and product market practices which do result in such a lack of rivalry that public intervention to reduce power or suppress particular types of behavior is in order.

Another reason why it is unnecessary to treat labor organization in detail is the extent to which such treatment would duplicate that accorded to milk markets. Here is a prime example of the truth of Taussig's observation that there are close analogies between some product markets and labor markets. Both milk and labor markets typically have large numbers of sellers; both are characterized by an absence of market leadership if individual sellers remain unorganized; in both, heterogeneous value systems tend to exist among sellers; the relevant number of buyers tends in each case to be small and tacit or formal organization among buyers has historically been commonplace.

The analogies, in fact, go beyond these primary structural similarities. The nature of both products — milk and labor services — cause peculiar difficulties when the available supply exceeds effective demand. Neither can be readily carried in inventory,[11] the price elasticity of market demand for each is low, and in both short-run supply may be quite inelastic or,

[11] I have purposely avoided referring to labor as a perishable product. Milk, of course, is perishable in the meaningful sense that a stock of it loses utility with age. Labor, however, is not perishable. As with other services, its production necessarily coincides with its use. An unused accumulation is impossible. Unemployed humans are theoretically more analogous to unemployed machines than to perishable products.

even worse, actually negatively inclined over some ranges. Both milk and labor services are supplied by an economic unit — the family — with objectives, values and behavior which are institutionally quite different from the conventional business firm. To the extent that this unit is like a firm, the ratio of fixed costs to costs variable with short-run changes in output is remarkably high. And in modern times, sellers of both milk and labor cluster in or about large cities. Milk cannot economically be transported great distances from the farm; labor services cannot economically be sold at great distances from the household. Neither farms nor households demonstrate much geographic mobility.

Historically, too, there are similarities in the efforts of laborers and milk producers to organize to bargain collectively. One can find, for example, aspects in the history of producers' associations which are counterparts of the three well-known theories of the labor movement. Perlman's theory,[12] emphasizing the recognition on the part of labor that job opportunities are limited, that laborers will not or cannot shift to other means of livelihood and that unions seek to control or "own" the job, would, if applied to milk farmers, stress the price inelasticity of demand for milk, the occupational immobility of farmers and the efforts of producers to control milk markets and eliminate outside sources of supply through co-operation, united bargaining and forward vertical integration. The theory of Tannenbaum[13] would point instead to the disintegration of the farm as a stable social unit and the loss of social and economic security after mid-nineteenth century as the rise of industry and cities and persistent technological changes severed the farmer from the consumer and caused the breaching of both the economic and political status of the farmer. The Webbs, whose theory is not unlike the more recent and more general theory of countervailing power, might

[12] Selig Perlman, *A Theory of the Labor Movement* (New York, 1928).
[13] Frank Tannenbaum, *A Philosophy of Labor* (New York, 1951).

have found parallels between the rise of the factory system and the rise of the city milk distributor.[14] In both, organized buyers arose between producer and consumer and in both the deterioration of economic conditions led to collective action.

It is not difficult to see, then, that it can be consistently argued that some type of sellers' organization is necessary to good performance in both milk and labor markets. Perhaps it was just such consistency which led to the inclusion of labor and agricultural organizations in the exemptions from the antitrust laws given by Section 6 of the Clayton Act. But even if this were granted, closer examination of the history of sellers' organizations in the respective markets and of the market problems faced in each demonstrates that the organizational problems of labor markets are far more complex than are those of milk markets.

It is not solely because of the great numbers involved that organizing labor markets proved so difficult. Of equal or greater import is the vast heterogeneity of labor — heterogeneity in views concerning the benefits and propriety of organization as well as heterogeneity in skills, strength, sex and market posture relative to employers. The history of successful unions during the nineteenth century is the story of comparatively small, homogeneous craft groups. When the larger, more heterogeneous, less strategically situated groups attempted to gain recognition to bargain collectively, the force they had to muster — against unsympathetic fellowworkers as well as employers — was so great that it is little wonder that events such as the Homestead and Pullman strikes and decisions such as those in *Gompers v. Bucks Stove and Range Company*[15] and *Loewe v. Lawlor*[16] transpired. The wonder is that the social discontent was not greater.

The exemption from the antitrust laws accorded by the

[14] Sidney Webb and Beatrice Webb, *Industrial Democracy* (London, 1926).

[15] 221 U.S. 418 (1911).

[16] 208 U.S. 274 (1908).

Clayton Act did little more than invite the accumulation of private power in unions to clash head on with the enormous power on the other side of the market. So long as the latter remained — as it did despite the anti-injunction provisions of the same Act — the gaining of collective bargaining by the growing group of industrial workers would have required a veritable private army and such threats to persons and property that no court could well constrain its injunctive relief. The approach of the Act — tending generally to encourage union power and to reduce the power of employers — has much to recommend it. And in an age other than that in which the labor provisions were interpreted, judicial definition of the injunctive provisions and of the "lawful" and "legitimate objects" of labor might well have altered the common law in labor's favor. But such was not the case.

To remain viable, an organization must be effective, efficient, or both.[17] By the early twenties, industrial unions were neither and even the craft unions had lost much of their ability to achieve material results. The strange spirit of the times was partially responsible for this, of course. So too were the attitudes of the courts as expressed in *Duplex Printing Press Co. v. Deering*.[18] But of primary importance — as they had been in stimulating the union movement for over a century — were technological changes and the nearly inexplicable refusal of the A.F. of L. to alter its organizational arrangements in the face of changing conditions.[19]

[17] Chester I. Barnard, *The Functions of the Executive* (Cambridge, Mass., 1938). Effectiveness refers to the accomplishment of group goals; efficiency to the accomplishment of the subgoals of its members.

[18] 254 U.S. 443 (1921).

[19] This is a good illustration of an organization which develops goals at variance with those of its members. The old way of doing things seemed more important than the old goals themselves. To a lesser degree, the inflexibility of the A.F. of L. continued in the next decade. See, for example, the interesting account in Herbert Harris, *Labor's Civil War* (New York, 1940), reprinted in E. Wight Bakke and Clark Kerr, *Unions, Management and the Public* (New York, 1948), pp. 63–64, of the organizer who set up 19 locals in one plant "despite the counter-evidence of conveyor-belts."

At the level of the firm and industry, the lack of balance between the market power of employers and that of employees accounted for rather meager increases in real wages and perhaps some feeling of social injustice. This theoretically could have been remedied by giving employee organizations more power or by removing some of the power of employers. At the macroeconomic level, however, the choice between the two methods is not unimportant and, during the twenties, the failure to attempt either approach had rather pronounced effects. In the aggregate, wages account for an important part of personal income and, on the expenditure side, of total demand. There is surely no magic — either ethically or economically — about wage increases precisely commensurate with increases in output per man-hour. Still, the failure to pass on productivity gains in the form of either wage increases or price decreases for several years is likely to undermine the purchasing power base on which prosperous business depends. Thus, because of its major importance in the whole economy, the organizational imbalance of the post-World War I period had ramifications beyond those of market rivalry and good performance in a microsector.[20]

The sudden and drastic reversal in public policy in the following decade is historically not difficult to understand, especially when the crisis environment in which it occurred is considered. The difficulties it has led to — at the microlevel since the resumption of relatively full employment and at the macrolevel since the monetary excesses of World War II financing were absorbed in a growing economy — are becoming more clear and are probably no less severe than those of the 1920's.[21] Much of the problem, it seems, arises from legisla-

[20] Careful reading of this paragraph should serve to distinguish the views expressed from others which suggest that increasing the power on the weaker side of the market is universally the appropriate equilibrating device. While it is necessary to orderly markets, power is not necessarily equilibrating or justifiable. It appears in degrees.

[21] See James R. Schlesinger, "Market Structure, Union Power and Inflation," *Southern Economic Journal* (January 1958).

tive and judicial inability to grant the need for formal, powerful labor organizations and, at the same time, the need to curb that power under some circumstances.

The closed shop issue provides a good illustration of the inability to strike a middle ground. At common law the majority opinion was that the closed shop was not a legitimate union objective — largely because it tended to cause the dismissal of nonunion employees.[22] A minority of courts took a contrary view, arguing that "unity of organization is necessary to make the contest of labor effectual." [23] Depending on the circumstances, either view could be correct. But under the Wagner Act, instead of permitting the closed shop when its effects were good, the minority common law position was adopted without qualification. And under the Taft-Hartley Act, the policy was again reversed to the older, majority view.

The closed shop may have much merit under certain conditions. It is not unusual for both employers and employees to advocate its use.[24] Again, in other circumstances it works much harm to employers and quite possibly to the public at large. Both the Wagner and the Taft-Hartley approaches, then, were bound to encounter enforcement difficulties because of the attempts they embody to take a general stand on a practice which has varying import in actual market situations.[25] The closed shop problem is too complicated to be decided on the basis of a single categorical imperative. The practice does infringe on individual liberties, yet public policy is replete with instances in which freedom — which can never be absolute in a stable, governed society — is compromised in the

[22] See, for example, *Berry v. Brown,* 188 Mass. 353 (1905).

[23] Justice Holmes, in dissent, *Plant v. Woods,* 176 Mass. 492, 505 (1900).

[24] Harold F. Browne, *Studies in Personnel Policy No. 12,* National Industrial Conference Board (1939), reprinted in Bakke and Kerr, *Unions,* pp. 122–123, provides a list of reasons given by employers for favoring closed shop arrangements.

[25] The Taft-Hartley Act has an obvious lack of symmetry in its treatment of the closed shop-union shop-open shop issue. It permits states to choose between the national policy of union shops and a state policy of open shops but refuses to state the choice between closed shops and union shops.

interest of greater security. Similarly, the closed shop problem can hardly be settled by determining that it gives unions the power to restrict supply and monopolistically to enhance wage rates. The very reason for unionism itself is to grant some private group control over labor supply conditions because particular market characteristics demand such control for acceptable market performance. Thus, as both Lester and Mason have pointed out, picking a particular union practice such as the closed shop and condemning it as monopolistic tends "to confuse rather than shed light on, the significant issues." [26]

Industry-wide bargaining presents somewhat the same type of problem. Criticisms of multiple-employer bargaining run from charges that it promotes cartelization and monopoly of employers to the argument that it destroys purchasing power; others find that it tends to reduce strikes and to produce more sensible and farsighted wage patterns.[27] But in any case, a definite limitist rule seems impossible to formulate. The breadth of the bargaining unit is only one of many factors which influence the ability of the union to obtain concessions from employers. And given the ambiguity of the definition of an industry, any rule other than one which would limit a union from bargaining with more than one employer would be imprecise as well as inappropriate to the organizational problems of various labor markets.

Union power may, of course, be abused and result in poor performance at both the micro and macrolevels of the econ-

[26] Richard A. Lester, "Reflections on the Labor Monopoly Issues," *Journal of Political Economy* (December 1947), as quoted by Edward S. Mason, "Labor Monopoly and All That," *Industrial Relations Research Association* (December 1955), reprinted in Walter Galenson and Seymour M. Lipset, *Labor and Trade Unionism* (New York, 1960), pp. 124–125.

[27] John V. Van Sickle, *Industry-wide Collective Bargaining and the Public Interest,* American Enterprise Association (Washington, 1947), and Richard A. Lester and Edward A. Robie, *Wages Under National and Regional Collective Bargaining* (Princeton, 1946), both reprinted in Bakke and Kerr, *Unions.*

omy. But because of the heterogeneity of labor and of labor markets and because the power may arise from truly infinite varieties of union structures and practices, simple uniform rules cannot cope with the public policy issues.

CHAPTER V

UNITED STATES v. ADDYSTON PIPE AND STEEL COMPANY[1]

INTRODUCTION

Viewed nationally, the market structure in the cast-iron pipe industry in the late 1880's came as close to the conditions hypothesized in the theory of perfect competition as one can imagine in a heavy-goods industry. There were a substantial number of sellers and a large number of buyers. There was little if any technical product differentiation. Prices were apparently made independently and no single firm enjoyed a size sufficient to wield the power of an effective market leader. Market knowledge of both prices and raw material costs was quite broad and entry and exit from the market were extraordinarily free. Performance, however, both prior and subsequent to the agreement among the Addyston group to limit price competition, was far from ideal.

The *Addyston* case illustrates the operation of a market in which an older and apparently efficient interfirm organization was upset by the entry of new firms. The latter developed an organization to challenge the older one and, in the process, established patterns of behavior which not only eliminated rivalry internal to the group but also set up an extremely discriminatory pricing system aimed ostensibly at maximizing joint profits. The case demonstrates the difficulty of rationalizing competition through even formal organizations in a particular structural situation and the eventual change in that

[1] 171 U.S. 614 (1899), 85 F. 271 (6th Cir. 1898).

structure when it became apparent that an organization of formality sufficient to keep the existing firms in business was also sufficiently restrictive to constitute a clear violation of the Sherman Act. There is also in the case the suggestion of horizontal rivalry between the two groups of firms — the older ones in the northern part of the country and the Addyston group — which, while it might prevent the charging of exorbitant prices, made more concentration in the industry an attractive means for asserting market leadership.

THE STRUCTURE OF THE MARKET

The suit of 1896 was brought against six firms: Addyston Pipe and Steel Company, of Cincinnati, Ohio; Dennis Long and Company, Louisville, Kentucky; Howard-Harrison Iron Company, Bessemer, Alabama; Anniston Pipe and Foundry Company, Anniston, Alabama; South Pittsburg Pipe Works, South Pittsburg, Tennessee; and Chattanooga Foundry and Pipe Works, Chattanooga, Tennessee. Despite the fact that cast-iron pipe had been in production in quantity for nearly a century, the defendant firms were relatively new entrants. Chattanooga Foundry and Pipe Works was organized in 1881; South Pittsburg, in 1887. Anniston went into operation in 1889 and the Howard-Harrison Iron Company was started in 1888.[2] Save for Howard-Harrison, which was organized by the Schickle, Harrison and Howard Iron Company of St. Louis, all six firms were independent enterprises. Anniston began as the Anniston Pipe Foundry and became insolvent shortly after operations had begun. It was operated for a time by the Radford Pipe and Foundry Company but was sold by bondholders and operating independently again by 1895.

[2] For the general historical background, see William D. Moore, "Development of the Cast Iron Pressure Pipe Industry in the Southern States," Newcomen Address (1939), Richard Moldenke, "Cast Iron Pipe Manufacture in the South," *Iron Age* (September 18, 1924), and James Bowron, "The History of the Iron and Steel Industry in the South," *Yearbook of the American Iron and Steel Institute* (1914).

By the mid-1890's, the six firms had a total capacity of about 220,000 tons of pipe per year.[3] Howard-Harrison, Dennis Long, and Addyston were each rated at 45,000 tons, Chattanooga at 40,000, Anniston at 30,000, and South Pittsburg at 15,000 tons. Nine other producers in what the Addyston group regarded as "pay territory" had an aggregate annual capacity of 170,500 tons, but these firms were scattered in Ohio, Michigan, Missouri, Texas, Oregon, Colorado, and Wisconsin. The largest of these, Lakeshore Foundry in Cleveland, had a daily capacity of 200 tons per day or, using 300 working days per year, 60,000 tons annually.

The production center of the nation was in New Jersey, Pennsylvania and New York. There were at least nine firms in these states with a total capacity of 332,000 tons per year. In addition, there was one firm in Virginia, also outside of "pay territory," with capacity of 16,000 tons per year. The largest firm in the nation was apparently R. D. Wood and Company, with plants in Millville, Florence, and Camden, New Jersey. Its total capacity was 400 tons per day or about 120,000 tons annually. Thus the largest firm could hardly have accounted for more than 16 per cent of the nation's capacity.

The main source of demand for cast-iron pressure pipe was from municipalities and utility companies for the distribution of water and gas. Since the population was heavily concentrated in the northeastern part of the country, this section was the most important market. A second important consuming area was the mid-West, especially in and around Chicago and St. Louis. Cities in other areas also demanded pipe, however, and transportation costs from the northeast were high. Small, local foundries tended to rival the northeastern firms in supplying such places in earlier years but by the 1880's, with improved transportation, the smaller foundries were disappearing or turning to specialty products.

[3] The 1894 and 1896 agreements were based on this figure but provided for shipments in excess of it.

Pig iron and coke were relatively inexpensive in the area of the Addyston group. The firms were in a geographical position which gave them a substantial transportation cost advantage over northern foundries for delivery to cities in the less densely populated southeast and southwest. Moreover, with lower raw material costs, they expected to be able to absorb freight costs and compete successfully with the northern manufacturers, especially in the mid-West market.

The pipe being made by all the companies was essentially the same from a technical point of view. It was made to the specifications of purchasers with the deep-pit casting method. None of the producers had adopted the technique of centrifugal casting so whatever product differentiation existed was due primarily to locational features of the market and to personal and business relations among buyers and sellers.

Market knowledge of both raw material costs and pipe prices was quite good. The price of pig iron, the most important input, was volatile and openly quoted. Announcements of the awarding of pipe contracts by municipal governments provided a reliable, though discontinuous, stream of pipe price information. In fact, information on raw material costs, pipe prices and production methods was so widely spread, and costs of entry so small, that during the period up to 1890 new pipe shops sprung up whenever demand was high and closed again when profits disappeared.[4] The larger, less adaptable, and therefore more permanent shops were denied to some extent the profits of periods of strong demand by the freedom of entry, yet burdened with the losses occasioned by heavy fixed charges during times when demand was weak.

The geographic dispersion of the firms and the high transportation costs were important for they gave rise to the familiar duopoly-oligopoly problem. The whole market took on geographical characteristics such that some parts of it were distinctly closer in terms of costs to one firm than to any other.

[4] Moldenke, "Cast Iron Pipe Manufacture," pp. 697–698.

In other places, two firms were, on the same basis, closer than the rest, and so on to locations which, from a cost basis, could be served equally well by increasing numbers of firms. The nature of the price-fixing agreement entered into by the southern foundries and, later, the formation of the United States Cast Iron Pipe and Foundry Company were influenced by this geographical pattern.

A final point on structural aspects of the market concerns the nature of demand. While it is true that there were a large number of municipalities buying pipe over the years, all of them were not in the market at the same time. St. Louis, for example, asked for bids three times in 1892, none in 1893, once in 1894, and three times in 1895 and again in 1896. Jobs for a large city on which a bid was submitted might be of sufficient magnitude to keep a shop operating for weeks or months. The fine adjustments within each firm which would allow variations in output according to revenue and costs so as to maximize profits were impossible. In the absence of agreement among firms, the outcome of the bidding made the difference between operating and not operating for a substantial period of time. The firm with excess capacity, bidding on a large job, would be prone to submit any price so long as it was in excess of the incremental costs of filling the order. And in view of the sporadic and large-sized jobs, some one of the several firms was apt to have the excess capacity created by a few unsuccessful bids.

MARKET PERFORMANCE AND FIRM BEHAVIOR

There is insufficient information to describe well the performance and behavior of the market and its firms prior to the formation of the association in 1894. What little can be pieced together, however, suggests that competition was intense. Note was made above of the ease of entry and exit of small firms. The Anniston plant, which was first put into operation in

1889, was, according to Moore,[5] "the largest pipe foundry in the world at the time of its building," and, "modern and up-to-date in every respect." Yet it remained solvent for only eighteen months and was being leased by bondholders to the Radford Pipe and Foundry Company at the time of the 1894 agreement. Even prior to 1894, Anniston had been associated with Howard-Harrison, Chattanooga and South Pittsburg in the Southern Associated Pipe Works, but whatever co-operative venture was involved was either inadequate or too late to prevent its bankruptcy. Moldenke,[6] without specifying the years involved, speaks of cast-iron pipe being sold in "dull times . . . at a few dollars a ton over the selling price of the pig iron used" and maintains that, "The history of pipe making, in the United States, is a checkered one — the mortality of plants is high and, from the nature of the industry, plants must be large to live." Counsel for the defendants, in a demurrer, stated that, "Previous to December 28, 1894, [the defendants] had bid on such occasions against each other and other companies proposing to take such contracts, and the competition provoked by this mode of dealing, secured to said gas, water, and municipal corporations the advantage of ruinous competition to the bidders, while said bidders had no other market in which to dispose of their product." [7]

The southern industry developed in the 1880's and early 1890's. These were generally, though not without exception, good years for cast-iron pipe sales. Until the 1880's, pipe had been either imported from northern foundries with high transportation costs or produced in non-specialized and inefficient foundries. The emergence of the southern industry — of the firms involved in the *Addyston* case — reflects the freedom of entry that existed. Pipe prices in the South were probably

[5] Moore, "Development of Cast Iron Pipe Industry," p. 19.

[6] Moldenke, "Cast Iron Pipe Manufacture," p. 697.

[7] *Records and Briefs in United States Cases,* U.S. Supreme Court, October Term, 1899, no. 51, p. 29.

higher than the costs of production of efficient specialty shops located in the area.

The southern firms had hardly entered the market when the demand for pipe slackened. A recession started in late 1890, and deepened through 1891, 1892 and 1893. Full prosperity was not restored until 1896 or 1897. In addition to the depression, the Wilson-Gorman tariff of 1894 is said to have forced price reductions in the southern iron industry. This, at least, was the reason given for attempts to reduce wages and for a resulting strike of coal miners in Birmingham.[8] These conditions were undoubtedly the immediate cause of the Addyston combination. The defendants maintained that their shipments in 1896, when recovery was well underway, amounted to less than 100,000 tons, or about 45 per cent of capacity.[9] The plan was aimed very directly at eliminating internal group rivalry which, in a high fixed-cost industry with market territories defined by transportation advantages, must have been severe as the firms actively sought contracts wherever they could be had. Without some rationalizing of rivalry, it is not inconceivable that all of the southern firms would have had the same fate as the "modern and up-to-date" Anniston plant. Too, whatever the means used among the northern foundries for reducing rivalry, it seems clear from the nature of the Addyston agreements that the southern firms either would not or could not join the older group.

THE ADDYSTON AGREEMENTS

There were at least three agreements among the southern producers after 1890. The first involved just four firms — Anniston, Howard-Harrison, Chattanooga, and South Pittsburg. The date of its commencement and its terms are not indicated, though it seems probable that it started after 1890

[8] Bowron, "History of Iron and Steel Industry."

[9] *Records and Briefs,* October Term, 1899, no. 51, p. 30.

and involved terms similar to those of the second agreement. The significant thing about the first agreement is that the four firms which were parties were located fairly close together, Howard-Harrison and Anniston in Central and East Central Alabama, respectively, and Chattanooga and South Pittsburg, in or near Chattanooga. The rail distance between the two furthest apart is about one hundred sixty miles. Addyston and Dennis Long, considerably further to the north, were not members.

In December of 1894, when recovery from the Depression of '93 had begun but while the recession was still severe, the second agreement was consummated. This was more extensive, bringing Dennis Long and Addyston into the fold. The agreement had two main parts. One "reserved" to each of the companies the business of the gas and water companies of certain cities. These jobs would not be bid on by the other firms, though bids could be submitted on other business in the same cities. The method of reserving these cities was not haphazard at all. Each firm generally reserved the cities in the immediate area of its plant or cities to which it was closer than the others. The only exceptions to this were the reservations of New Orleans to Chattanooga, Omaha to South Pittsburg, and St. Louis to Howard-Harrison. The latter, of course, was done so that orders could be filled by Schickle, Harrison, and Howard, the parent company of Howard-Harrison which was located in St. Louis. The pattern of reservations is consistent with the hypothesis that prior to the decline in demand each company had areas surrounding it in which it was the sole or, at least, principal supplier due to locational advantage. Under the agreement of 1894, each firm was required to pay $2.00 per ton to the Southern Associated Pipe Works, the formal name for their group, for all shipments to the reserved cities.

The second part of the 1894 agreement related to "pay territory," all of the states and territories west of New York and Pennsylvania and south of Virginia, and including the nongas, nonwater company business in the reserved cities. Prices for pipe in this territory were not fixed. Instead, the members of the Association could bid for work at whatever prices they wished subject only to a compulsory reporting of shipments to an auditor of the Association and payment to the Association of pre-established bonuses. The effect was to add an amount ranging from $1.00 to $4.00 a ton, depending on location, to the costs of the successful bidder. Bonuses thus collected were distributed to the members of the Association on the basis of both the respective tonnages of capacity for various sizes of pipe and the total sales by all members, both in and out of "pay territory."

The 1894 bonus agreement was obviously aimed at reducing price competition among the member firms. The added cost levied on the successful bidder should have had the effect of raising the minimum price each firm would submit. In addition, since the unsuccessful bidders received some revenue from each job, the impact of idle capacity on profits was reduced. This was not the only objective of the plan, however. Its detail shows clearly the importance of rivalry from shops outside the Addyston group — and a desire to meet it — as well as the desire for reducing competition within the group. In general, bonus payment were low where transportation costs from nonmember firms would be low.[10] Georgia coast points, the Texas coast, Mobile, Florida, North Carolina, and South Carolina, all of which were accessible to the northern foundries through inexpensive water transportation, had the minimum bonus of $1.00 per ton. Oregon, Washington Territory and West Virginia, all of which were located close to nonmember producers, also had the minimum bonus. Alabama (other than the cities of Birmingham, Anniston, and Mobile) had a bonus of $3.00 per ton and was not close cost-

[10] The transportation cost advantage of the defendants in "pay territory" ranged from $2 to $6 per ton over shops in the Northeast. See *U.S. v. Addyston Pipe and Steel Co.*, 85 F. 271, 277 (6th Cir. 1898).

wise to nonmember firms. Arizona Territory, Indian Territory, Middle and West Tennessee, Nevada, Oklahoma, the interior of Texas, Louisiana (other than New Orleans), Montana, and Nebraska all had $3.00 bonuses. Only Wyoming and Mississippi had the maximum bonus of $4.00 per ton.

It seems probable that the definition of "pay territory" was itself predicated on transportation costs. That is, in the Northeast, where nonmember mills were at a cost advantage, no bonus at all was collected. In short, the idea of the bonus system in the 1894 agreement was to keep the delivered cost of the successful bidder nearly as high as the alternative delivered costs of nonmember firms.

The 1894 agreement did not accomplish the purposes for which it was designed. Five months after its adoption, the firms agreed that "the system . . . had not, in its operation, resulted in the advancement in the prices of pipe, as was anticipated, except in reserved cities . . ." [11] Even in St. Louis, a reserved city, the price of pipe was $19.85 per ton in March, 1895, contrasted with $25.48 in late 1892.[12] The failure of the scheme is not surprising. The bonuses, while they tended to increase the costs of the successful bidder to an equivalent of nonmember costs, were apparently conceived on the basis of the differences in the full costs of member and nonmember mills. To be effective in the short run in raising prices to full costs, the bonuses would have had to be great enough to take all the short-run quasi rents from the successful bidder, making short-run marginal costs for that firm equal to long-run average costs. Such a program, however, unless every firm in each market area joined, would have resulted in jobs tending to go to nonmembers rather than members. Still, it appeared that something might be done to eliminate at least the competition among the members in the nonreserved areas of "pay territory."

[11] 85 F. 274.
[12] *Records and Briefs,* October Term, 1899, no. 51, p. 66.

At a meeting on May 27, 1895, the mode of bidding and the bonus system in nonreserved "pay territory" were changed. Each firm appointed a representative to a board and, when bids were solicited, they were forwarded to the board. The board then determined the lowest price that would be bid and informed the member firms what this price was. Each firm was then given an opportunity to bid a bonus to the board for the privilege of submitting this lowest price, the firm offering the largest bonus receiving the job. The other firms might then go through the formality of submitting bids but, in order to protect the successful shop, such bids would be in excess of the price set by the board. In December of 1895, the status of reserved cities was changed. Thereafter, prices and bonuses for jobs in these cities were to be determined jointly at meetings of the member firms. In addition, only those tonnages shipped into "pay territory," rather than total tonnages wherever shipped, were used in computing bonuses.

The combination worked out by the Association by the end of 1895 obviously eliminated competition among the members. Unlike the earlier agreement, the 1895 plan provided buyers with no alternative supply sources from among the six member producers. On the surface, the appearance of alternatives was made by the submission of bids by more than one firm but in fact the low bid and bidder were pre-arranged by the board of representatives. The only real alternative for buyers was to purchase from nonmember shops and these, being poorly located with respect to "pay territory," could offer only an inferior alternative which denied to buyers the geographical cost advantages which might otherwise have been available to them.

The board probably attempted to establish prices just low enough to keep the bulk of "pay territory" jobs away from nonmember firms. A member firm would increase its profits so long as it bid up to, but not more than, the difference between the incremental production and delivery costs for a job and the incremental revenue to be obtained from the job. Because of the competition in bonus bidding, the successful bidder may have derived little additional profit from the jobs that firm actually handled. But viewing the Association as a group, the program made amazing sense. Prices were as high as could be obtained, given the degree of outside competition. The member firm with the lowest combined production and delivery costs would be in a position to bid the greatest bonus. Thus, from the group point of view, revenue was maximized, costs minimized, and consequently joint profits tended to be as large as possible. The scheme for dividing bonus money distributed these profits among the members on the basis of the capacities of each and the total shipments of all, without respect to the actual tonnage shipped by the respective members. The program came as close to a pure attempt at joint profit maximization as one could imagine.

One factor restricting the Association's ability to raise prices after 1895 was the influence of the supply of nonmember firms. So long as the latter remained independent some maximum price was set by the willingness of the independents to enter "pay territory." As would be expected, it seems that this willingness was determined by the level of demand. There was a revival from the depression in 1895, bringing a "boom in (the) iron and steel industry." [13] Optimism prevailed among the cast-iron pipe makers. A representative of the Chattanooga Company wrote that he estimated shipments from Association members in 1896 would "amount to fully 200,000 (tons) . . . ; more than that, probably overrun 240,000 tons, from the fact that the city of Chicago and several other places that annually use large quantities of pipe were not in the market last year or last season, from the fact that they were out of funds." [14] Between March, 1895, and February, 1896, How-

[13] Willard L. Thorp and Wesley C. Mitchell, *Business Annals* (New York, 1926), p. 137.

[14] 85 F. 276.

ard-Harrison's price for pipe to St. Louis rose from $19.85 to $24.00 per ton.[15] Howard-Harrison paid a bonus of $6.50 per ton for the latter contract.[16] These high prices could, of course, be attributed solely to the new agreement. Doubtless that was a factor, but the more important reason would seem to be the change in business conditions which made the non-member firms less willing to sell in "pay territory."

By the middle of 1896 it was clear that the optimism of 1895 had been misfounded. The economy slid back into a short depression. In the St. Louis bidding of July 28th, Howard-Harrison was again the successful bidder, but by this time the price was only $19.64 per ton. Since St. Louis was "reserved" to Howard-Harrison, the decline in price since the previous February cannot be ascribed to rivalry within the Addyston group. The more likely explanation is the increased competition from without the group as business conditions deteriorated.

Judge Taft was able to adduce from the evidence that the cost of production of pipe in Chattanooga, "together with a reasonable profit, did not exceed $15 a ton." [17] From this, he held in his decision that the prices being charged by the defendants were unreasonably high. Since no evidence was presented on production and freight costs, his conclusion is apparently based on the fact that the Chattanooga company "offered pipe in free territory" that netted them "from $13 to $15 per ton at their foundries." [18] Since the concluded unreasonableness of prices was of some importance in Taft's decision, it is worth noting that he was very likely in error. In 1896, for example, Bessemer pig iron averaged more than

[15] *Records and Briefs,* October Term, 1899, no. 51, p. 66.

[16] 85 F. 275.

[17] 85 F. 293.

[18] *Ibid.,* p. 277. In addition, the record contained a letter from a Mr. Thomasson of the Chattanooga company in which he states, "we have had our prices entirely too high, and especially do we believe this has been the case as to prices in 'reserved cities'."

$12 per long ton — or nearly $10 per short ton — in Pittsburgh.[19] A price in the same neighborhood probably prevailed in the South. With operations near capacity, it appears that profits would have been possible only when pig iron cost no more than half the price of finished pipe.[20] On this basis, a price of about $20 would have covered full costs, including transportation, in 1896 if the mills had been operating at relatively full capacity. Since operations were, in fact, far below this level, a charge that the general level of prices was exorbitant seems unjustified. The Addyston group was undoubtedly getting as much as it could under the circumstances, but the nature of their own agreement, competition from outside the groups and the general depression exercised important restraining influences. If the prices were unreasonable, it was in their extremely discriminatory pattern, not in their general level. Prices in the reserved cities probably did cover full costs and more when competition from the northern mills allowed it. Prices in other places, even those in "pay territory" when considered net of the "bonus" payments, may sometimes have been below even the variable costs of production.[21]

[19] *Wholesale Prices,* Bulletin No. 45, Bureau of Labor Statistics (1926).

[20] This is an admittedly rough estimate. United States Cast Iron Pipe and Foundry Co., whose development is noted below, paid dividends in only 1905, 1906, and 1907 during the first 27 years of its existence. The price of a ton of iron averaged almost exactly half the price of an equivalent amount of cast-iron pipe in the 3 years of dividend payments. Immediately prior and subsequent to these years, iron prices were more than half the price of iron pipe. In the profitable period of the 1920's, iron prices averaged less than 40 per cent of pipe prices, though by this time a new technology had been introduced and some of the inefficient plants contained in the Addyston group had been shut down. See Simon N. Whitney, *Antitrust Policies,* II (New York, 1958), 11–12, for data and a discussion of the ratio of iron and cast-iron pipe prices.

[21] In a letter dated January 2, 1896, the Chattanooga company spoke of other companies running the bonuses so high that it was better to "take the bonus" than to seek the jobs. Such a decision should be based on variable, not full costs. In the same letter, it was opined that the other companies were losing money and that one company would "wreck their shop in a few months."

THE DECISIONS AND THEIR AFTERMATH

Agreements with discriminatory characteristics as strong as those in the Addyston case cannot be long hid. During early 1896, when recovery had apparently started, the companies operating the Associated Pipe Works attempted to increase their prices. R. D. Wood & Co., a Philadelphia pipe manufacturer, underbid the Anniston Company on an Atlanta job. All bids were rejected by the city because they were too high and it was charged by persons in Atlanta that there was a "trust" or "combine." [22] On rebidding, Anniston received the job, but the damage had now been done. A secretary of the Associated Pipe Works, the agency of the companies through which the bids were determined and the bonuses distributed, agreed to make public the full method of operations in return for a share of the amounts that would be collected by the buyers from the pipe companies because of collusive overcharging.

Suit was brought in the Circuit Court of the United States for the Eastern District of Tennessee.[23] This Court found for the defendants on two main points. First, relying on the *E. C. Knight* case[24] it held that the combination was one which affected only manufacturing and was, hence, not within the interstate commerce provisions of the law. Second, even if it were within the law, the burden was on the government to prove the combination unlawful.

Justice Harlan and Circuit Judges Taft and Lurton heard the case on appeal. Taft's decision is a classic in the antitrust field and is regarded by some as the beginning of the per se illegality doctrine in price-fixing cases. Taft reasoned that "if the contract of association which bound the defendants was void and unenforceable at the common law because in re-

[22] See letter quoted, 85 F. 276.
[23] U.S. v. Addyston Pipe and Steel Co., 78 F. 712 (E.D. Tenn. 1897).
[24] U.S. v. E. C. Knight, 156 U.S. 1 (1895).

straint of trade, it is within the inhibition of the statute if the trade it restrained was interstate." [25] His conclusion was that, "we can have no doubt that the association of the defendants, however reasonable the prices they fixed, however great the competition they had to encounter, and however great the necessity for curbing themselves by joint agreement from committing financial suicide by ill-advised competition, was void at common law, because in restraint of trade, and tending to a monopoly." [26] He noted in addition that even if this were not the case the argument would have failed the defendants since their attempts to justify the combination on grounds of reasonableness had no foundation.

Recent studies indicate that Taft was incorrect in his assessment of the common law. John C. Peppin argues that, "The conclusion is inescapable that the American common law authorities prior to 1890 did not support the proposition that agreements directly fixing prices were unlawful *per se* . . . Not a single case had announced, even by way of dictum, the view declared by Taft to represent the common law, that all restraints on competition which are not ancillary to some other lawful contract are unlawful *per se*." [27] More recently, Donald Dewey has advanced the same interpretation. He suggests that misconceptions about the common law "persist because proponents of 'positive' programs for *laissez faire* persist in seeking the aid and comfort of history." "Peaceable combinations," he concludes, "were immune from legal harassment, however restrictive their practices. The enforcement of contracts imposing 'direct' restraints on trade turned upon their 'reasonableness'." [28]

Taft's decision was rendered in February, 1898. In May of

[25] 85 F. 271, 278–279.

[26] *Ibid.*, p. 291.

[27] John C. Peppin, "Price-Fixing Agreements Under the Sherman Anti-Trust Law," *California Law Review*, 28:350 (1940).

[28] Donald Dewey, *Monopoly in Economics and Law* (Chicago, 1959), pp. 137–138.

the same year, Howard-Harrison, Anniston Pipe and Foundry, the South Pittsburg Pipe Works and Chattanooga Foundry and Pipe merged to form the American Pipe and Foundry Company. These were the same companies which had formed the original agreement prior to 1894. In March of 1899, slightly more than a year after Taft's decision and prior to affirmation or reversal by the Supreme Court, the United States Cast Iron Pipe and Foundry Company was formed. It took in the American Pipe and Foundry Company, Addyston and Dennis Long — all of the Associated Pipe Works companies — and a number of other companies both in and out of the old "pay territory." The new company had total annual capacity of 450,000 tons which at the time was said to be 75 per cent of the entire output of the country.[29] The company did not include R. D. Wood & Co., until then the largest producer and, interestingly, the firm whose lower bid in the Atlanta market three years previous had triggered the entire antitrust proceedings. Two other firms located close to the Wood plants were included and these had combined capacity in excess of that of Wood. None of the nine firms with daily capacities of less than 100 tons was involved in the merger.

The structural characteristics of the market after the formation of United States Cast Iron Pipe and Foundry were radically different from those existing previously. The new company was by far the largest and the only one with production facilities close to all the major consuming areas. The next largest firm was perhaps one quarter as large and the third largest was about half as large as the second. After these, all the remaining firms were relatively small.

The Supreme Court, speaking through Justice Peckham, affirmed Judge Taft's opinion later in 1899 without reference to either of the mergers. Moreover, Justice Peckham avoided

[29] *Moody's Manual of Corporation Securities* (1903), p. 1672; *Commercial and Financial Chronicle* (February 4, 1899), p. 233. It appears that the estimate of the percentage of the nation's capacity was too high.

endorsing Taft's interpretation of the common law. Instead, he restricted the opinion to the application of the Sherman Act to the facts at hand and found the combination unlawful.

COMMENTS ON THE *Addyston* CASE

The *Addyston* case provides two important lessons. The first concerns the anomalies, inconsistencies and inadequacies of what appear to be the prevailing views on antitrust policy. The case, for example, is often cited as the first in a chain of decisions which led to the per se doctrine for price-fixing agreements. The complete absence of intra-group rivalry, the discriminatory prices and the acceptance of Taft's view that the prices were unreasonably high have made the case an example of the danger of permitting pooling arrangements of any kind.[30] At the same time, it is generally accepted that the mergers subsequent to Taft's decision were partially because of the striking down of the price-fixing agreement and, whatever the motives, that the formation of the United States Cast Iron Pipe and Foundry Company not only nullified the verdicts but extended the degree of monopoly in the industry as well. There can hardly be question of the illegality of such a merger under current interpretation of Section 7 of the amended Clayton Act.

To the views that the agreement should have been illegal and that the merger would now be prevented must be added a third. That is that because of the characteristics of the industry — high fixed costs, fluctuating demand, high transportation costs, product homogeneity and oligopolistic rivalry — price competition may be excessive to the point that bankruptcies extend to even the efficient firms in the industry.[31] With only slight exaggeration, one can conclude from these views that the policy recommended for such industries is to

[30] For a statement of this and the subsequent points, see Whitney, *Antitrust Policies* II, pp. 608 ff.

[31] *Ibid.*

disallow any agreements which tend to reduce price rivalry among the firms, to disallow any mergers of substance and, hence, to permit only those structural changes which result from true "survival-of-the-fittest" competition. After a few cycles in demand, the number of firms would be reduced sufficiently and new entrants adequately discouraged so that the remaining few firms — perhaps the remaining firm — could live in the market successfully.

The second lesson of the case is found in the paradox that the very things which the policies against agreements and against mergers are aimed at preventing occur anyway. To the extent that the policies are successful, firms are reduced not through mergers but rather through failures; agreements which restrain price rivalry exist not through formal agreement among a large number of firms but rather through implicit agreement and, perhaps, leadership, among a few firms. But the result is still the avoidance of excessive rivalry.

These remarks do not imply a justification of either the Addyston agreements or of the subsequent mergers. It is quite clear that the former were unreasonable in character and may have had unreasonable results. The mergers left so little rivalry that more than a decade passed before the resulting firm was pressed to become more efficient. The remarks are intended instead to demonstrate interrelationships between market structure, business behavior and market performance. The structure of the cast-iron pipe market — especially after the southern firms entered the industry — was such that market performance adequate to maintain efficient firms in business could be obtained only through some sort of restraining or collusive behavior. While it cannot be proved, it seems likely that the northern firms, led probably by the R. D. Wood Company, had a tacit or formal understanding concerning their behavior. The entrance of the new firms made this arrangement ineffective and, with the aggravating circumstance of a depression, cutthroat rivalry developed. It was inevitable that the final result would be less competition since, even if both mergers and formal agreements had been prevented, the structural changes occasioned by failures would have produced the same end.

The *Addyston* case, then, illustrates the point that formal interfirm organizations are alternatives to changes in market structure. Which of the two is the preferable way to reduce excessive rivalry while at the same time discouraging monopolization cannot be answered generally. But it is clear from this case that neither the formality of organization nor structural concentration can be carried to extremes without changing excessive rivalry into no rivalry. In later decades, the performance of the cast-iron pipe industry improved as concentration decreased through the entry of new firms. For a time, the inept and almost disinterested United States Cast Iron Pipe and Foundry Company provided leadership and stability through little other than its size alone. In this period, it was much like the United States Steel Company in the sister industry. As the number of firms increased again, however, more positive leadership was asserted; then a more formal organization emerged as a basing point pricing system was adopted. Thus the later history continues the alternating blend of organizational formality and concentration, with perhaps no period in which rivalry was again strong enough to produce the best performance possible in the industry.[32]

[32] See Whitney, *Antitrust Policies,* II, for a brief account of this history.

CHAPTER VI

ORGANIZATION AND THE BITUMINOUS COAL INDUSTRY

INTRODUCTION

One of the most dramatic of industrial histories is that of bituminous coal. As in the case of cast-iron pipe, there was a need for either organizational or structural change from at least the late nineteenth century. Unlike the pipe industry, however, and even apart from the Sherman Act's prohibitions, the bituminous coal industry was for years unamenable to privately sponsored organizational efforts and not susceptible to rapid or extensive structural changes. The poor performance of the industry caused an early recognition of the need for "an instrument of industrial order," or "a combination of devices and procedures," "composed of usages and habits, conventions and practices, taboos upon action and ways of doing things." [1] Even beyond this, it was recognized that this organization would have to emerge from the conscious efforts of interested persons. The coal industry demonstrated that "an industry does not automatically organize itself; there is no natural, immutable, indefeasible scheme of order . . . No self-maintaining, self-regulating scheme of order has ever existed." [2] Thus, since the structure was not capable of changing in response to poor performance, the alternative to that performance was more formal regulation. And that could be either privately or publicly imposed.

[1] Walton H. Hamilton and Helen R. Wright, *A Way of Order for Bituminous Coal* (New York, 1928), pp. 55, 64.

[2] *Ibid.*, p. 55.

THE PERFORMANCE OF THE BITUMINOUS COAL INDUSTRY

Beginning at least as early as 1890, the bituminous coal industry was troubled with excess capacity. Contrary to conventional theory, price competition did little toward mitigating it for at least thirty years. Between 1890 and 1923, excess capacity amounted to less than 30 per cent of production in only two years, 1917 and 1918, the years of World War I.[3] In the years 1893, 1894, 1895, 1896, and 1897, excess capacity was respectively 52, 82, 58, 60 and 57 per cent of production. It was over 50 per cent of production in 1904, 1908, 1909, 1914, 1915, 1919, 1921, 1922, and 1923, reaching an historic peak of 117 per cent in 1922. Despite this, however, the industry tended chronically to expand. In 1890, there were an estimated 192,000 workers in the industry producing 111,302,000 tons of coal.[4] By 1923, 703,000 workers produced 564,157,000 tons. The number of workers did not respond to conditions of employment. Between 1920 and 1922, for example, production declined from 568,667,000 tons to 422,268,000 tons. The number of workers increased from 640,000 to 698,000, with the average number of days worked by each declining from 220 in 1920 to 142 in 1922.

Both demand and technological progress were creating an opportunity to lessen the amount of human resources devoted to bituminous coal mining. In 1890, the output per man per day was 2.56 tons. By 1923, this had increased to 4.47 tons. The rising labor productivity was accompanied by an eightfold increase in the number of horsepower used per ton of coal produced.[5]

[3] Walton H. Hamilton and Helen R. Wright, *The Case of Bituminous Coal* (New York, 1926), p. 263. The data came originally from the U.S. Coal Commission, Part I, *Relief from Irregular Operation and Over Development,* and from the U.S. Geological Survey.

[4] *Ibid.,* pp. 260–261.

[5] *Ibid.,* pp. 270, 272.

Changes in mine capacity appear to have been quite unrelated to prices and to existing excess capacity. In the period 1915 to 1920, the average value of coal at the mine rose from $1.13 per ton to $3.75 per ton and capacity increased from 647,447,000 to 796,494,000 tons.[6] This, on a priori grounds, is perhaps not too surprising even with the existing excess capacity. In the period 1920 to 1922, however, the country as a whole was in a depression, the average value of coal at the mine fell to $3.02 per ton, and the number of days worked by each worker fell considerably. Even in the face of these conditions, mine capacity continued to grow from 796,494,000 to 915,900,000 tons.[7] With only 1895, 1911 and 1916 as exceptions, mine capacity grew year after year regardless of the conditions of the industry.

By the 1920's, there were more than seven thousand firms mining soft coal, not counting certain short-lived "fly-by-night" operations.[8] The largest firm accounted for no more than 3 per cent of total output and the two-hundred largest companies produced only 50 per cent of total output. There was a large trade association, the National Coal Association, and quite a few smaller ones in various districts, but they did not exercise any perceptible influence on prices.[9] Some of the larger, more modern firms mining good veins made large profits, especially during years of national prosperity, but the losses accruing to others did not seem to deter capacity expansion or to weed the inefficient mines from the industry. Bankruptcy was frequent, but so was reorganization and the entry of new firms.[10] When a firm failed, its stockholders and bondholders might lose money, but the mine shafts remained. Unlike the plants and buildings of manufacturing, which might

[6] *The Case of Bituminous Coal,* p. 273.
[7] *Ibid.*
[8] *Ibid.,* p. 41.
[9] *Ibid.,* p. 49.
[10] *Ibid.,* pp. 62–66.

be shifted to the production of other goods, the mine was useful for but one purpose and it tended to stay in the industry until the seams ran out.

There were factors other than the highly specialized form taken by physical capital which encouraged chronic excess capacity and virtually profitless operations for most of the firms. Rich deposits, for the most part controlled by firms in the industry, tended to be brought into use at the first opportunity even though profitable operation was likely to be ephemeral. Frequently there was sufficient lapse of time between the decision to open a mine and its actual operation that the opportunity for profits had disappeared before the first coal was sold.[11]

Another factor is the "joint cost" supply conditions. Most coal is screened into size classifications prior to sale rather than sold as run-of-the-mine. Consequently the production of one size necessarily results in the production of several other sizes, the mixture depending on the particular mine and the methods used in extraction. While some mines had sizes which were primary in their production, none could specialize fully and each always had some amounts of sizes primary to other mines. It was a frequent practice to get rid of nonprimary sizes at whatever the market would bring, resulting in a tendency for each mine progressively to underbid the others.[12] This so-called "distress coal" had permanent and significant depressing effects.[13] The practice of "pyramiding" sales through dealers, the lack of well-defined size standards, the power of large buyers to force price concessions and, particularly after 1920, the growing use of substitute fuels all added to the industry's plight.

[11] *Report of the Committee on Prices in the Bituminous Coal Industry*, National Bureau of Economic Research (New York, 1938), pp. 13–14.

[12] *Ibid.*, p. 16.

[13] Appalachian Coals, Inc. v. U.S., 288 U.S. 344, 362–363 (1933).

PLANS TO ORGANIZE THE COAL INDUSTRY

There were many proposals for changing the conditions of the coal industry. In 1922, in a pamphlet called *How to Run Coal,* the United Mine Workers of America suggested a form of nationalization.[14] The plan called for public ownership and statistical accounting control through a Federal Interstate Commission on Mines. The head of the Commission would be the Secretary of Mines, a member of the cabinet, and there would be ten other members — five appointed by professional and industrial associations[15] and five, in addition to the Secretary, appointed by the President. While the Commission was to determine price and output, actual administration of operations was to be in the hands of a National Mining Council with regional counterparts. These councils were to be comprised of administrative personnel, miners and consumers.

In its final report of 1925, the U. S. Coal Commission recommended "use of the powers of the Federal Government . . . , recognizing that . . . a substantial part of the responsibility rests on the State and local governments . . . and that an even larger part rests on the industry itself and the public which it serves." [16] A "coal division" in the Interstate Commerce Commission was recommended which would, among other things, issue licenses to ship and sell coal in interstate commerce, readjust long and short haul freight rates to discourage overdevelopment caused by widening market territories, distribute railroad cars during times of shortage, encourage the "consolidation, grouping, or pooling of bituminous coal operations" and, like a large trade association, publish facts on costs, profits, wage rates and working and

[14] Most of the text is reproduced as Appendix C in Hamilton and Wright, *A Way of Order for Bituminous Coal,* pp. 340–348.

[15] Like many of the proposals advanced, provision was made by the union for an important voice for engineers and other professionals. Thus, even in coal, where there surely was no contrived shortage arising from a "conscientious withdrawal of efficiency," technocracy had its influence.

[16] Reprinted in *A Way of Order for Bituminous Coal,* Appendix B, p. 319.

living conditions of miners. The report recommended that communities license retailers, organize co-operatives and establish municipal fuel yards. It also asked somewhat piously that the operators "realize their duty as citizens and their interest in establishing such a spirit of co-operation as will promote the prosperity of the industry with direct benefit to the public" and that the United Mine Workers accept "the principle that the public interest is superior to that of any monopolistic group, whether of employers or employees."

Senator Watson introduced a bill in Congress in 1928 to control the industry. It provided for a Bituminous Coal Commission appointed by the President, the setting of minimum and maximum prices as proposed by marketing pools of producers and approved by the Commission, licensing of producers, production control through approval of new rail sidings and a system of fines and penalties for failure to comply with its regulations.[17]

Hamilton and Wright, after having written a book on the problems of the industry,[18] wrote another on alternative ways of organizing the industry.[19] The choice, they felt, reduced to these alternatives: the then present unregulated industry, some form of monopoly or a commission regulated industry. The first was rejected, despite its ideological appeal, because of its poor record. A monopoly controlled by either business or the union was rejected because of the likelihood of irresponsible control. Commission regulation seemed a weak possibility because the commission would be comprised of persons who "choose to bother themselves with coal," rather than of those to whom coal must be a concern. The final preference of Hamilton and Wright was a single, unified control through

[17] The bill is summarized in Waldo E. Fisher and Charles M. James, *Minimum Price Fixing in the Bituminous Coal Industry,* National Bureau of Economic Research (Princeton, 1955), pp. 22–23, 26.

[18] *The Case of Bituminous Coal.*

[19] *A Way of Order for Bituminous Coal.*

a Federal Bituminous Coal Company which was to be owned and operated jointly by consumers and mineworkers.

Appalachian Coals, Inc.

Nothing was done for coal despite the plethora of proposals. From 1924 until the great depression, the performance of the industry followed lines suggested by the theory of competition. Production, employment and the number of mines in operation declined. Aggregate net income in the industry was negative, with more firms reporting losses than reporting profits.[20] After several meetings with government officials had borne no results, the operators held a general meeting in New York in October, 1931. A committee was appointed to make suggestions and, at another meeting in December, it recommended the setting up of regional sales agencies in the industry. Less than a month later, on December 30, 1931, one hundred thirty-seven producers in the Appalachian territory — in the states of Virginia, West Virginia, Kentucky and Tennessee — incorporated a new company, Appalachian Coals, Inc. It was to be the exclusive selling agent for all coal produced by them except that outstanding on existing contracts and that used in the operation of the mines or sold to employees.

Ownership of the new corporation was made proportional to the historical production of the several firms. The corporation was to establish standard-size classifications, apportion orders among the owning firms if all production could not be sold, guarantee accounts receivable for sales made by it and, in return, receive a 10 per cent commission on orders it sold directly and a 2 per cent (net) commission on orders taken by subagents which were, in fact, the existing sales outlets. The "best prices obtainable" were to be gotten by Appalachian Coals. The corporation was also to study the demand and

[20] Fisher and James, *Minimum Price Fixing,* pp. 14–19.

marketing system for coal, embark on an advertising campaign, provide an engineering and maintenance department to demonstrate the advantages of coal as a fuel, and set up a research department to study the efficient use of coal so the producers could better compete with substitute fuels.

The one hundred thirty-seven producers mined about 12 per cent of total bituminous coal production in 1929. They produced nearly 75 per cent of all noncaptive coal in the Appalachian territory and 64 per cent of coal from that territory and the immediately surrounding region in the same year. While these shares of the market might not constitute a monopoly, even under the rule of Judge Hand in the *Alcoa* case,[21] the agreements to sell only through Appalachian Coals, Inc. clearly was aimed at eliminating price competition among the 137 producers.

The United States sought an injunction before the plan was put into operation. Judge Parker, writing for a three-judge court, rendered an opinion[22] in the tradition of the *Potteries* decision. He wrote:

It will be observed that the act itself draws no distinction between loose combinations resulting from agreements between independent dealers and the combination which results from normal corporate organization. It is clear, however, that the distinction must be drawn when the rule of reason laid down by the Supreme Court is applied . . .

. . . There is a vital distinction in principle . . . between a bona fide corporate organization resulting from normal growth and development and an agreement eliminating competition between independent dealers; and the distinction is so clearly recognized in recent decisions of the Supreme Court that we have no choice but to follow them.

Corporate organization is ordinarily the product of natural economic forces; and, so long as there is no intention to monopolize

[21] U.S. v. Aluminum Company of America, 148 F. 2d 416, 424 (2nd Cir. 1945).

[22] U.S. v. Appalachian Coals, Inc., 1 F. Supp. 339 (W. D. Va. 1932).

and no attempt to exercise monopolistic control of the market or unreasonably to restrain trade, there is no substantial danger of injury to the public or reason for interference by the state. Such organizations have grown large ordinarily because the economic law of increasing returns is operative — because internal economies and the elimination of duplication and waste make operation on a large scale more profitable than in small units . . . In addition to this, there is the practical consideration that, where a corporation has grown large by natural processes, even though absorption of competitors be involved, it is almost a matter of impossibility to dissolve it without injury to the public interest. No method of 'unscrambling eggs' has as yet been discovered.

Combinations of independent producers, on the other hand, organized to fix uniform prices . . . or to eliminate competition among themselves, are artificial agreements designed to limit the operation of natural economic laws . . . In dealing with such combinations, moreover, the courts face no such difficulties as in dealing with corporate organization where the fusion of interests has become a fact accomplished. The free competition which it is the policy of the law to promote can be restored by the simple expedient of forbidding the independent dealers to operate under their agreement.[23]

Judge Parker undertook a review of the law from 1890 up to date. It is much like a sequel to Taft's *Addyston* decision, with considerable attention to and quotation from that case, and concludes with a reaffirmation of *Trenton Potteries* and the granting of an injunction.

There can be scant doubt that Judge Parker was correct in his interpretation of the law at that time and, for that matter, of the law as it exists today. At the same time, his opinion illustrates the inconsistencies of that law. The incorporation of separate and horizontally related firms eliminates price competition even more positively than does a so-called "loose combination." In the former, it is as impossible (and more unlikely) for the unified firms to unscramble the eggs as it is for the law to do it. In the case of agreements in restraint of

[23] 1 F. Supp. 343–344.

trade — and some of the cases in subsequent chapters are in point — the agreement may be abandoned and competition restored by the actions of a single trader. The incorporation gets the poorer score from the standpoint of maintaining competition.

More important, however, is the distinction drawn between the "natural economic forces" which lead to merger and consolidation and the "artificial" and ostensibly sinister forces which give rise to agreements in restraint of trade. Who is to say, for example, that the mergers of the cast-iron pipe producers in 1898 and 1899 were more or less a response to "natural" forces than the Appalachian agreement? The pipe mergers did reduce freight cross hauls, develop engineering standards and encourage research,[24] but Appalachian Coals, Inc. intended to do and probably was as well-equipped to do precisely the same things. The roles of internal economies and increasing returns in the pipe mergers are not clear, for it was not until twenty-five years after the mergers that U. S. Cast Iron Pipe and Foundry Co. began shutting down inefficient and poorly located plants.[25] The dichotomy of "natural" and "artificial" forces is itself artificial. The clear thing about the cast-iron pipe mergers and the formation of Appalachian Coals, Inc. is that the firms in both cases wished to mitigate the intensity of competition. For pipe, merger was one way out; in bituminous coal, the task of consolidating even the one hundred thirty-seven firms was probably so prodigious that it could not be a seriously considered alternative. Had it been possible it presumably would have been legal, despite the fact that it would have had even more restricting effects on rivalry than did the joint selling agency.

The opinion of the Supreme Court, parts of which are quoted in Chapter X, below, is difficult to understand. Apart from bits of the *Sugar Institute* decision,[26] the Court has not

[24] Whitney, *Antitrust Policies,* II, 8.
[25] *Ibid.*
[26] Sugar Institute, Inc. v. U.S., 297 U.S. 553 (1936).

used similar language since the per se rule was clarified in the *Trenton Potteries* case. One can but wonder how influential the 1930 appointment of Chief Justice Hughes was. Hughes, who wrote the *Appalachian Coals* opinion, was no novice to antitrust law. Indeed, it was he who argued the *Trenton Potteries* case before the Supreme Court in 1926.[27] To him, perhaps more than to any of the other justices, the fact recognized by even the District Court that the coal companies had been "acting fairly and openly, in an attempt to organize the coal industry and to relieve the deplorable conditions resulting from overexpansion, destructive competition, wasteful trade practices, and the inroads of competing industries" [28] argued strongly against the application of a per se rule which was blind to structural, performance and organizational characteristics of the market.

The *Appalachian Coals* case presented a problem of enormous importance. Both the District Court and the Supreme Court concluded that the proposed organization would "affect" market prices. This would be especially likely if similar selling agencies were established in other districts as appeared probable,[29] for such a development would radically have changed the structure of the industry. In broad terms, the problem was whether through an agreement which falls short of corporate consolidation a group of competitors can change the structural-organizational characteristics and hence the performance characteristics of a market.

The same problem had, in fact, been before the Court on many occasions but never quite so boldly. No one denied in the *Chicago Board of Trade*[30] case that the "call" rule adopted did "affect" prices. Quite obviously it did, not just during the period between the close and the opening of the sessions but during the sessions as well. Moreover, though

[27] 273 U.S. 393 (1927).
[28] 1 F. Supp. 341.
[29] 288 U.S. 364–365.
[30] Board of Trade of the City of Chicago v. U.S., 246 U.S. 231 (1918).

that case does not get to this point, there was a host of other rules governing trading on the exchange some of which affected prices and the general performance of the market to a substantial degree. It was these very rules which allowed the exchange to operate as an *organized* market. For the sake of consistency, it would have been necessary to declare the agreements establishing the exchange unlawful if the Court had held the "call" rule a violation. Every rule, every custom, every mode of behavior influences market prices, yet somehow the law has set aside for special consideration those which result from agreement.

Justice Hughes' opinion faced this issue. It distinguished between an agreement which influences prices and an agreement which fixed prices. He clearly would not have condoned the fixing of prices. Neither would he have approved of all agreements which affect prices, for some such agreements are reasonable and some unreasonable. More pointedly — and beyond the question of reasonableness — he saw that some agreements are necessary to allow competition to work. Thus included in the decision are the following:

> A co-operative enterprise, . . . which carries with it no monopolistic menace, is not to be condemned as an undue restraint merely because it may effect a change in market conditions, where the change would be in mitigation of recognized evils and would not impair, but rather foster, fair competitive opportunities . . .
>
> . . . Putting an end to injurious practices, and the consequent improvement of the competitive position of a group of producers is not a less worthy aim and may be entirely consonant with the public interest, where the group must still meet effective competition in a fair market and neither seeks nor is able to effect a domination of prices.[31]

The Court was satisfied that Appalachian Coals, Inc. was not a monopolistic menace and could not dominate prices.

[31] 288 U.S. 373–374. Note Hughes' emphasis here on the intent and power of the parties to the agreement.

Although it had been considered by the operators prior to the agreement, there was no attempt to limit production. Production limitations, they decided, would be neither legal nor practical.[32] Moreover, even if there had been a production limitation, it seemed improbable that the selling agency could enhance the price very much. The bulk of its coal was sold outside of Appalachian territory, in the area east of the Mississippi and north of the Ohio rivers. In this area there would be competition from the coal of other territories. In addition, the existing excess capacity of mines in the territory and owned by persons other than the defendants plus the ease of starting new mines made it appear to the court that there was little danger that the public would suffer from unreasonably high prices.

The real danger of monopoly and price-fixing came not from Appalachian Coals itself but from the probability that the selling agency plan would become more general. The Court noted that operators in other districts were holding their plans in abeyance pending the outcome of this case. If the Appalachian plan were approved, it would be expected that the other districts would follow suit. It might also be expected that both in Appalachian territory and in the others efforts would be made to bring new operators into the plan or, at least, to see that nonmembers behaved in a way which would not defeat the purposes of the selling agency.[33] Still, with so many producers and with the existing freedom of entry into the business, even these developments might present the consumer with little danger.

A monopoly, of course, despite its dangers to the public and perhaps to labor, would have had certain advantages for the coal industry. As Hamilton and Wright noted in 1928, a monopoly "would obviously provide the unity which the coal

[32] *Ibid.*, p. 367.

[33] The original plan set an upper limit of 80 per cent of the commercial tonnage in the territory because "greater control might unduly restrict competition."

industry demands . . . A single board of directors and managerial staff responsible to them . . . could attack the problem of capacity with little difficulty."[34] But this points out exactly why Appalachian Coals, Inc. was not a great public danger. Even though it would have been the exclusive agent for all the coal of the one hundred thirty-seven operators, it would have had neither the unified view nor the control over production and capacity of a textbook monopolist. High prices would encourage more output *by its own members* and, as stocks built up through the opportioning of orders, the individual members would pressure the selling agency for lower prices or, what is even more probable, violate the agreement and sell directly. Thus there is some reason to doubt whether the agreement would have been as fruitful as the operators wished when it was established.

EVENTS AFTER THE DECISION

The Supreme Court's decision was given on March 13, 1933, some fourteen months after Appalachian Coals was incorporated. In the meantime, two bills had been introduced in the Congress, both of which provided for the setting of minimum prices by the operators and, directly or indirectly, the control of production. Neither bill was passed.[35]

Appalachian Coals, Inc. was put into operation after the decision even though the sanction given it by the Court was not unequivocal. In September, however, the N.R.A. Code of Fair Competition for the Bituminous Coal Industry was approved. It provided for marketing agencies similar to Appalachian Coals and allowed such agencies to set "fair market prices." Certain unfair trade practices were prohibited but no production quotas were established.[36]

[34] *A Way of Order for Bituminous Coal,* pp. 142–143.

[35] Fisher and James, *Minimum Price Fixing,* pp. 22–27. These bills were far more monopolistic in their design than was the Appalachian Coals plan.

[36] *Ibid.*

Appalachian Coals operated under the N.R.A. Code. Now, rather than having simply a voluntary agreement, the terms of the code had the strength of law. Violations were punishable as misdemeanors and fines of $500 could be levied on the violators for each offense. Long before the N.I.R.A. was declared unconstitutional, "violations of the minimum pricing structure were occurring widely and frequently, and by the early months of 1935 the structure had all but collapsed." [37] This suggests that the Appalachian Coals plan, which without the N.R.A. would have had virtually no authority to compel behavior compatible with its objectives, could hardly have been successful in raising prices.

The Bituminous Coal Conservation Act of 1935 was passed shortly after the demise of the N.I.R.A. It, too, was declared unconstitutional and was succeeded by the Bituminous Coal Act of 1937. Under the latter law, minimum and maximum prices were proposed by district boards of operators and approved by the National Bituminous Coal Commission. The operators had less freedom in setting prices since they were to be based on the weighted average costs of the mines in each district and since the Commission had authority to set maximum prices and to modify or revise the minimum prices suggested by the district boards. Membership in the plan was "voluntary," but nonmembers paid a tax of 19½ per cent on all coal sold. The Commission was empowered to issue cease-and-desist orders for violations. Violators could be suspended from membership and subject to the 19½ per cent tax. Minimum prices were not established until October, 1940, and these remained in effect for only thirty-five months. Violations of the code, though not unusual, were less frequent and less disturbing than during the N.I.R.A.[38]

The Bituminous Coal Act expired in 1943. Since then government regulation and enforcement of minimum prices

[37] Fisher and James, *Minimum Price Fixing,* p. 28.
[38] Fisher and James, pp. 282–306, 391–395.

have not been in effect. Their termination did not, however, signal the resumption of competitive price-cutting and demoralizing conditions. In part this was due to the general prosperity of the war and immediate post-war years. Probably even more important than the prosperity was the change in the organization of the industry which transpired during the 1930's and early 1940's. Significant among these changes is the almost complete unionization of labor in the industry. One important reason for the severe and relentless price-cutting of the earlier period was the persistent attempts by the non-unionized southern operators to expand their markets by moving into the markets which geographically were more proximate to unionized operators. This they could do by cutting prices and, sometimes, cutting wages so they could cut prices still more.[39] General unionization, by equalizing wage rates and by enforcing similar terms for the introduction of labor-saving machinery in the mines, has tended to make the cost of production more uniform among the mines. And the more uniform costs are, the easier it is for the industry to maintain its prices. Costs, that is, are important in the value systems of the firms.

The union has also made itself the instrument of production limitation and allocation of production among the several mines. This it accomplishes by control of the length of the work week.[40] Even though the number of mines and the amount of excess capacity rose after 1943, this control on production has prevented these events from reviving the price wars of the 1920's and 1930's.

The influence of the *Appalachian Coals* decision and of the organization given the operators by the subsequent governmental regulation cannot be minimized. Bituminous coal con-

[39] *Ibid.*, pp. 326–327, and Hamilton and Wright, *The Case of Bituminous Coal*, pp. 224–227.

[40] Clair Wilcox, *Public Policies Toward Business* (Homewood, 1955), p. 471, and James M. Henderson, *The Efficiency of the Coal Industry* (Cambridge, Mass., 1958), pp. 109–112.

tinued to be sold by regional selling agencies after 1943.[41] In addition, the operators — especially the larger ones — had had by then more than a decade of experience of working together on the district boards and of making joint requests and proposals to the National Bituminous Coal Commission. Under the Act of 1937, following the experience with the N.R.A. Code, market areas were defined which were to be supplied by particular producing districts. Similarly, regulations were adopted for the pricing of "distress" coal, for standardizing the classification of coal and for controlling coal distribution. After the years of working together with such regulations it would not be surprising if many elements of the former control were retained as customs and practices.

The industry's performance after 1945 was very different from that of the 1920's. Yet its structure was not radically different. The reason for the different performance is not that the basic demand conditions had been altered. Excess capacity and the declining relative importance of coal as an energy source continued. The explanation of the different performance is in the change in market organization.

CONCLUDING OBSERVATIONS

The organizational aspects of the bituminous coal industry have been emphasized to show the importance of them to the industry's performance. There has been no intention to hold them up as an ideal form. It should be noted, however, that the coal industry is strapped with one structural characteristic which distinguishes it from most manufacturing industries. By the very nature of the resource and the conditions imposed by technology, the industry must have a large number of geographically scattered plants (mines). Physical consolidation of plants is impossible. This obviates the possibility of achieving the operating economies caused by increasing re-

[41] Appalachian Coals, Inc., for example, was operating at least as recently as 1959. See *Coal Age* (February 1959), p. 26.

turns to scale and, hence, one factor which has tended to encourage consolidations and mergers in manufacturing industries. By the 1890's there were thousands of operators who had been brought into competition with one another both by the improvements in transportation and by the concentration of industrial demand in the large manufacturing areas of the nation.

The consolidations which occurred in manufacturing were impossible in the coal industry. While it would have been conceivably possible for a few large firms to emerge, the lack of promised economies and the sheer magnitude of the number of firms which would have had to be merged before effective market control could be achieved argued against this development.[42] Thus the production of coal, like the production of agricultural goods, did not become markedly more concentrated. Coal became instead a "sick" industry.

It should not go unnoticed that the very conditions of the coal industry which satisfy the conditions of perfect — or pure — competition were the conditions responsible for the industry's poor performance.[43] Of course, all the conditions necessary for such competition, especially good market knowledge and freedom of exit, were not present, nor could they be in the absence of better organization. Further improvement in the performance of the industry is not likely to result from the traditional approach of reducing concentration and preventing more formal interfirm organizations. Just the opposite, in fact, appears the more promising policy. Entry needs to be discouraged, miners and their families need to be aided in transferring human resources to other lines of production, public or private control of production is required, and more

[42] There has been an increase in concentration in recent years, but not nearly commensurate with that in manufacturing. In 1950, the largest 15 groups of companies or companies — whichever was the producing organization — produced 21.7 per cent of the national total. By 1959 the largest 15 accounted for 39.2 per cent. See *Coal Age* (February 1960), p. 74.

[43] See Henderson, *The Efficiency of the Coal Industry*, pp. 98–99.

efficient geographical allocation of supply to demand would be desirable.[44]

The ease with which many manufacturing industrial structures changed when their markets experienced excessive rivalry is also seen in a different light when compared with the difficulties of industries such as coal. Increasing concentration in manufacturing brought with it many problems. In some industries it was carried to such an extreme that excess monopoly power was created. It did, however, bring one generally unrecognized benefit. It reduced the need for formal organization among firms. The growth in concentration, by reducing the number of firms, by creating positions of market leadership, and by causing the development of explicit and implicit market rules and patterns of behavior, simplified the task of market organization.

Without the growth in concentration, the demands for private interfirm organizations and the demand for government regulation would have been far greater. The performance of unconcentrated, informally organized industries is characteristically so poor that formal organizations, immunities from the antitrust laws, or government regulations usually appear. In this light, then, modern oligopoly seems not so inconsistent with realistic forms of market rivalry and "administered prices," at least to some degree, appear desirable as well as unavoidable.

[44] See *ibid.,* pp. 102–105.

CHAPTER VII

THE HARDWOOD CASES[1]

INTRODUCTION

The *American Column and Lumber* and *Maple Flooring* cases provide interesting insights into the theory of interfirm organization. The activities of trade associations in the hardwood lumber industry are in themselves good illustrations of the influences of relatively formal organizational efforts directed toward tempering the rivalry characteristic of large-number, complex market interdependence. And the antitrust cases allow observations on the importance of differences in numbers and differences in the homogeneity of value systems in two markets with more or less similar interfirm organizations.

The discussion of these cases has fundamental importance for the subsequent policy conclusions. Perhaps unwittingly, and abetted by major changes in its membership, the Supreme Court appears to have been influenced by short-term price behavior records in its decisions in these cases. Even a cursory examination of performance in an appropriate theoretical context suggests very strongly that a violation of the Sherman Act was found in the case in which rivalry was the greatest and that acquittal resulted in that in which rivalry was more restrained. The cases at once demonstrate the ease with which uncritical, nonanalytical performance tests can mislead antitrust policy and the need for theoretical explanations rather than just descriptions of performance.

[1] *American Column and Lumber Co. v. U.S.*, 257 U.S. 377 (1921), and *Maple Flooring Manufacturers' Association v. U.S.*, 268 U.S. 563 (1925).

HISTORICAL BACKGROUND

Until shortly after the Civil War, the northeastern states — New England, New York, and Pennsylvania — were the principal sources of lumber in the United States.[2] Improved canal transportation between the Great Lakes region and the eastern markets, plus the growing scarcity of extensive stands in accessible locations in the Northeast, led to the development of the Lake States as the main source of supply during the 1870's and 1880's. Following this, rail transportation opened the South and Southwest and, by the late 1890's, more lumber was produced in this area than in any other section of the country.

The growing production in places remote from the populous eastern market effected an important change in the structure of the industry. Its "local" characteristics, which had begun to break down as early as 1820,[3] gave way to more regional and national influences. Each consuming center could potentially be supplied by any of the thousands of mill operators scattered broadly over a great geographical area. Unlike the former local industry with but a few mills in close proximity, the sellers of lumber in the 1890's had little knowledge of who their rivals were and virtually no knowledge of the prices at which these rivals might be offering lumber.

Trade associations in the lumber industry were organized at least as early as 1883.[4] The early associations included the Missouri and Arkansas Lumber Association, the Southern Lumber Manufacturers' Association (later the Yellow Pine Manufacturers' Association and, still later, the Southern Pine Association), the Georgia Sawmill Association, and many others. Apparently without exception, the associations were

[2] Wilson Compton, *The Organization of the Lumber Industry* (Chicago, 1916), chaps. i and ii, George R. Hall, "The Lumber Industry and Forest Policy" (unpublished PhD thesis, Harvard University, 1959), pp. 152–163.

[3] Hall, p. 156.

[4] Ralph C. Bryant, *Lumber*, 2nd. ed. (New York, 1938), p. 299.

organized on a geographic or on a species of tree basis, or some combination of both. This suggests that the trade associations of this period were attempting to do on a formal basis for large numbers of rivals no more than the tacit association of the few sellers in each local market had done in previous decades. In any case, it is clear that the objectives of the associations included exerting a stabilizing and rationalizing influence on prices. The 1892 platform of the Southern Lumber Manufacturers' Association contained as goals the following:

> 3. To establish a ratio of prices between various grades and lengths as well as an open official form of list, and recommend at regular intervals a schedule of prices which shall be in accord with market conditions present and prospective.[5]

The National Association of Hardwood Lumber Manufacturers was formed in 1891. In 1902, the Hardwood Manufacturers' Association was started. The Gum Manufacturers' Association was organized in 1913 and the American Oak Manufacturers' Association began in 1917.[6] The Oak and Gum Manufacturers' Associations merged in January, 1919, to form the American Hardwood Manufacturers' Association and, in December of the same year, the Hardwood Manufacturers' Association merged with the latter organization.[7] The resulting organization represented 400 producers of many varieties of hardwoods with mills stretching from New York to Texas.[8]

Another of the early associations was the Maple Flooring Manufacturers' Association. It apparently originated sometime in the 1890's, had seven member firms at the start, and may have accounted for as much as 95 per cent of the maple

[5] *Southern Lumberman* (August 15, 1892), p. 9, as quoted by Bryant, p. 310.

[6] Nelson C. Brown, *The American Lumber Industry* (New York, 1923), p. 244.

[7] *Ibid.*, and Bryant, *Lumber*, pp. 304–305.

[8] 257 U.S. 391.

flooring production in the United States by 1901.[9] This association was unincorporated and, though the name remained unchanged, was reorganized several times before 1922.[10]

It is difficult to assess the precise influence of the early associations on the performance of the industry. A few points are clear, however. One is that price stabilization or, more forcefully, price control and output restrictions were one of the more important reasons for the formation of the associations. The by-laws and quotations from the trade press reproduced in the more extensive histories cited make this amply evident. Similarly, it is clear that despite this intention the prices of the various species fluctuated with respect to one another and, when averaged together, moved much as one would expect of competitive prices with varying demand.[11] For example, indexes of oak prices and of general lumber prices based on Compton's data are juxtaposed with cyclical peaks and troughs in Table 1. The association between lumber prices and general business conditions is obvious. This general pattern of price behavior continued through World War I and in the post-war inflation the rise in lumber prices was marked. Table 2 shows the extent of hardwood price increases found by Bryant during the year 1919. The increases in individual items were sometimes much greater than the averages indicate.[12]

The lumber trade associations were involved in legal proceedings as early as 1881.[13] Until 1906, however, the suits typically involved the enforceability of association agreements

[9] *The Lumber Industry,* Bureau of Corporations, Department of Commerce and Labor (Washington 1913–1914), part iv, pp. 878–882.

[10] 268 U.S. 566.

[11] See Compton, *The Organization of the Lumber Industry,* chaps. iv and v; R. C. Bryant, "Lumber Prices," *The Annals,* American Academy of Political and Social Science, 89:78–98 (May 1920); *The Lumber Industry,* pt. iv, pp. 878–882; *Historical Forestry Statistics of the United States,* Statistical Bulletin No. 228, U.S. Dept. of Agriculture (Washington, October 1958).

[12] 257 U.S. 409.

[13] Bryant, *Lumber,* 2nd. ed., pp. 323–345.

TABLE 1

LUMBER PRICES INDEXES AND THE BUSINESS CYCLE, 1897–1912

(Index based on 1901–1903 = 100)

	Peaks and Troughs of:		
Year	Oak price index[a]	Lumber price index[a]	Cyclical turning point[b]
1897	80.9	64.5	Trough, 2nd quarter, 1897
1900	98.2	96.8	Peak, 3rd quarter, 1899
1901	93.9	84.3	Trough, 4th quarter, 1900
1903	109.7	107.6	Peak, 4th quarter, 1902
1904	106.8	97.5	Trough, 3rd quarter, 1904
1907	139.2	150.3	Peak, 2nd quarter, 1907
1908	119.2	112.2	Trough, 2nd quarter, 1908
1912	153.0	145.3	Peak, 1st quarter, 1913

[a] Based on Compton, *The Organization of the Lumber Industry*, p. 83.

[b] Arthur F. Burns and Wesley C. Mitchell, *Measuring Business Cycles* (New York, 1946), table 16.

TABLE 2

HARDWOOD PRICE INCREASES DURING 1919[a]

Specie	Per cent Increase in Price
Hard maple	114%
Gum	92
Oak, plain	87
Ash	65
Hickory	60
Yellow poplar	58
Chestnut	53
Birch	40

[a] Bryant, "Lumber Prices," p. 87.

among the parties to the agreement, refusals to deal with certain wholesalers and retailers, and related trade practices. Members of the Mississippi Valley Lumbermen's Association were indicted for allegedly violating the Sherman Act in 1892 but the indictment was quashed.[14] An extensive investigation of the entire industry was begun in 1907 after the Senate directed the Department of Commerce and Labor to inquire "into the cause or causes of the high price of lumber" and to ascertain "whether or not there exists . . . any combination, conspiracy, trust, agreement or contract intended to operate in restraint of lawful trade." [15]

In 1911, two years before the report of the Department of Commerce and Labor was published, the Attorney General sought an injunction against the Eastern States Retail Lumber Dealers' Association.[16] Nearly two years later, in January, 1913, the District Court permanently enjoined the defendants from "combining, conspiring, or agreeing together to distribute, and from distributing" official reports concerning wholesalers who sold directly to consumers.

It was also in 1911 that the Lumber Secretaries' Bureau of Information was indicted for publishing information about manufacturers and wholesalers who sold to mail-order houses, co-operatives, contractors and consumers.[17] This case was dismissed in 1913. Shortly thereafter, civil suits were filed against the Michigan Retail Lumber Dealers' Association, against the Northwestern Lumbermen's Association and against the Colorado and Wyoming Lumber Dealers' Association.[18] The Lumber Secretaries' Bureau of Information was made a co-defendant in each of these cases. A permanent in-

[14] *Ibid.*, p. 325.

[15] *Ibid.*, p. 327, quoted from the *American Lumberman* (December 22, 1906), p. 29.

[16] U.S. v. Eastern Retail Lumber Dealers' Association, 201 F. 581 (S.D.N.Y. 1913).

[17] Bryant, *Lumber*, 2nd. ed., p. 332.

[18] *Ibid.*, p. 333.

junction was issued in 1917 against the publication of lists of wholesalers and manufacturers who sold directly to consumers.

It is interesting that the date of the suits and investigations coincide with the dates of high lumber prices. The lumber investigation of the Department of Commerce and Labor began in 1907, not long before the panic of the same year. Of the panic year, Bryant says, "The era of high prices culminated . . . and the rapid drop in value during this period led to many financial failures and to general demoralization in the industry." [19] In April, 1907, the *American Lumberman* could report that "Maple is one of the most active woods. The recent advance of $1 has made no apparent difference in demand." [20] In November it reported, "Maple flooring cannot be termed firm as sales have been heard of at considerably under list." By February, 1908, it reported that, "The maple flooring men of Michigan feel that competition is so fierce in these dull times that it would be advisable to combine all stocks under one selling agency, probably located in Chicago." The 1911 and 1913 suits also came during a period of relatively high lumber prices.

THE *American Column and Lumber Co.* CASE

Lumber production, both of hardwoods and soft, reached its historic peak in 1906 and 1907.[21] Hardwood production in these years amounted to about 11,100 million board feet per year. Production declined after this, reaching about 7,500 million, 8,500 million, 6,700 million, 6,200 million, 7,100 million and 7,400 million board feet in the years 1915, 1916,

[19] Bryant, "Lumber Prices," p. 80.

[20] This and the following quotations are taken from *The Lumber Industry,* part iv, p. 891.

[21] *Historical Statistics of the United States, 1789–1945* (Washington, 1949), tables F 109, 110, 111, p. 125. Other sources, including the National Lumber Manufacturers' Association's *Lumber Industry Facts* (1957), p. 15, cite 1909 as the peak year.

1917, 1918, 1919 and 1920, respectively. Averaging all hardwoods together, prices tended to decline slightly from 1906 to 1915, then rose through 1920.[22]

The American Hardwood Manufacturers' Association was formed, as noted above, from a merger of two other associations in January, 1919. The new association adopted the uniform grading rules of the Hardwood Manufacturers' Association and took over the statistical reporting of all three of the associations eventually merged together.[23] Headquarters were in Memphis where an office staff and a "Manager of Statistics" occupied a substantial amount of space.

Two years prior to the formation of the American Hardwood Manufacturers' Association, the Hardwood Manufacturers' Association declared that:

> The purpose of the plan is to disseminate among members accurate knowledge of production and market conditions so that each member may gauge the market intelligently instead of guessing at it; to make competition open and above board instead of secret and concealed; to substitute, in estimating market conditions, frank and full statements of our competitors for the frequently misleading and colored statements of the buyer.
>
> This plan does not contemplate anything illegal or anything which might be developed into illegal acts. There is absolutely no agreement as to prices, either real or implied. There is no obligation, either real or implied on the part of any member to reduce, increase, or change the character of his production in any other manner than he himself may think best. The plan will, however, furnish information to enable each member to intelligently make prices and intelligently govern his own production.[24]

In the rest of the statement, a specific plan was outlined. Each member was to report on production, sales, shipments, stocks, price lists and lumber inspection every two months on

[22] *Historical Statistics,* table F 122, p. 125.
[23] Bryant, *Lumber,* 2nd. ed., p. 305.
[24] *Ibid.,* p. 335. The Supreme Court, 257 U.S. 392, quotes the first, but not the second, paragraph of this statement of purpose.

forms provided by the Association. There were to be monthly reports on production, stocks and price lists and daily reports on sales and shipments, including the names and addresses of the buyer and the kind, grade, and quality of the lumber involved.[25] The Manager of Statistics was to collect these data and return to the members monthly summaries of production by type of lumber, weekly reports of all sales, showing each sale and price and the name of the purchaser, and another weekly report of each member's shipments. In addition, monthly stock reports and monthly reports on price lists were to be sent out. Finally, the Manager was to distribute a "market report letter" on "changes in conditions both in the consuming and producing sectors." [26]

This plan, though a new one for this association, was not novel in the industry. The Southern Lumber Manufacturers' Association had agreed in 1892 "to collect, tabulate, and distribute . . . information regarding the output, shipments and stock-on-hand." [27] Moreover, there was nothing at all secret about the plan. It was adopted on January 31, 1917, published in full in the *Hardwood Record,* February 10, 1917, applied first to oak beginning March 1, 1917, and discussed, of all places, in the June, 1917, issue of the *American Economic Review.*[28] The plan was extended to poplar on July 1, 1917; to cottonwood, July 15, 1917; to chestnut, August 15, 1917; to ash and basswood, September 15, 1917; and to other hardwoods, March 1, 1918.[29]

In the meantime, an inflationary prosperity had begun in the entire country. Private construction increased from $2,482,000,000 in 1918 to $3,770,000,000 and $4,779,000,000 in 1919 and 1920, respectively.[30] Currency and deposits rose

[25] Bryant, *Lumber,* 2nd. ed., p. 335–336 and 257 U.S. 394–395.

[26] 257 U.S. 396.

[27] Bryant, *Lumber,* p. 310.

[28] *Ibid.,* pp. 335–336, and H. R. Tosdal, "Open Price Associations," *American Economic Review,* 7:331–352 (June 1917).

[29] Bryant, *Lumber,* 2nd. ed., p. 336.

[30] *Historical Statistics 1789–1945,* table H 3, p. 168.

rapidly and the BLS Wholesale Price Index (1926 = 100) increased from 85.5 in 1916 to 117.5 in 1917, 131.3 in 1918, 138.6 in 1919, and 154.4 in 1920. The price index for building materials rose from 67.6 to 150.1 during the same period.[31]

Hardwood prices had been rising gradually since 1915 but during 1919 the rise in some varieties was spectacular. On February 16, 1920, the U. S. Attorney General sought an injunction in the District Court in Memphis to restrain the year-old American Hardwood Manufacturers' Association, its Manager of Statistics and its members from continuing the "open competition plan" begun by the Hardwood Manufacturers' Association in 1917 and taken over a year previously by the new Association.[32] The full statistical program had been in operation for two years and, while the original plan called for monthly meetings in each of four districts in the Southwestern territory, forty-nine smaller meetings — approximately one per week — were held between January 31, 1919 and February 19, 1920.[33] The summaries of the weekly sales reports and the monthly market letters prepared by Mr. F. R. Gadd, the Manager of Statistics, were discussed at these meetings.

The consolidated American Hardwood Manufacturers' Association made a concerted effort to get all its members to join the plan. It told the potential participants among other things, that:

Knowledge regarding prices actually made is all that is necessary to keep prices at reasonably stable and normal levels.

. . . By keeping all members fully and quickly informed of what the others have done, the work of the Plan results in *a certain uniformity of trade practice*. There is no agreement to follow the practice of others, *although members do follow their most intelli-*

[31] *Ibid.,* tables L 15 and 22, p. 233.

[32] U.S. v. American Column and Lumber Co., et al. 263 F. 147 (W.D. Tenn. 1920).

[33] 257 U.S. 397.

gent competitors, if they know what these competitors have been actually doing . . .

Competition, blind, vicious, unreasoning, may stimulate trade to abnormal activity, but such condition is no more sound than that medieval spirit some still cling to of taking a club and going out and knocking the other fellow and taking away his bone.

The keynote to modern business success is mutual confidence and co-operation. *Co-operative competition, not cutthroat competition.* Co-operation is a matter of business, because it pays, because it enables you to get the best price for your product, because you come into closer *personal contact with the market.*

. . . For the first time in the history of the industry, the hardwood manufacturers are organized into one compact, comprehensive body, equipped to serve the whole trade in a thorough and efficient manner . . . More members mean more power to do more good for the industry. With co-operation of this kind we will soon have enlisted in our efforts practically every producing interest, *and you know what that means.*[34]

Mr. Gadd continued his efforts to "sell" the plan to the industry — to keep existing members and to bring in new ones. On April 23, 1919, Gadd wrote members asking them to detail their experience with the Plan.[35] The June 7th weekly sales report provided excerpts of the replies. A few of these follow:

We believe we have profited from $500 to $1,000 during the past 30 days by being correctly informed relative to the prices stock is really being sold at.

The very first report which we received under this plan enabled us to increase our price $6 per thousand on a special item in oak.

At a recent Memphis meeting it developed our company was carrying an unusually large stock in thoroughly dried gum, and seemed to be the only one among those present who had it. Within two weeks from date of this meeting, where it developed there was

[34] 257 U.S. 393–394. Italics are in this source. It is not indicated whether italics are in the original being quoted.

[35] *Ibid.*, pp. 407–408.

a big shortage of red gum items, we found a most unusual demand at prices we had not hoped for.

There seems to be a friendly rivalry between members to see who can get the best prices, whereas under the old plan it was cutthroat competition. Now it is a pleasure to sell because *we know* what we are doing and have information at our finger tips that enables us to know these things before the other fellow does.

Our experience has been that the open competition plan has been absolutely accurate, but instead of apparently stabilizing the market, it has caused a runaway market.[36]

Mr. Gadd's comments on market conditions in his weekly letters may be indicative of the spirit he was attempting to instill in the membership. In the third letter issued, that of February 8, 1919, he noted:

Buyers who have been looking for a downward revision of prices are going to be disappointed . . . It is no longer merely a question of who can, or will, hold out the longest — that condition no longer exists. Buying has been resumed after a period of waiting and uncertainty, and it is confidently expected that the move in this direction will long be continued . . . Stocks remain below normal. Total stocks on hand in the Southern territory are two million feet less, all grades combined, as compared with last month . . . Production in the Eastern territory, however, is not more than sixty per cent. of normal at the present time . . . It must be apparent that the outlook on the whole is favorable for a strong market for all the lumber that can be produced during the coming months.[37]

On March 1, 1919, Gadd reported "a situation we believe is unparalleled in the hardwood industry." Stocks, it appeared, had decreased tremendously between January 1, 1919, and February 1, 1919. The report continued:

The chief factors contributing to this situation are curtailed production and increased volume of sales . . . At this rate, it will

[36] 263 F. 154–155. Some of the same quotes and some additional ones are at 257 U.S. 408–409.
[37] 263 F. 153.

not be long before there is a famine of hardwood lumber. We hear a great deal about the waiting attitude of the buyer, with the expectation of a price recession; but with such conditions as are above recited it is difficult to understand why holders of hardwood lumber need worry as to the future . . . With stocks low and ill-assorted, and with no prospect for restoring them to even last year's meager quantities, the outlook for strong prices on all hardwoods could not be better.[38]

On March 8, Mr. Gadd reported production "is at the present time only fifty-six per cent. of normal. . . . Certainly in any other industry the buyer could never expect anything but an advance in price when the supply is below normal, the production is far below normal, and the demand is improving." [39] Nonetheless, he observed at the same time:

There has been a long drawn out and desperate effort to break the hardwood market by withdrawal of demand; but, be it said to the eternal credit of the hardwood producers, *they have maintained a stout heart and stiff backbone,* with the result that there has been exhibited a strength in the market which has been little short of remarkable in the face of the light demand and the vigorous efforts which have been steadily made *to hammer down prices* . . .

With this known information before him it is difficult to see how any intelligent hardwood manufacturer can entertain any hesitation as to *the proper course for him to pursue* in selling his lumber.[40]

By March 29th, the weekly letter noted that "a firm market for the balance of the year, with prices moving upward," was indicated. Mr. Gadd could find "no reason to cut prices." [41] Now there was no mention of efforts of buyers to "hammer down prices." In the April 26th letter, issued three days after Gadd had asked members to describe their experience with the Plan, it was pointed out "that stocks were less than 75 per cent. of normal, that production was about 60 per cent. of

[38] *Ibid.*
[39] 263 F. 153–154.
[40] 257 U.S. 405.
[41] *Ibid.*, pp. 405–406.

normal and that demand was far in excess of supply." [42] The "light demand" of two months previous had disappeared and, according to Mr. Gadd:

If ever there was a time when rich rewards awaited the producer of hardwood lumber, now is that time. *There are glorious opportunities ahead* . . . Supply and demand must necessarily govern prices. The demand is with us, the supply inadequate, therefore *values must increase, as our competition in hardwood is only among ourselves.*[43]

Subsequent letters, much in the same vein so far as demand conditions, warned of the danger of overproduction. The May 17th sales report noted that:

The lumbermen have gone through several lean years, but we are confronted with the possibility of killing the goose that laid the golden egg. *Overproduction will spell disaster,* as it should always be borne in mind that the maximum productive capacity of the sawmills of the country is much in excess of any demand the country has ever known.[44]

Similar warnings against overproduction and "running day and night" appeared in other letters and this same topic was discussed at some of the meetings. By February 16, 1920, 365 of the 400 members of the American Hardwood Manufacturers' Association had joined the plan. These operated 465 of the "more than 9000 hardwood lumber mills in that part of the United States," [45] and produced about one third of total U.S. hardwood output.

In the decision of the District Court, Judge McCall noted that the facts were undisputed. There were, he said, only two questions. The first was whether there was "in the minds of two or more of the defendants a design to accomplish by and through the plan a common purpose." And his answer was clear. "It cannot be with reason denied . . . by the de-

[42] *Ibid.*, p. 406.
[43] 257 U.S. 406.
[44] *Ibid.*, p. 403.
[45] Dissenting opinion of Justice Brandeis, 257 U.S. 413.

fendants, that they formed an association, a combination, or an agreement, to promote the interests of the members of the plan." [46]

Having answered this affirmatively, the legality of the plan depended on the answer to the second question. "Did and does this combination or association restrain trade in interstate commerce, within the meaning of the law?" [47] To this the answer was less obvious for, according to the Judge:

> It would serve no useful purpose to analyze the evidence, or to enter into a discussion of the decided cases, which have hitherto arisen under the Sherman Act; each case must be decided on its own facts, and if these facts establish the proposition that the combination entered into unreasonably restrains trade in interstate commerce, by suppressing competition in prices, it falls within the condemnation of the act. Competition and co-operation by and with those engaged in the same business is (sic) not necessarily inconsistent. Successful business will likely result from a proper balance of the two, but too much of either may lead to disaster. Competition without co-operation means destructive competition. Cooperation without competition means the destruction of competition — price-fixing. The latter is the state of the open competition plan, as disclosed on this record.[48]

And thus a temporary injunction was granted on March 16, 1920, and made permanent by an agreement in order to hasten appeal on April 21st. The case was heard by the Supreme Court on October 21, 1920, reargued on October 12th and 13th, 1921, and a decision was rendered on the following December 19th. The majority opinion posed "only the question whether the system of doing business adopted resulted in that direct and undue restraint of interstate commerce which is condemned by this antitrust statute." [49] Again the answer was affirmative. The American Hardwood Manufacturers' Association was dissolved shortly thereafter.[50]

[46] 263 F. 151–152.
[47] *Ibid.*
[48] 263 F. 156.
[49] 257 U.S. 400.
[50] Bryant, *Lumber,* 2nd. ed., p. 338.

THE *Maple Flooring* CASE

In the early years of its operation, the Maple Flooring Manufacturers' Association represented nearly all the maple flooring manufacturers in the country and was active in establishing prices, discounts, commissions and output.[51] Members had a deposit with the Association which, on violation of the rules or agreements, might be forfeited. In spite of having so large a portion of total production, of having but a few members located in a relatively small geographic area, and of their frequent meetings, agreements, and fines, the Association was not always able to maintain the listed prices. In the Fall of 1903, during a cyclical downswing, the *American Lumberman* reported that "the famous 'maple trust' seems to be a thing of the past." [52]

By 1913, after a series of reorganizations of the maple and hardwood trade associations in the Lake regions, direct agreements on prices and output had disappeared, though the issuance of list prices continued. In addition, in articles of the Association dated January 1, 1913, a system of allotment of total production among the members was devised and apparently kept in operation until March, 1920.[53] During 1916, a "minimum price plan" was adopted. Minimum prices of maple, beech and birch flooring were to be prepared based on the average cost of the members to manufacture and sell, with 10 per cent added for "profit." It is not clear that this plan, which included penalties for violation, was ever put into effect but in any case it was abandoned as an explicit objective of the Association in 1920 or 1921.[54]

The prices of maple rose in a manner similar to other hardwoods in 1918 and 1919. Bryant's index of hard maple prices, with 1913–1914 = 100, increased from 135 in the first

[51] *The Lumber Industry*, pt iv, pp. 878–892.
[52] Quoted in *The Lumber Industry*, pt iv, pp. 880–881.
[53] 268 U.S. 576.
[54] *Ibid.*, pp. 572, 576.

quarter of 1918 to 310 by the fourth quarter, 1919.[55] From late 1920 to early 1922 — the period following the new plan for maple — lumber prices fell quite sharply.

In March, 1922, following the decision in the *American Column and Lumber* case, the Maple Flooring Manufacturers' Association was reorganized. The new group had twenty-two corporate members, about half of which produced rough lumber and manufactured it into flooring. The other half purchased rough lumber for flooring manufacture. There were in that year at least seventeen other manufacturers of the same maple, beech and birch flooring in the states of Illinois, Michigan, Minnesota and Wisconsin and more than thirty-one additional manufacturers in other states.[56] The defendant corporations accounted for 70 per cent of total maple, beech and birch flooring production in 1922,[57] of which about 90 per cent was maple.[58] Defendants worked only 2 per cent of the total stand of these types of lumber in the country and it was estimated that there were 4,767 other manufacturers of maple products who could, with small expense, convert to the production of maple flooring.[59]

The government filed a bill in equity on March 5, 1923, asking for injunctive relief. The principal contention of the government was that although the old "minimum price plan" had been formally abandoned an effective substitute had in fact been devised. The substitute consisted, so it was alleged, of the computation and distribution of the average cost of the various grades and dimensions of flooring and of a freight rate booklet.

The cost computation was done as it had been under the

[55] Bryant, "Lumber Prices," p. 89.

[56] 268 U.S. 565. In a deposition, Mr. Edward B. Gordon, an expert witness, estimated the total number of nonmember producers at 70. *Records and Briefs in United States Cases,* U. S. Supreme Court, October Term, 1924, no. 342, p. 626.

[57] 268 U.S. 565.

[58] Deposition of Mr. Edward B. Gordon, *Records and Briefs,* p. 630.

[59] *Ibid.,* pp. 628, 632, 633.

"minimum price plan." At the time the suit was brought, instead of adding 10 per cent for "profit" and calling the result a minimum price, with penalties for violation, the Association added 5 per cent for "contingencies" and called the sum "average cost." The contingency amount was dropped in July, 1923, prior to the hearing of the case.[60]

The freight rate booklet showed rail freight rates for flooring from Cadillac, Michigan, to more than 5,000 points in the United States. Members usually sold on a delivered price basis and used the rates shown in the booklet for this purpose. Under the old "minimum price plan," the entries in the rate booklet were the minimum price plus freight but this practice was abandoned in March, 1920. Still, the defendants quoted delivered prices after 1920 by using freight rates from Cadillac despite the fact that actual shipment was from mills located in other places. Evidence was introduced to show that the aggregate of actual freight cost was only nominally different from those based on Cadillac for the factories located in Michigan and Wisconsin.[61] No mention was made of whether the company located in Illinois and that located in New York also quoted freight from Cadillac and, if so, how much difference there was between actual and quoted rates in these instances. Failure to cover this point makes it difficult to assess whether the defendants used the rate booklet because of delays in getting rate quotation from local freight agents, as they claimed, or whether the booklet was used to maintain more uniformity in delivered prices, as argued by the government.

The Maple Flooring Manufacturers' Association, like the American Hardwood Manufacturers' Association and many others in the industry, collected and distributed statistics on sales, prices, production and unfilled orders. Neither the names of purchasers nor a geographic breakdown of pur-

[60] 268 U.S. 568–570.
[61] *Ibid.*, p. 571.

chases was reported and, after July, 1923, the reporting mill was no longer identified. The Association did not at the time of the suit publish any reports dealing with current and future market conditions.[62]

Members of the Association did meet monthly and it was admitted that trade conditions, market prices and manufacturing and market conditions were discussed. These discussions, at least prior to June, 1923, when *U.S. v. American Linseed Oil Co.*[63] was decided, included mention of "the trend of prices and future prices." [64]

The District Court decided that the government had proved its case; that the activities of the Maple Flooring Manufacturers' Association fell within the rules of the *American Column and Lumber Co.* and the *American Linseed Oil Co.* cases. The dissolution of the Association was ordered and an injunction granted because, in the words of the court, "it cannot be doubted that the association exercised its power wrongfully and that the agreements and methods, at all times, have had a compelling tendency to impede the operation of the economic laws of supply and demand, to increase prices and to stifle competition." [65]

On appeal to the Supreme Court, the decision of the District Court was reversed on June 1, 1925. Now Justices Brandeis and Holmes, who had dissented along with the now retired Justice McKenna in *American Column and Lumber,* joined in the majority opinion of the recently appointed Justice Stone. Justice McReynolds, a member of the majority in *American Column and Lumber,* joined Chief Justice Taft and Justice Sanford in dissent.[66] Apart from the change in its make-

[62] 268 U.S. 573–574.

[63] 262 U.S. 371 (1923).

[64] 268 U.S. 575.

[65] Quoted by Bryant, *Lumber,* 2nd. ed., p. 340.

[66] The change in the membership of the Court between 1921 and 1925 is an interesting side light of the two cases. Justices Day, Pitney and Clarke, who were with the majority in *American Column and Lumber,* were replaced by Justices Sutherland, Butler and Sanford. Thus two of the three

up, the Court found that recent maple prices were declining or stable, not rising rapidly as had been the case in the previous suit.

COMMENTS ON THE HARDWOOD CASES

Most comment on the *American Column and Lumber* and *Maple Flooring* cases revolves around the question of whether the two are consistent. The view of the District Court in the latter case was that the facts were sufficiently similar to warrant a verdict for the government. Justice Stone was unable to convince Justices Taft, McReynolds and Sanford of material differences.

The same question has been debated by economists. In a paper written shortly after the *Maple Flooring* decision, Sharfman could argue that:

> . . . there appears to be no adequate ground for considering the opinion . . . in *Maple Flooring* . . . a reversal of the earlier decisions. Justice Stone . . . clearly distinguished between the two . . . In the Maple Flooring case . . . Justice Stone developed carefully the following chain of reasoning: that each case under the Sherman Act must necessarily be determined on its own facts; that in order to succeed, the government must bring its complaint within the rule of the Hardwood and Linseed cases; that the characteristic feature of those cases consisted in their involving concert of action; that such concert of action was entirely lacking in the [Maple Flooring] proceeding; that while the collection and dissemination of trade information might be made a basis or instrument of concert of action, there was no necessary tendency for such an outcome to follow.[67]

Myron H. Watkins, in a comment on this view, was of an opposite opinion. Speaking of the *American Column and Lumber,* the *Linseed Oil,* the *Maple Flooring* and the *Cement* cases, he said:

---

new members voted to reverse the District Court in *Maple Flooring.* Justice Stone had been appointed to fill Justice McKenna's place after the latter retired in January, 1925.

[67] J. L. Sharfman, "The Trade Association Movement," *American Economic Review,* 16:217-218 (March 1926).

True, the Court relates numerous circumstances calculated to support its interpretation of the record in each of these four instances. But I think I am correct in stating that not in a single respect are the facts specified in support of one of these decisions in harmony with the comparable facts in the other case decided the same way and contrary to the situation disclosed in the two cases decided in the opposite way. Thus, in respect to the character of the statistical data interchanged, it was at least as detailed, or 'intimate,' in the Cement case as in either the Hardwood Lumber or Linseed Oil cases. In respect to the publicity given the information assembled, none of the four defendant associations stood in a better light than the Hardwood Association. If the Linseed Crushers' Council operated secretly, so also did the Cement Manufacturers' Association. In respect to the reporting of so-called 'future prices,' or prices current, the Hardwood Association appears to have been no more miscreant than the Maple Flooring group, and the Cement Association no less reprehensible than the Linseed Crushers' Council, if this be considered an element in the latters' offense . . . And it might be well not to overlook the fact that the trial court in the Maple Flooring case found, in connection with the association meetings, what the Supreme Court was unable to find, evidence of the exertion of the pressure of group opinion to induce conformity to the policies deemed mutually advantageous. Finally, in respect to the existence of agreements, . . . if there is no evidence of express commitments in the recent cases, neither is there in the earlier cases . . .

The real explanation of the contrary decisions in 1921 and in 1925 . . . is not that in examining the respective records the Court saw different things, but that it saw things differently. Fundamentally, the change in general business conditions accounts for the opposite view taken in the earlier and in the later cases . . .[68]

Rather curiously, a study by R. C. Bryant of the War Industries Board, published in 1920 prior to the *American Column and Lumber* decision, explained the increase in lumber

[68] Myron H. Watkins, Comments on "The Trade Association Movement," *American Economic Review,* 16: 233–235. While Watkins claimed it was not his purpose to inquire whether the rule of reason which produced these results was good or bad, it is clear from his discussion that he leaned toward the view that it was not very good.

prices in 1919 as the result of the resumption of demand following a period of uncertainty concerning government contracts, a prolonged period of bad weather, and labor and transportation tie-ups.[69] Actually, since the Hardwood Association was formed only in January, it is a bit difficult to imagine that the new organization was so effective as to cause the noted drastic depletion of stocks in the very first thirty to sixty days of its operation.

This brings up a most important point — one that neither the courts nor those commenting on the cases appear to have noticed. There were in *American Column and Lumber* three hundred sixty-five participating firms. The firms produced a wide variety of hardwoods, some presumably specializing in one, some in another. The businesses of the firms ranged from cutting down trees to manufacturing logs into lumber and to selling to manufacturers and to wholesale and retail dealers. Again, it is unlikely that all the firms were fully integrated across these lines. More likely, while some may have been so integrated, the bulk of the firms were principally in some one stage of this vertical process. In addition, the firms were members of three separate associations until 1919. They had had little time to get well acquainted. In summary, the American Hardwood Manufacturers' Association was a *large, heterogeneous group with no historically established pattern of behavior.*

Contrast this with the Maple Flooring Association — almost exclusively one kind of wood, only two types of activity (producing lumber and producing flooring), a much smaller number of participants, and a long history of co-operation with one another. In relation to the Hardwood Association it was *small* and *homogeneous.*

Attempts to demonstrate the consistency of the Court in these two cases are bound to fail. Distinguishing *American Column and Lumber* from *Maple Flooring* on the basis of Mr.

[69] Bryant, "Lumber Prices," pp. 82–90.

Gadd's comments concerning the future and the danger of overproduction simply ignores other aspects in which *Maple Flooring* involved far more restraining influences. It is, in the first place, most unlikely that Gadd's comments would long have affected the behavior of the individual firms. So long as they comprised a small percentage of total output and a still smaller percentage of total mills, output restrictions would have worked to the advantage of nonmember firms and "chiselers" to the agreement, thus causing the output restrictions to be abandoned. And in the second place, the freight rate booklets and delivered pricing system of the Maple Flooring group would, with so few, quite geographically concentrated firms, be far more effective in preventing independent rivalry. The historic use of the delivered pricing system effected a strong, implicit agreement. As Smith pointed out, a conspiracy can be effective only so long as every individual trader continues of the same mind — and even establishing, let alone maintaining, the same mind among the many Hardwood Association producers would have been most difficult. In contrast, the Maple Flooring group had substantially similar values. Or again, as Smith observed, it is more difficult for several persons in the same trade to conspire than for a few, thus the restraint on rivalry in *Maple Flooring* was easier to maintain than was the case in *American Column and Lumber*.

The consideration of number and homogeneity of sellers is as important as the formality of the interfirm organization in realistically evaluating restraint of trade cases. An organization which, with a small number of homogeneous firms, results in a complete absence of interfirm rivalry may, with larger numbers of more heterogeneous firms, be no more than adequate to produce conditions of workable rivalry.

CHAPTER VIII

THE TRENTON POTTERIES CASE[1]

INTRODUCTION

U.S. v. Trenton Potteries Co. is at once a well known and an almost neglected case in the price-fixing area of antitrust policy. Its legal aspects are familiar to all. Mr. Justice Stone's famous decision, which declared that contracts fixing uniform prices "by those controlling in any substantial manner a trade or business" were per se illegal regardless of "the reasonableness of the particular prices agreed upon," [2] is a landmark in the history of antitrust litigation.

The forgotten aspect of the *Potteries* case is not its legal importance. It is the economic situation which gave rise to the case. Since the Supreme Court's decision in 1927 it has been largely forgotten that the evidence of an agreement to fix actual prices was primarily circumstantial; that the case, like *American Column and Lumber* and *Maple Flooring,* concerned the activities of a trade association and its members; that the period of time during which the illegal activities were said to have occurred was, again like the Hardwood cases, the years 1919 through 1922; that the defendants, rather than being content with a stable and profitable arrangement restraining trade to their advantage, were bickering among themselves and suffering losses even during years of prosperity; and that prices, rather than being fixed and uniform, rose and fell with the tides of business and displayed through-

[1] U.S. v. Trenton Potteries Co., 273 U.S. 392 (1927).
[2] *Ibid.*, p. 398.

out large variability both within and among the defendant companies.

It should not be inferred from these comments or those that follow that it is being argued that the *Trenton Potteries* group should not have been found in violation of the Sherman Act. It was quite within reason that the jury should have found an agreement among the firms to fix prices even while it is as clear that the firms did not succeed in this endeavor. The only criticism of the legal aspects of the case that are of concern here is the extent to which economic questions were ignored through the rulings of the bench. And conclusions with respect to these are deferred to the last chapter.

The importance of the case at this point is the excellent illustration it provides of the problems inherent in effecting a working conspiracy in a market with more than a few sellers, an absence of leadership and a modest degree of heterogeneity in value systems. Economists, it seems, are too prone to believe that collusion is easy to accomplish. Perhaps this is because it can be shown theoretically that collusive behavior results in greater joint profits than does independent behavior. Whatever its origin, however, the tendency to independent action is often stronger than has been appreciated, providing an atmosphere in which rather formal attempts to suppress rivalry fail in their missions. The *Potteries* group was attempting to stall a change in industrial structure which both their internal price behavior and technological conditions were forcing on them. And their organization, whatever treatment it received under the antitrust laws, was incapable of stemming this tide.

THE *Potteries* CASE

In the early years of the present century, the production of vitreous enamelware was centered in New Jersey along the Delaware River. One group of firms specialized in sanitary pottery fixtures for use in bathrooms and lavatories. The largest of these was the Trenton Potteries Company, of Trenton, New Jersey, which had been incorporated in 1892 and which, by the 1920's, had a plant of thirty-six kilns representing perhaps 11 per cent of the total capacity in the country.[3] The next largest firm was Thomas Maddock's Sons Company, also of Trenton, with twenty-one kilns. In the same area were the Sanitary Earthenware Specialty Company, with fourteen kilns, some in Trenton and some in Columbus; Ohio; the Keystone Pottery Company of Trenton, with thirteen kilns; John Maddock and Sons Company, with eleven kilns in Trenton; the Universal Sanitary Manufacturing Company, of New Castle, Pennsylvania, with eleven kilns; and at least six other firms with a total of thirty-eight kilns.[4]

These firms belonged to the Sanitary Potters' Association, a trade organization with offices in Trenton. Other members included the Standard Sanitary Manufacturing Company, with twenty-seven kilns in Kokomo, Indiana, and Tiffen, Ohio; the Bowers Pottery Company in Mannington, West Virginia, which had seventeen kilns; the Pacific Sanitary Manufacturing Company, Richmond, California, with twelve kilns; the Eljer Company, of Cameron, West Virginia, and Ford City, Pennsylvania, with ten kilns; and seven other scattered firms with a total of fifty-two kilns.[5]

The twenty-three corporations represented 82 per cent of the industry's output in 1922. Their association, which had

[3] Data on the individual companies are from *Records and Briefs in United States Cases,* U.S. Supreme Court, October Term, 1926, no. 27.

[4] These firms were the Acme Sanitary Pottery Company (Trenton), the B.O.T. Manufacturing Company (Trenton), the Camden Pottery Company (Camden), Cochran-Drugan and Company (Trenton), Lambertville Pottery Company (Lambertville, N.J.) and the Resolute Pottery Company (Trenton). There were several other firms which were not indicted.

[5] These firms were the Abington Sanitary Manufacturing Company (Abington, Illinois), The Chicago Pottery Company (Chicago), the Kalamazoo Sanitary Manufacturing Company (Kalamazoo), the Kokomo Sanitary Pottery Company (Kokomo), the National-Helfrich Potteries Company (Evansville, Ind.), the Wheeling Sanitary Manufacturing Company (Wheeling) and the Horton Pottery Company (Chillicothe, Ohio).

been in existence for at least a decade and of which the president was Mr. A. M. Maddock, head of the Thomas Maddock's Sons Company, was an active one. It worked on standardization of design and parts, was encouraging the adoption of a uniform system of cost accounting, held frequent meetings for members, operated a statistical collection and reporting service and published and distributed an "official" price list for the various items produced by the members. The association exhorted its members not to sell so-called "Class B" goods — seconds with slight imperfections — on the domestic market and kept a file of dealers to whom the members regularly sold "Class A" ware.

On August 8, 1922, a federal grand jury returned an indictment against these twenty-three firms and as many of their officers and officials of the Sanitary Potters' Association. It was charged that:

> defendants in pursuance of a common plan, agreement, and undertaking among them so to do, and in order effectively to carry out the aims, objects, and purposes of the aforesaid combination and conspiracy, by common and concerted action did arbitrarily fix, establish, maintain, and exact uniform, arbitrary, and non-competitive prices . . . and further did refrain from engaging in competition with each other as to the prices at which the said sanitary pottery should be sold, and . . . did, further, secure and exact the uniform, arbitrary, and non-competitive prices so fixed by them from time to time . . .[6]

In addition to this count, the indictment also charged that the defendants had conspired and agreed to sell only to certain "legitimate" jobbers and had uniformly refused to sell to others. All of this, it was alleged, was accomplished with the Sanitary Potters' Association as the vehicle.

The statistical reporting had begun in 1916. Each month the members reported the numbers of the various items of sanitaryware that had been ordered from them, the prices at

[6] *Records and Briefs,* October Term, 1926, no. 27, p. 9.

which these orders were taken and the geographic zone in which the purchaser was located. For the latter purpose, the United States was divided into six zones. Zone 1, for example, consisted of the states of New York, Connecticut, Rhode Island, Massachusetts, Vermont and Maine.

The Secretary of the Association summarized the original reports, destroyed them, and distributed copies of the summaries to whatever members had co-operated in reporting. Nothing on the summaries identified the seller or the buyer, and the zones were used solely to show generally where the buyers were located. The reports did not cover production, stocks on hand, or market conditions.[7]

The Association appointed a price list committee from time to time to review and recommend changes in the list. The list was a printed form which gave, in dollars and cents amounts, a figure for each item produced by the members. While there were some variations in shapes and weights, the items fell into rather broad design, type and size categories. The individual firms then prepared "bulletins" which showed the list prices and the discounts off the list prices which were applicable to the various items. After discounting off list, the practice was then to add "surcharges" on invoicing. It was largely through changes in the surcharges that the general level of prices was raised or lowered. Thus the surcharge rose from 5 per cent in July, 1917, to a cumulative 50 and 30 per cent in late May, 1918.[8]

The Association itself was not involved in the pricing process beyond the publication of the price list. The price bulletins were prepared by the separate companies and bore their identification. When correspondence was addressed to the Association concerning the bulletins and actual prices, the secretary's answer always emphasized that pricing was a matter for the individual companies and noted that were this

[7] *Ibid.*, pp. 24–44.
[8] *Ibid.*, pp. 317ff.

not so a violation of the law might be involved. This, however, was undoubtedly a formality both from an economic and from a legal point of view. It was admitted that prices were discussed among the members at their frequent meetings, though the minutes of the meetings did not report the exact nature of the discussion. In addition, the correspondence among the members — frequently in the form of a complaint because some firm had sold at low prices — suggested strongly that discounts and surcharges were discussed and that at least some of the firms felt that an understanding on these had been reached.

In the light of the activities of the Association and the meetings and correspondence among the defendants, the actual behavior of prices is at first surprising. If each member had used the same price list and applied uniform discounts and surcharges, their resulting net prices to customers would, of course, have been identical. Since the price list was prepared by the Association, this was identical for all firms. The discounts announced, however, were less uniform. In a study of five of the principal articles, a witness for the government testified somewhat ambiguously that 80.58 per cent of the announced discounts were identical in 1918, 84.25 per cent were identical in 1919, 87.55 per cent in 1920, 70.05 per cent in 1921 (a depression year) and 84.61 per cent during the first six months of 1922.[9] The same witness showed that the announced surcharges, the main means of price change, were even more identical, at least up to the middle of 1918. On these there was complete uniformity save for one firm.[10]

The similarity in announced discounts and surcharges lent support to the allegation of the indictment that there was not only an agreement but, further, that the defendants did in practice "fix, establish, maintain, and exact uniform, arbi-

[9] *Records and Briefs,* 1926, no. 27, pp. 317ff.
[10] *Ibid.*

trary, and non-competitive prices." But a defense witness, a buyer, testified:

> . . . in the nineteen years of my business I have very seldom paid the bulletin price . . . We do not go by the bulletin. We give them the specification for what we want and ask their price. After that the lowest man, providing the goods are equal, gets the business . . . I dealt with the Trenton Potteries Co., the Camden Pottery, Lambertville Pottery, Cochran-Drugan, Standard Sanitary Mfg. Co., Ironsides Pottery Co., the Sanitary Earthenware Specialty Co., and some the Kalamazoo Mfg. Co . . .[11]

Another buyer asserted:

> . . . I received their bulletins . . . I did not make use of the bulletins except to put them in the waste basket, because I went around shopping and bought just as I found the market ripe to buy. My prices were not affected or controlled by these bulletin prices that I know of . . .[12]

Still another said:

> . . . I paid non-bulletin prices a great deal oftener than I paid bulletin prices. I obtained concessions all the way from 5 to 25% . . .[13]

The defendants produced many similar statements from other customers. Even so, these could have been isolated cases of large buyers. An accountant who appeared for the defendants dispelled this possibility. In a study of actual invoice prices of twenty of the defendant companies, he found that deviations from the announced prices were the rule, not the exception. During the period from June 1, 1918, through July 31, 1922, 476,317 tanks, or 64 per cent of all those sold, were sold at less than the announced net prices. In the same period, 196,335, or 26 per cent, were sold at bulletin prices and 77,698, or 10 per cent, were sold for more than bulletin

[11] *Records and Briefs,* 1926, no. 27, pp. 421–423.
[12] *Ibid.,* p. 439.
[13] *Ibid.,* p. 448.

prices. For bowls, 68 per cent were sold below bulletin prices, 28 per cent at bulletin prices, and 4 per cent above. And the differences in prices were not slight. During the months between January and June, 1919, when 68 per cent of the tanks were sold below bulletin prices, the announced price was $12.56 or $12.57, depending on the rounding of a fractional cent. There were sixty-three actual invoice prices less than the announced $12.56 which ranged from $7.50 to $12.54, and there were thirty-eight prices above $12.57 ranging from $12.60 to $18.00. This was not an uncommon period but one fairly typical of the whole time to which the indictment pertained.[14]

Evidence brought forth on the second count of the indictment was not nearly as extensive as that on the first. It appears that the defendants did generally refuse to trade with anyone who was not a "legitimate jobber." In practice this meant that plumbers and retail outlets could not purchase directly from the manufacturers but instead had to deal through wholesalers. There was no evidence that any wholesaler was denied goods by the manufacturers; some evidence that occasionally a large order would be accepted directly from plumbing contractors.

The evidence on the agreement to sell "Class B" goods only for export suggests that one method of price cutting used by the firms was to use a "Class B" label on what were in fact "Class A" goods. In addition, there was ample evidence that real "Class B" goods found their way into the domestic market.

LEGAL ASPECTS OF THE *Potteries* CASE

Certain of the legal aspects of the case are so intriguing that they require brief comment even while the principal conclu-

[14] *Records and Briefs,* 1926, no. 27, pp. 560ff. These data come from oral testimony of the witness. The charts from which he was testifying are not contained in the *Records and Briefs.* The charts covered each of the 20 companies for which data were available and were divided into several time intervals between June 1918 and July 1922.

sions to be drawn below are economic, not legal. Counsel for both the defense and the government entered objection after objection throughout the efforts of the other to elicit evidence. Rather strangely, few if any of defense counsels' objections were sustained; few, if any, of the governments' objections were not sustained. Legally this has, apparently, no significance. To the economist, many of the questions overruled were especially relevant. When defense counsel asked, "What is a price list?" the objection of government counsel was sustained.[15] Similar rulings were made to such questions as, "Is it not a fact . . . that the prices stated in these things [price lists] were not intended nor understood by anyone to be the selling price?" and "What was the method used in quoting prices when a manufacturer was asked by a jobber or other customer to quote prices?" [16] The question of whether a witness "observed or noted competition" may be too general and may call for conclusions from the witness,[17] but questions of the former kind are necessary to understand how the market operated.[18]

Defense counsel was granted an exception to these many rulings. He did not in any place attempt to justify the conspiracy on the grounds that the prices fixed were reasonable. Instead it was argued, especially in the requests to charge and in the exceptions to the charge, that the language of *Chicago Board of Trade* was the proper charge. Defendants wanted the jury told that "the legality of an agreement or regulation cannot be determined by so simple a test, as whether it re-

[15] *Records and Briefs,* 1926, no. 27, p. 177.

[16] *Ibid.,* p. 178.

[17] 273 U.S. 406.

[18] For example, in *Tag Manufacturers Institute v. Federal Trade Commission,* 174 F. 2d 452 (1st Cir. 1949), the court distinguished between price lists which were 96.8 or 97.5 per cent uniform and actual sales prices which were 75 per cent uniform (p. 459). It also defined the nature of a price list and concluded that "from the nature of things it is reasonably to be expected that off-list sales would be the exception rather than the rule, even where no price-fixing exists" (pp. 453–454).

strains competition . . . The true test of legality is whether the restraint imposed is such as merely regulated and perhaps thereby promotes competition or whether it is such as may suppress or even destroy competition." [19]

Judge Van Fleet refused to charge with a "rule of reason." And it was right here that the remainder of the legal treatment of the case was divorced from both the case facts and from economic analysis. There was nothing in the defendants' request to charge which maintained that the jury ought to be instructed that a conspiracy that fixed prices reasonably was not illegal. Nonetheless, the courts' charge did go to this question, pointing out that the fixing of prices was the crime and that the reasonableness of the prices, if they were fixed, was immaterial.[20] In an argument concerning exceptions of the defense to the charge, this interpretation of the law was not contested. It was argued, however, that "if low prices were charged there would be strong evidence that no conspiracy had been entered into." [21]

On appeal, the trial court was held to have erred in several respects. Most important to the Circuit Court was that it could find no jurisdiction for the courts of the Southern District of New York.[22] Also, it maintained that the lower court was wrong in refusing the request to charge with a rule of reason.[23] Finally, the appeals court thought there were minor errors in the lower courts' sustaining of government objections and in its overruling certain defense objections.[24]

The Supreme Court upheld the trial court in its decision of February 21, 1927. Now the appellant was the government

[19] *Records and Briefs,* 1926, no. 27, pp. 666–685. Several of the requests to charge are quotes from *Board of Trade of the City of Chicago v. U.S.,* 246 U.S. 231 (1918), *U.S. v American Tobacco Co.,* 221 U.S. 106 (1911) and *Standard Oil Co. v. U.S.,* 221 U.S. 1 (1911).

[20] *Records and Briefs,* 1926, no. 27, pp. 698–699.

[21] *Ibid.,* p. 724.

[22] Trenton Potteries Co. v. U.S., 300 F. 550, 552 (2nd. Cir. 1924).

[23] *Ibid.,* p. 553.

[24] *Ibid.,* pp. 554, 555.

and the questions raised related only to the rulings of the Circuit Court that the jury should have been charged with a rule of reason, that there was a lack of jurisdiction in the Southern District and that there were errors in the admission and exclusion of evidence. The questions of whether there was or was not an agreement among the pottery manufacturers and the subjects to which the agreement, if there were one, related were not reviewed by the Supreme Court. It accepted quite properly the jury's finding that there had been an agreement to fix prices. Had the Court stopped at this point by merely reaffirming the ruling of the trial judge that "agreement itself is a violation, even though nothing is ever done toward carrying it out," [25] with the qualification that the agreement referred to was one to fix prices — *actual market prices* — there could be little cause to comment. But the Court did not stop here and much of the rest of the decision has, therefore, little relevance to the case tried.

In the decision Justice Stone treated at length the question of fixing reasonable prices. Speaking of the use of a rule of reason, he concluded that:

> . . . [I]t does not follow that agreements to fix or maintain prices are reasonable restraints and therefore permitted by the statute, merely because the prices themselves are reasonable . . . Our view of what is a reasonable restraint of commerce is controlled by the recognized purpose of the Sherman Law itself. Whether this type of restraint is reasonable or not must be judged in part at least, in the light of its effect on competition, for, whatever difference of opinion there may be among economists as to the social and economic desirability of an unrestrained competitive system, it cannot be doubted that the Sherman Law and the judicial decisions interpreting it are based upon the assumption that the public interest is best protected from the evils of monopoly and price control by the maintenance of competition . . .

The aim and result of every price-fixing agreement, if effective, is the elimination of one form of competition. The power to fix

[25] *Records and Briefs,* 1926, no. 27, p. 695.

prices, whether reasonably exercised or not, involves power to control the market and to fix arbitrary and unreasonable prices. The reasonable price fixed today may through economic and business changes become the unreasonable price of tomorrow. Once established, it may be maintained unchanged because of the absence of competition secured by the agreement for a price reasonable when fixed. Agreements which create such potential power may well be held to be in themselves unreasonable or unlawful . . .[26]

Justice Stone's decision makes no distinction whatever to the difference between agreed upon price lists and agreed upon prices. His decision suggests very strongly that the facts of *Trenton Potteries* disclosed a lack of rivalry when there was, in reality, strong competition in the market. To Justice Stone, the low and reasonable prices were the result of an agreement so to fix them, when in reality the low prices were the result of independent rather than collusive behavior. To Justice Stone, there was power among the pottery manufacturers to control the market when, in reality, the evidence pointed repeatedly to a lack of power, both individually and collectively, among the defendants. To Justice Stone, the Sanitary Potters' Association seemed an effective monopolistic device when, in reality, it was an impotent effort to restrain what

[26] 273 U.S. 396–397. It is difficult to explain why Justice Stone gave such emphasis to the question of reasonably fixed prices. The Circuit Court had not confused the rule of reason with reasonably fixed prices. The latter played no part in its decision. In *Brief for Respondents* (requesting denial of certiorari), pp. 8–9, it was pointed out that, "The Circuit Court of Appeals did not hold . . . that the agreement may be reasonable unless the public is injured. [*It*] did hold that the essence of the law is injury to the public and that it is not every restraint of competition . . . that works injury to the public." After certiorari had been granted, a later *Brief for Respondents,* pp. 21–22, mentions the reasonableness of prices but in no way argues that an absolute defense could be established on the basis of prices alone. The closest the defense came to suggesting that reasonable prices, even though fixed, could be the basis for acquittal was in a specific request to charge that it was not illegal for one defendant to agree with two others to refrain from selling below cost in a particular instance. This, in an inconspicuous place among more than one hundred requests to charge, could hardly have been the basis for Justice Stone's attention.

was apparently quite unbridled competition. There was between 1919 and 1922 no price actually "fixed today" to become "the unreasonable price of tomorrow."

ECONOMIC COMMENT ON THE *Potteries* CASE

Evidence of the kind presented by the defense casts substantial doubt on that part of the allegations which asserted that a conspiracy had been made effective. It also raises some question of whether, even if the defendants had actually sat together and each affirmed his intention to charge a uniform price, there would have been an agreement in the sense that minds had really met and there was — even instantaneously — the intention to translate words into deeds. But there are for the economist more perplexing problems than these.

The *Trenton Potteries* case presents all the elements which have traditionally been viewed as favorable to an effective conspiracy. The number of firms was not large, they had a formal organization which comprised practically the entire industry, their products were relatively standardized, they held frequent meetings and had ample opportunities for communication, the reconciliation of conflicts, and agreement. Why was their combination, in an economic sense, not effectively collusive?

The testimony of the individual defendants that they had not attempted to fix prices was unconvincing. Some of them, at least, did everything in their power to bring about an effective conspiracy. They perhaps succeeded in getting everyone to nod his head affirmatively to their suggestions, but then each went his own way. The most revealing communication in this regard is that of Mr. A. M. Maddock, president of the Association. On December 28, 1918, he sent a letter to each of the member firms. In it he hoped that each would adopt a "New Years resolution" to co-operate and hold prices at the levels announced in the bulletins. He wrote in a rather sad tone, commenting that he was "ashamed" of the poor profit record of his own firm, even during the years of prosperity, and added sincerely that:

> . . . It has been mighty hard at times to keep faith with our competitors, and it has been very discouraging to find some concerns who took very lightly the bulletins of prices . . . I have been surprised to find how easy it was for some manufacturers to deviate from their published prices.[27]

This points to the difficulty of the pottery manufacturers. Here was the president of their Association, the president of one of the largest and oldest firms in the industry, pleading with the others to be honorable in their pricing. This attitude, coupled with the persistence of price cutting, the lack of any evidence of threats, coercion or pressure on any member, demonstrates that no one in the market had enough power to lead the group effectively. There was never a penalty beyond a certain "social stigma" attached to being a price cutter. Even this stigma probably was not great for, as Judge Magruder noted in the *Tag* case, "an odor which is common to all is offensive to none." Each firm found reasons of its own for cutting prices. To the Resolute Pottery Company, getting a sale was more important than keeping prices up. "We endeavored to get our bulletin prices," an official testified, "but we could not always get them." [28] The Acme Sanitary Pottery Company felt its market position made identical prices impossible. A representative of that company said that, "It has been our experience years ago that we could not get the prices that they [the other firms] could for their ware. They advertise. They carry a complete line and we are at a disadvantage . . . all we can put in is a tank and a bowl . . . I told our salesmen, 'Get the price you can.' " [29]

[27] *Records and Briefs,* 1926, no. 27, Government Exhibit no. 122, pp. 922–926. Note that the letter does not chide the members for breaking an agreement. It is directed instead to prices which deviated from the bulletins and the latter *might* have been issued independently by the several firms.

[28] *Records and Briefs,* 1926, no. 27, p. 377.

[29] *Ibid.*, pp. 381–392.

Nothing was done about these deviations from published prices. The manufacturers never recognized a set of group objectives which might override the importance of individual firm objectives, never attempted to police or penalize the recalcitrants to agreements, and none of the individual firms had the power or the will to force such recognition and penalties for "anti-group" behavior on the others. The market was, in fact, quite disorganized, with too many firms for tacit reconciliation of interfirm conflicts, an association too weak to act as arbitrator, and no firm dominant enough to insist on a particular course of behavior.

Economic theory largely neglects organizational aspects of markets, emphasizing instead structural characteristics. Competitive markets in particular are defined in theory in terms of their structure, not their organization, by reference to the number of firms, the homogeneity of the product, freedom of entry, etc. This is curious since the markets of the real world which are used as illustrations of competitive price setting are not unorganized, unregulated meetings of buyers and sellers. They are organized to rather extreme detail. The *organized* stock and commodity markets, for example, limit direct access to the exchanges to selected brokers, regulate commissions, list and de-list issues by established standards, set quality standards, require brokers to stabilize the market under certain conditions, regulate conduct, and supervise the collection and distribution of market information. The market, itself, is in fact the "book" of the specialist and is operated by human endeavor and ingenuity.

In the *Trenton Potteries* case, the members of the industry were attempting to regulate rivalry through organizational means. This failed, partly perhaps because of the antitrust laws, but more because the leadership required to establish an effective market organization was lacking. And in addition to the pressure put on the existing market structure by the intensity of competition, there was a major technological change occurring at the same time, with new tunnel kilns beginning to replace the less efficient beehive kilns.

No effort has been made to trace in detail the changes in the structure of the industry since the decision of the lower court in 1922. It appears, however, that of the original twenty-three corporations indicted, eight have gone completely out of existence, most of them before 1933 or 1934.[30] Another firm, while still in existence, is producing other vitreous products[31] and no information was discovered about two others.[32] Of the remaining twelve firms, two were merged in 1925 [33] and later these and one other[34] were brought together in the American Radiator and Standard Sanitary Corporation. Two others were purchased by Sears, Roebuck and Company.[35] The Crane Company purchased the Trenton Potteries Company in 1924. Three companies have only recently been combined with other firms,[36] leaving at most only three of the original companies.

The present industry has about the same number of establishments as the industry of 1922. Their ownership, however, is concentrated with the American Radiator and Standard Sanitary Corporation, the Crane Company, the Eljer Division of the Murray Corporation and Kohler and Kohler. With this structure, firms are few enough and the power lodged in the larger firms is great enough so that no formal organization is required to prevent excessive rivalry.

[30] These firms are Acme Sanitary Pottery Co., B.O.T. Manufacturing Co., Cochran-Drugan and Co., Keystone Pottery Co., John Maddock and Sons Co., Resolute Pottery Co., Sanitary Earthenware Specialty Co., and Wheeling Sanitary Manufacturing Co. The Cochran-Drugan plant was closed after purchase by Kohler and Kohler.

[31] Lambertville Pottery Co.

[32] Kalamazoo Sanitary Manufacturing Co., and the Horton Pottery Co.

[33] Standard Sanitary Manufacturing Co. and Pacific Sanitary Manufacturing Co.

[34] Thomas Maddock's Sons Co., purchased in 1929.

[35] Camden Pottery Co., and Universal Sanitary Manufacturing Co.

[36] Abington Sanitary Manufacturing Co. (Briggs Manufacturing Company), Kokomo Sanitary Pottery Co. (Gerber Industries) and the Eljer Co. (Murray Corporation).

CHAPTER IX

THE PLATE GLASS MIRROR CASE[1]

INTRODUCTION

The *Trenton Potteries* case pointed to certain of the difficulties involved in rationalizing competition through interfirm organizational efforts. The *Plate Glass Mirror* case discussed in the present chapter affords the opportunity to treat these difficulties in more detail. The case is similar to the *Potteries* case in its legal, antitrust aspects and because of this these will not be treated at length.

BACKGROUND OF THE CASE

The case concerns prices for plate glass mirrors sold to manufacturers of furniture by a small group of mirror manufacturers in southern Virginia and North Carolina. There were about twelve mirror plants in this area in 1954, not counting the mirror shops of a few of the larger furniture manufacturers which manufactured their own mirrors. These plants accounted for perhaps 40 per cent [2] of plate glass mirrors manufactured in the United States and probably a still higher percentage of such mirrors sold to furniture manufacturers.

The sizes of the mirror manufacturing firms varied con-

[1] U.S. v. Pittsburgh Plate Glass Co., Carolina Mirror Corporation, Galax Mirror Co., Inc., Mount Airy Mirror Co., Stroupe Mirror Co., Virginia Mirror Co., Inc., Weaver Mirror Co., Inc., and three individuals, Criminal Action no. 5790 (W.D. Va. 1957). The subsequent appeals are reported in *Pittsburgh Plate Glass Co. v. U.S.*, 260 F. 2d 397 (4th Cir. 1958), 360 U.S. 395 (1959).

[2] Indictment, par. 9.

siderably. Of the seven firms indicted in 1957, the Carolina Mirror Corporation was the largest in the relevant market, with 1954 sales of more than half the total plate glass mirror sales of all defendant companies.[3] The Virginia Mirror Corporation, the next largest, sold about 15 per cent of the total. The smallest of the indicted companies, Weaver Mirror Company, Inc., had less than 5 per cent of these sales. The relative sizes of the mirror manufacturers which were not indicted cannot be determined from the record. At least three of them — the Lenoir Mirror Company, the O. W. Slane Glass Company and the Logan Porter Mirror Company — were of substantial size, however, though undoubtedly smaller than the Carolina Mirror Corporation.[4]

The Pittsburgh Plate Glass Company, which was the principal defendant corporation, had a relatively minor role in the supply of mirrors to furniture manufacturers. During 1954, its mirror sales to these customers through both its High Point, North Carolina, and Roanoke, Virginia, warehouses amounted to about 5 per cent of total defendant mirror sales to furniture manufacturers, ranking it along with the Weaver Mirror Company as one of the very smallest in the furniture-mirror market. Pittsburgh Plate Glass Company did sell mirrors to other types of customers, as did the other defendants, but its chief position among defendants was as a supplier of plate glass, not as a direct competitor. This supply position was shared with the Libby-Owen-Ford Company and, to an unknown extent, with importers of plate glass made in Belgium, France, Germany and England.[5] The domestic concerns, PPG and LOF, priced on a "freight equalization to the nearest mill" basis so that no differences existed in their prices for plate glass save for relatively short periods when one or

[3] Record, Government Exhibits nos. 15, 23, 27, 28, 36 and 42 and Defendants' Exhibit no. 15.

[4] The importance of the Lenoir Mirror Company in the market is developed below in the discussion of the case.

[5] Record, p. 1088.

the other of these companies had initiated a price change which had not been followed by the other.

There was some interlocking ownership among the mirror manufacturers. The Galax and Mount Airy companies were owned and controlled by the same family. In addition the same family owned two furniture manufacturing concerns which purchased mirrors from the Galax and Mount Airy plants.[6] The owners of the O. W. Slane Glass Company owned a substantial interest in the Lenoir Mirror Company.[7]

With the exception of the Pittsburgh Plate Glass Company, all the defendant corporations were members of a nationwide trade association, the Mirror Manufacturers Association.[8] PPG had resigned its "associate membership" sometime prior to 1950 and the participation of that company and of LOF at association meetings since that date were restricted to acting as hosts at banquets and cocktail parties and in co-operating in panel discussions relating to plate glass.[9] PPG representatives who attended these meetings were concerned with plate glass sales and had no direct connection with the manufacture and sale of plate glass mirrors in that company.[10]

The activities of the trade association were typical. In 1954, there was a Committee on Mirror Information, a Committee on Trade Practices and Standards, a Membership Committee, a Market Development Committee, a Cost Manual Committee, a Packaging and Traffic Committee, and some others.[11] Each committee held meetings and some made reports at the annual meeting of the entire Association. There were, in addition, exhibits of suppliers, speeches, cocktail parties, banquets and golf. The Association performed no statistical reporting services.

[6] *Ibid.*, p. 930, Government Exhibits nos. 16, 23, 24, 25 and 27, and Indictment, par. 3.

[7] Record, p. 866.

[8] *Ibid.*, pp. 532–535.

[9] *Ibid.*, pp. 534–536, 541–546.

[10] *Ibid.*, pp. 430–435.

[11] Record, Government Exhibit no. 64.

The Association occasionally appointed a List Committee to study and suggest revisions in a booklet of list prices. In 1954, all of the defendant companies except PPG were using a set of list prices from a booklet dated April 1, 1950, the most recent revision of the list. The PPG list was identical to the others save for the date and a few unimportant printing errors.[12] The lists contained dollar and cents for more than two thousand standard sizes of plate glass mirrors but, unlike the lists of the old Maple Flooring group, these figures were not selling prices. While there is no direct evidence on this point, it seems probable that they were instead indexes of what the committee had regarded as the *relative* costs of a typical manufacturer in producing the respective sizes.[13] In any case, the dollar and cents amounts expressed in the booklet were far greater than actual selling prices. The latter were obtained by applying a discount to the listed figures. Thus, for example, a company quoting a discount of 80 per cent off list would be offering to sell at amounts equal to 20 per cent of the list amounts. The higher the discount announced, the lower were the actual prices. This method of price quotation had been used in the flat glass industry for many, many years and was not at all novel to the mirror manufacturers.

In 1950, the Mirror Manufacturers Association had turned the new list over to a printer who, in turn, printed books to order for the member firms. The latter had their own names printed on the cover and distributed them widely among their customers. The April 1, 1950 list came into use during late spring and early summer of that year, the dates of adoption for the several companies being spread over several months.

The defendant mirror companies sold to more than one

[12] Record, Government Exhibit no. 61, and Record, pp. 450–452, 611–613.

[13] The cost of producing a mirror is not strictly proportional to its area. Plate glass waste, breakage and packaging costs vary with differing shapes and sizes.

hundred fifty furniture manufacturers. Most of these were in the states of North Carolina, South Carolina, Virginia and Tennessee, but some were as distant as Oregon and California.[14] Most of the furniture manufacturers bought from but one mirror manufacturer, but some of the larger ones purchased from two or three of them. There was no evidence that territorial market division existed. The Carolina Mirror Corporation, for example, had six customers in Lenoir, North Carolina, the home town of the Lenoir Mirror Company, three customers in Mount Airy, Virginia, the location of the Mount Airy Mirror Company, two customers in Galax, Virginia, home of the Galax Mirror Company, one customer in Roanoke, where PPG had a warehouse, and one customer in Martinsville, Virginia, where the Virginia Mirror Company was located.[15] The Galax Mirror Company, in turn, had customers in the home towns of the Virginia Mirror Company, of a PPG warehouse, and of the Carolina Mirror Corporation.[16]

In general, business had been good for the mirror manufacturers after World War II. In early 1953, however, furniture production declined rapidly. The demand for furniture, like that for other consumer durables, fell off with the 1953–1954 recession. Until early 1953, most, if not all, of the mirror manufacturers had announced discounts off the list of 79 per cent [17] but, because of the development of price-cutting as early as 1952,[18] many sales were going at prices less than those announced. Announced discounts rose from 79 per cent off list to 80 per cent in late 1953, and then to 80 and 10 per cent (cumulatively) off list. Still, by May, 1954, even though

[14] Record, Government Exhibits nos. 14, 24, 27, 28, 36, 42 and 55.
[15] Record, Government Exhibit no. 14.
[16] Record, Government Exhibit no. 24.
[17] Record, Government Exhibits nos. 22 and 40, Defendants' Exhibit no. 12.
[18] Record, p. 641.

announced prices had dropped by more than 13 per cent, more than 70 per cent of the combined furniture manufacturer sales of PPG, the Galax Mirror Company, the Mount Airy Mirror Company and the Weaver Mirror Company were at prices below those announced.[19] Some sales went for as low as 83 per cent off list.[20]

Effective June 1, 1954, the defendant companies raised their announced prices to 80 per cent off list. While this date was identical for all the firms which sent out announcements, notification to customers of the increase began in the previous March and the several companies announced the change on different dates between March and June. Furniture production began to increase after June, 1954, and by August and September, the demand for mirrors had become more brisk.

In early September there was a hurricane which caused a large replacement demand for plate glass windows.[21] At about the same time, the production of 1955 model automobiles began and these, with "wrap-around" windshields, required far more plate glass than former models.[22] Then, in October, LOF experienced production difficulties which led them to wire their customers that there would be little or no plate glass available.[23] Thus, with demand rising, the mirror manufacturers were faced with a threatened shortage of plate glass and the likelihood that the glass manufacturers would be forced to allocate supplies.[24]

[19] From data compiled in an invoice study conducted by A. M. Pullen and Co., Certified Public Accountants. Data for the three other companies are not available for this date.

[20] *Ibid.*

[21] Record, p. 938.

[22] *Ibid.*

[23] *Ibid.*, pp. 1056–1057, 1074.

[24] *Ibid.*, pp. 631–632, 732, 742–745, 936–941, 988–991, 1000–1002, 1056–1065, 1074–1075 and 1087–1088.

THE CONSPIRACY TO RAISE PRICES

On March 26, 1957, an indictment was returned against the mirror manufacturers. It charged that:

> Beginning in or about October, 1954, . . . and continuing thereafter, the defendants, the co-conspirators and others to the grand jurors unknown, have been engaged in a combination and conspiracy in unreasonable restraint of . . . trade . . .
>
> The . . . combination and conspiracy has consisted of a continuing agreement, understanding and concert of action . . . , the substantial term of which has been that they agree to stabilize and fix prices for the sale . . . of plain plate glass mirrors to furniture manufacturers by the following means and methods:
>
> (a) By agreeing upon and using identical list prices covering a range of over two thousand sizes of plain plate glass mirrors as a base for the quotation of prices for such mirrors; and (b) by agreeing upon and applying in pricing plain plate glass mirrors a uniform discount from said list prices, the amount of which discount, from time to time, has been changed by agreement among the defendants and the co-conspirator mirror manufacturers.[25]

On trial, the Government presented direct evidence to support the indictment. There had been a meeting of the Mirror Manufacturers Association from October 24 to October 27, 1954, in Asheville, North Carolina. Carolina Mirror Company, Galax Mirror Company, Mount Airy Mirror Company, Stroupe Mirror Company, Virginia Mirror Company and Weaver Mirror Company — all members — had representatives there. Among the nonmembers registered were representatives of both LOF and PPG.[26]

On Monday evening, October 25, Mr. Kenneth Hearn, of the Virginia Mirror Company, and Mr. Robert Stroupe, of the Stroupe Mirror Company, were dining together when Mr. John Messer, Sr., President of both the Galax and the Mount Airy Mirror Companies, joined them. According to Mr.

[25] Indictment, pars. 11 and 12.
[26] Record, Government Exhibit no. 65.

Stroupe, there was a short discussion of the plate glass shortage "and Mr. Messer said that it was his plan to send out a letter announcing a price change to 78." [27] The initial reaction of Mr. Stroupe was one of disbelief.[28]

Mr. Hearn, Mr. Stroupe and Mr. Ralph Buchan, of the Carolina Mirror Corporation, apparently discussed this further the next day,[29] and at least Mr. Hearn accepted Mr. Messer's word that he intended to raise prices.[30] By Wednesday, it seems that Mr. Messer's statement was well known to those attending the meetings. Mr. Gordon, one of the PPG representatives, had heard about it and when asked if he thought Messer was "trying to shoot for too high a price" said, "It sounds like it to me." [31] Another PPG representative, after hearing from Stroupe that the mirror manufacturers were losing money and would lose more if there were a shortage of glass, told Stroupe that he should get his prices up.[32]

On Wednesday evening, Hearn, Stroupe and Buchan placed a call to Mr. A. G. Jonas, of the Lenoir Mirror Company, to tell him that "it had been generally rumored around that they were willing to raise prices." Hearn told Jonas that if he "didn't come along, prices wouldn't be raised. There would not be any increase if [Jonas] didn't agree to do so." [33]

Mr. Jonas "was amazed that there was conversation that Mr. Messer was willing to raise prices." He didn't know whether he could believe Hearn and Stroupe and "wasn't sure whether the boys were trying to pull something" on him.[34] To check this, Jonas asked them to have Mr. Gordon, a "close personal friend," call him so he could find if there were any

[27] *Ibid.*, p. 732.
[28] *Ibid.*, p. 733.
[29] Record, pp. 619, 629–630.
[30] *Ibid.*, p. 643.
[31] *Ibid.*, p. 742.
[32] *Ibid.*, p. 745.
[33] Record, p. 793.
[34] *Ibid.*, p. 794. See also p. 641.

truth in the matter. Gordon called him back in just a few minutes to confirm that, "In some of the rooms I heard the fellows saying they would like to get their prices increased." [35] Jonas told Gordon he was not inclined to raise prices and Gordon replied, "I don't have anything to do with what you do about your business. That is entirely up to you." [36]

After this conversation, Hearn called Jonas back to ask if he would attend a meeting to "go into the matter further." [37] Jonas considered this overnight and called Hearn back early Thursday morning. Jonas told Hearn he hadn't decided yet about raising prices, but agreed to meet with a group of mirror manufacturers the following day.

Mr. Jonas met Buchan, Mr. Grady Stroupe, and Mr. Messer on Friday at a lodge on the Blue Ridge Parkway. They lunched and then went to a bedroom to discuss prices. Jonas went into this meeting with the feeling that "it all hinged on me, . . . It looked like to me that if I didn't agree to raise my prices, the prices would never be raised." [38] He was, in addition, "fed up with John Messer cutting prices." In his own words:

> . . . I had never expressed myself to him, my actual feelings at all times. So when we got in this meeting . . . and I could see where Mr. Messer apparently had had a change of heart and wanted to raise the prices . . . I just decided to tell him, 'John, you are the one that started this price war to begin with.' I can't recall just the exact things that took place, but he as much said I was a damn liar, that I started it. I said, 'What do you mean, I started it, Mr. Messer?' He said, 'You shipped mirrors into Galax, Virginia. You started it.' I said, 'I have never shipped a square foot of mirrors into Galax, Virginia, and I want you to retract and quit accusing me of starting this price war, when you are the one that did it.'

[35] *Ibid.,* p. 795.
[36] Record, p. 796.
[37] *Ibid.,* p. 797.
[38] Record, p. 804.

I might add further that . . . Mr. Messer turned so red I thought he was going to have a stroke . . .[39]

Buchan testified that Jonas and Messer got into a terrific hassle. His recollection was:

. . . I thought they were going to come to blows. The luncheon meeting had been very congenial, but after the first two or three minutes in this meeting . . . it looked like there might be a free-for-all break out at any time.

Jonas jumped on Mr. Messer and said he was the worst price cutter there was living, or words to that effect, and couldn't believe a word he said, he was undependable. Then Mr. Messer took the conversation back again and got on Mr. Gardner and went into a long harangue about what kind of a fellow he was.[40]

Mr. Grady Stroupe's impression of the meeting was much the same:

. . . Mr. Messer told us of his conversation at Asheville . . . that he was going to send out a letter lowering the discount to 78 . . . About the time he made that statement, Mr. Jonas and Mr. Messer got into a hassle. I never was sure what it was about, but there were some very heated words. Mr. Messer got very red in the face. Frankly, I thought he was going to have a stroke. During that time we were all talking at one time.[41]

Somehow the meeting quieted down and discounts were discussed. There was mention of discounts of 79, 78 and 77 per cent, but Mr. Messer insisted the new price be 78.[42] He also insisted that all the companies send letters to that effect. When Mr. Stroupe objected because of the different "economic situations" of the firms and because of "appearances," Jonas told him that "Mr. Messer was calling the rules of the

[39] *Ibid.*, pp. 875–876. It is interesting to note that while the Lenoir Mirror Company was not selling in Galax, the Carolina Mirror Corporation, the Virginia Mirror Company and the Weaver Mirror Company were.

[40] Record, p. 671. Mr. Gardner, President of the Carolina Mirror Corporation, was not present.

[41] *Ibid.*, pp. 760–761.

[42] *Ibid.*, pp. 761, 807.

game and we would have to play by them." [43] Jonas, Messer and Stroupe apparently agreed to write letters dated October 29 changing the discount to 78 per cent[44] and Buchan, who had been sent to the meeting as an "observer," agreed to recommend the same action to Mr. Gardner of Carolina Mirror Corporation.[45]

Jonas also recalled that there was some understanding reached that those present at the meeting would notify the rest of the mirror manufacturers about the outcome of the meeting. He had the responsibility of telling the O. W. Slane Glass Company and the Union Mirror Company and told the others he "would report the outcome of the meeting to Pittsburgh Plate Glass Company." [46]

Before the meeting broke up, however, there may have been a resumption of the earlier argument, for Buchan remembered that as they were leaving "Mr. Messer said, the substance of it was that we could all go to hell, he was going to raise his price to 78 and we could do what we wanted to." [47] Mr. Stroupe described a similar statement.[48]

Mr. Jonas testified that he did call Sam J. Pritchard of PPG, Mr. Gordon's subordinate, and that he told Pritchard of the meeting. In his own testimony, Pritchard acknowledged that calls from Jonas regarding plate glass orders were not unusual, but denied that Jonas ever mentioned the meeting to him. Jonas also called Mr. Gardner to be sure that Carolina "would be agreeable." [49] Then, in letters dated October 29, 1954, Carolina Mirror Corporation, Galax Mirror Company, Mount Airy Mirror Company, Virginia Mirror Company and Weaver Mirror Company changed the announced discount to 78 per cent. The letter of the Stroupe Mirror Company was

[43] Record, pp. 671, 763–765.
[44] *Ibid.*, p. 807.
[45] *Ibid.*, p. 765.
[46] *Ibid.*, p. 809.
[47] Record, p. 690.
[48] *Ibid.*, p. 783.
[49] *Ibid.*, pp. 810–814, 923–928.

dated October 30, and the PPG letter was dated November 1.[50]

The instructions to the jury were very similar to the instructions in the *Trenton Potteries* case. In particular, the jury was told:

> Those who engage in an unlawful combination or conspiracy to fix prices violate the law merely by entering into such an agreement or understanding, and it makes no difference whether or not the objectives of such conspiracy or agreement are carried out in whole or in part . . .
>
> Since all conspiracies to fix or stabilize prices are prohibited by the Sherman Act, it is immaterial whether any particular price-fixing scheme resulted in higher or lower prices, or whether the scheme is wise or unwise. Whether there was a glass shortage or whether there was a price war or whether there existed competitive evils in the mirror manufacturing industry are not defenses to price fixing . . .
>
> . . . The very gist of the offense . . . is any agreement to fix prices, and if any such agreement or understanding is entered into, it does not matter what the effects or the business were; and it does not make any difference what the defendants did thereafter . . .
>
> . . . While this testimony as to the prices which they charged in November, which was immediately following the date of this alleged agreement, is admissible as bearing on whether or not they did enter into an agreement, it is for that purpose only, and if you believe that the agreement was entered into at Asheville or consummated up there on the parkway, then it does not make any difference what happened afterwards . . .[51]

The jury found all the defendants guilty, with the exception of PPG's Gordon, who was acquitted by the court at the conclusion of the Government's case in chief.

COMMENT ON THE *Mirror* CASE

The price information mentioned in the instructions to the jury is summarized in the chart reproduced on page 190.

[50] Record, Government Exhibits nos. 8, 16, 25, 30, 37, 51 and 57.
[51] Record, pp. 1338–1344.

It shows that in the month following the agreement the defendant companies received one hundred-twenty orders for mirrors from furniture manufacturers and that, of these, eighty-two were charged less than 78 per cent off list with a 2 per cent cash discount.[52] The two companies controlled by Mr. Messer — Galax and Mount Airy — received thirty-seven orders and charged less than the announced price on twenty-two of them. Stroupe Mirror Company received twelve orders and of these five were for less than the announced price. The Carolina Mirror Company, which was also represented at the second meeting where the agreement was reached, received forty-seven orders and charged the announced price or more on only seven of these. Virginia Mirror Company, which was not represented at the last meeting but, like the rest, sent out an announcement, charged 78 per cent off list on only two of its eleven orders during November. On five orders, Virginia charged 78 & 10 & 10 off list, a price roughly equivalent to 83 per cent off list, or more than 22 per cent less than the agreed upon price.

Now, in summary, there were not many firms involved — not more than a dozen including both the defendant companies and the coconspirators. Demand was picking up, the existing level of prices was unprofitable for at least some of the companies,[53] and there was a shortage of glass. With this increase in demand and reduction in supply, there would tend to be an increase in price without any conspiracy or collusion. Any of the mirror manufacturers, even the smallest one, could feel secure in raising his prices since his customers, were they to turn to other manufacturers for mirrors, would have found no alternative source of supply. This point is well illustrated

[52] The cash discount is indicated on the chart by the figure following the dash. Thus, the figures 78 & 10–5 indicates a discount of 78 off list, plus another 10 per cent off with a cash discount of 5 per cent. Since a 2 per cent cash discount was customary — and, in fact, announced by Galax, Mount Airy, Virginia and PPG — anything less than 78–2 is regarded as less than the agreed upon price.

[53] Record, pp. 935–937, 940, 1079, Government Exhibit no. 37.

DISCOUNTS OFF LISTS ON ORDERS RECEIVED FROM FURNITURE MANUFACTURERS BY DEFENDANT COMPANIES NOVEMBER 1954

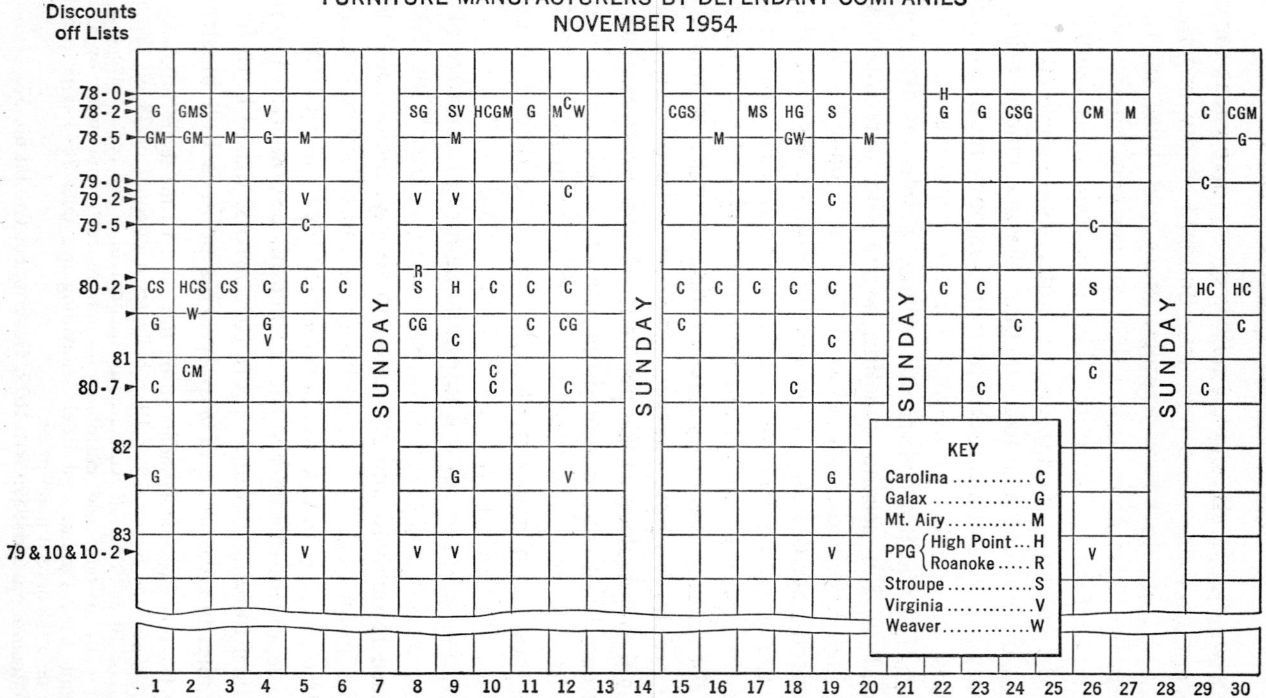

Note: Eighteen different discounts were given on orders received during November, 1954. These were 78–0, 78–1, 78–2, 78–5, 79–0, 79–1, 79–2, 79–5, 80–1, 80–2, 80–5, 78 & 10–2, 78 & 5 & 3 & 5–0, 80–7, 78 & 10–5, 81 & 2–0 (or 80–7), 80 & 10–2 (or 82–2), and 79 & 10 & 10–2.

by the response of Mr. Weaver, who insisted that he raised prices without knowledge that the others were doing likewise, to questions asked by the judge:

The Court: You did hear at Asheville that these other manufacturers were going to 78 per cent discount?

The Witness: No, sir. I didn't even know it then until all this came out.

The Court: Mr. Weaver, if you were such a small concern, how did you expect to raise prices and leave yourself at the mercy of these bigger companies who would not raise prices?

The Witness: I was just taking a chance. I didn't have very many furniture customers at that time. The ones I had are pretty loyal.

The Court: You think they would remain loyal if they had to pay you more for mirrors than they had to pay somebody else?

The Witness: I was banking a lot on this glass shortage taking care of that, sir, because everybody's customers were crying for mirrors, the furniture business had boomed a little, and there was a shortage of glass all over. I knew they were having a hard time supplying —

The Court: You mean you felt they could not readily get mirrors from your competitors even if the competitors' price was lower than yours?

The Witness: That is right, sir.[54]

It is not true, of course, that factors such as customer loyalty would never prevent price increases in the face of increased demand and shortages. But in the present case, with some of the firms apparently losing money at the existing price levels, with customers aware of the history of price changes in response to general business conditions, and with prices in the Virginia-North Carolina area lower than those to the north and west, such factors do not seem to apply. The whole picture of price behavior is something of an enigma. Standard methods of economic analysis would lead to the conclusions that (1) the prices of the several manufacturers should have tended to equality because of the homogeneity of the product

[54] Record, pp. 1080–1081.

and the market knowledge of the buyers and (2) prices should have risen in the fall of 1954 without the need to resort to collusion. Yet, while prices rose, they were not uniform and did not, in general, rise to the level established after a most belabored effort at conspiracy.

As in the *Addyston* case, there is nothing to suggest that the firms in the northern and western branch of the industry had such tendencies to periodic price wars or, more important, that they resorted to overt conspiracy to avoid such behavior. That is, other firms with much the same structures, products, trade association activities and market demand characteristics, succeeded in mitigating the degree of rivalry without formal conspiratorial organization. The southern part of the mirror market was being influenced by factors which go beyond those usually included in economic analysis. The price behavior is more readily understood by viewing the firms in the market as individuals in a small group. In this instance, the members of the group were much at odds with one another, and market performance, which reflects the adjustment of the group to its economic environment, was indicative of this fact. The members of the group were not of the same mind and there was no effective means for reconciling their differences. The conflicts in subgoals were too great for even formal organization and express agreement to overcome. In short, the extreme heterogeneity of their value systems created such intense interfirm rivalry that there were not only barriers to effective conspiracy, but also barriers to stable and workable competition.

One important fact in explaining the price behavior appears to be that the sellers simply did not trust one another. Mr. Messer, with the reputation of a "price-cutter and a double-crosser," [55] is a perfect illustration of this. No one had faith in either his word or in the consistency of his behavior and, judging from his accusations of Jonas, he apparently recipro-

[55] Record, p. 1296.

cated in kind. The history of price wars in the industry reflects these feelings. The mutual animosity of the mirror manufacturers was periodically rekindled. In a psychological sense, it is doubtful that these men were capable of agreeing on anything. There would always be mental reservations which precluded a true meeting of the minds.

This lack of mutual trust is important in explaining market performance for it meant that, unlike the organized exchanges, there were no "rules of the game" governing individual behavior. Individual competitive behavior is effective in setting prices only if a market organization exists which establishes some individual tactical actions as "acceptable" and others as "unacceptable." Individual action, that is, has to be tempered by the organization. With such an organization, which in most markets develops informally through custom, an individual competitor knows certain limits to the reactions of his rivals to his own moves. The very organization of the market rationalizes competition and creates an atmosphere of assurance which promotes rather than deters individual decision-making. The *Mirror* case illustrates the results of a lack of market organization even more forcefully than does the *Trenton Potteries* case.

It is somewhat strange that the mirror market lacked organization. It would appear that the Carolina Mirror Corporation, had it been so disposed, could have exercised its position in the market to provide the leadership necessary to establish a more rational market organization. Too, it would seem that the suppliers of plate glass might have tempered the behavior of the mirror manufacturers. At the time of the case, however, such leadership was not being supplied.

Certain elements in the structure of the market undoubtedly made a stable organization of the group difficult to achieve. One of these is the likelihood that there were significant differences in costs among the southern mirror manufacturers. No evidence was introduced in the trial which would make it certain that such differences did exist. But the price chart indicates that the two largest companies generally had lower prices than the smaller ones. One reason for this could be differences in costs and, if this were true, there may have been no single price which would have come close to being the "best" — or even satisfactory — for each firm.[56] Firms with lower costs, based on a desire either for more sales or more profits, might persistently seek a lower price than firms with higher costs. Such a conflict in interests would be difficult for a very formal organization to reconcile.

Another structural characteristic of the market which would have made organization difficult was in the distribution of buying power among the furniture manufacturers. The large number of buyers belies the skewness in their size distribution. Each of the mirror manufacturers had one or two large customers which accounted for large proportions of their sales. Even if the mirror manufacturers had, in good faith with one another, reached an agreement to raise prices, the concentration of buying power might have been great enough to break down the agreement.

Related to this whole problem of sellers' organization and the behavior of prices is the amount of imperfection in buyers' knowledge. No conscious effort on the part of the mirror manufacturers to withhold knowledge from buyers appeared in the evidence. On the contrary, by supplying furniture manufacturers with the books of list prices and by openly announcing discounts from the lists, the mirror manufacturers made it easier for buyers to shop among alternative sources of supply and to break down an agreement if one existed. Nonetheless, even though cost differences explain why the various mirror manufacturers might wish different prices and so make market organization difficult, the persistence of dif-

[56] Another reason, of course, might be that the larger firms were attempting to force others from the market.

ferences in actual prices suggests that some buyers did not know the prices that others were paying. Such a premise, while not inconsistent with the notion that concentrated buying power would tend to disrupt an agreement among sellers, implies that the price concessions would not necessarily be given to all the buyers.

Finally, mention should be made of the use of the books of list prices and the relation of this to efforts at conspiracy. While it is certainly possible that the list could be used as part of a conspiracy in restraint of trade, it probably operated in the opposite direction in this market. The use of the list increased the knowledge of both buyers and sellers. If one seller discovered, for example, that a competitor was quoting, say, 78 & 10 per cent off list he immediately had adequate knowledge to meet or to beat his competitor's prices on all of the two thousand-odd sizes of mirrors. This is quite different from knowing only that his competitors quoted, say, $19.10 for a 50″x60″ plain mirror. Net price quotations in dollars and cents would have made it far more difficult for one seller to discover the competitive tactics of his rivals. Conspiracy requires only occasional and, perhaps, clandestine communication among the participants; rivalry requires continuous and open communication of the very sort facilitated by the open use of the books.[57]

In both the *Trenton Potteries* and in the *Mirror* cases, the juries found illegal conspiracy. But there was effective economic collusion in neither. In fact, these cases raise the question of whether it is not more likely that overt conspiracies of this kind occur in markets in which rivalry is severe rather than in markets in which competition is stifled.[58] So long as there are no strong tendencies toward independent behavior

[57] In a consent judgment dated December 29, 1959, the defendants were ordered to discontinue the use of the April 1950 list prices.

[58] Walton Hamilton and Irene Till, *Antitrust in Action,* T.N.E.C. Monograph no. 16 (Washington, 1941), pp. 19–20.

— that is, so long as firms are few, have homogeneous values, are endowed with leadership, face impotent buyers and comprise an efficient organization — the need for express agreement does not exist.

PART THREE

SOME COMMENTS ON PUBLIC POLICY

CHAPTER X

THE DEVELOPMENT OF THE PER SE RULE

INTRODUCTION

As was noted in Chapter IV, exemptions from the antitrust laws — or, the establishment of per se legalities — have arisen from specific legislative action. Per se illegalities, however, are the result of judicial interpretation of the relevant statutes. The purpose of the present chapter is to trace the development of this interpretation in order to provide a chronological background for the policy conclusion of the next chapter.

The decisions of Judge Taft in the *Addyston Pipe*[1] case and of Justice Douglas in the *Socony-Vacuum*[2] case would lead one to believe that the per se rule has made contracts to fix prices either void or illegal for well over a century. Taft noted that:

> It is true that there are some [common law] cases in which the courts, mistaking, as we conceive, the proper limits of the relaxation of the rules for determining the unreasonableness of restraints of trade, have set sail on a sea of doubt, and have assumed the power to say, in respect to contracts which have no other purpose and no other consideration on either side than the mutual restraint of the parties, how much restraint of competition is in the public interest, and how much is not.[3]

[1] U.S. v. Addyston Pipe and Steel Co., 171 U.S. 614(1899), 85 F. 271 (6th Cir. 1898).

[2] U.S. v. Socony-Vacuum Oil Co., 310 U.S. 150 (1940).

[3] 85 F. 283–284.

But after a careful review of the cases and of the nonancillary aspects of the restraints imposed by the companies involved in the *Addyston* agreements, he concluded that:

> . . . we can have no doubt that the association of the defendants, however reasonable the prices they fixed, however great the competition they had to encounter, and however great the necessity for curbing themselves by joint agreement from committing financial suicide by ill-advised competition, was void at common law, because in restraint of trade, and tending to a monopoly.[4]

Taft reasoned that any restrictive agreement which was void and unenforceable at common law was surely prohibited by the Sherman Act.[5]

Justice Douglas' opinion in *Socony-Vacuum* was delivered to overrule an opinion from the Circuit Court of Appeals[6] which had held it necessary to show that the agreement among several oil companies was in unreasonable restraint of trade before a violation of the Sherman Act could be found. Douglas held this view to be erroneous and defined the per se price-fixing rule quite clearly. The following, he wrote, are all subject to the per se treatment:

1. "price-fixing agreements" [7] regardless of both the substantiality of the trade controlled by the parties[8] and conditions of "ruinous competition, financial disaster, evils of price cutting and the like" [9]
2. "any combination which tampers with price structures" [10]
3. "agreements to raise or lower prices whatever machinery for price-fixing was used" [11]

[4] *Ibid.*, p. 291.

[5] *Ibid.*, pp. 278–279.

[6] Socony-Vacuum Oil Co. v. U.S., 105 F. 2d 809 (7th Cir. 1939).

[7] 310 U.S. 218.

[8] *U.S. v. Trenton Potteries Co.*, 273 U.S. 398 (1927), qualified the per se rule to those controlling trade "in any substantial manner." Douglas cites this approvingly but drops the qualification.

[9] 310 U.S. 221.

[10] *Ibid.* Note how broadly this might be interpreted.

[11] 310 U.S. 222.

4. agreements setting "the range within which purchases or sales will be made" [12]
5. combinations "formed for the purpose and with the effect of raising, depressing, fixing, pegging, or stabilizing the price of a commodity" [13]
6. all or any of the above, even though, "The alleged conspiracy is not to be found in any formal contract or agreement" and hence must be "pieced together" [14]

Justice Douglas maintained that the Supreme Court "for over forty years . . . consistently and without deviation adhered to the principle that price-fixing agreements are unlawful per se under the Sherman Act." [15] A review of the cases demonstrates that the Court was hardly as consistent as Douglas asserts; some doubt attaches to even Taft's view that nonancillary price-fixing agreements were void at common law.[16] Instead, the courts have been of varied opinions, even recently, though there is no doubt that since *Socony-Vacuum* the per se rule has been applied rather consistently.

THE COMMON LAW

Common law prior to 1890 divided contracts in restraint of trade into two categories — those which were ancillary to the principal purpose of a contract and those whose principal purpose was to provide restraints on competition. An agreement by the seller of a business not to compete with the purchaser is an example of an ancillary restraint and the question of the reasonableness of the restraint in view of the principal purpose of the contract was determining in establishing its legality. Price-fixing agreements, on the other hand, are

[12] *Ibid.*
[13] 310 U.S. 223.
[14] *Ibid.*, p. 177.
[15] *Ibid.*, p. 218.
[16] Peppin states flatly that, "Judge Taft was pretty clearly wrong." See his "Price-Fixing Agreements Under the Sherman Antitrust Law," *California Law Review*, 28:297, 667 (1939–1940).

one type of nonancillary agreements. The establishment of restraints on competition is their primary purpose. While Judge Taft regarded such contracts as void per se at common law in the majority of jurisdictions, there were two other views. In one, price-fixing agreements among competitors were legal even though competition among the parties was eliminated so long as there was competition in the market as a whole. Under this rule, the extent of market control provides the criterion of reasonableness. Under the third view, price-fixing agreements among all competitors in a market were upheld so long as the market power thus created was not abused. The reasonableness of the prices and the kinds of market conditions the agreements were designed to rectify were the criteria used in judging them.[17]

THE SHERMAN ACT

Even though the common law now appears to have been vague at the time, it is generally agreed by historians that the intent of Congress — that is, what legislators thought they were doing — in passing the Sherman Act was to codify the body of common law and to provide the Federal courts with jurisdiction in such restraints as involved interstate commerce.[18] But when *U.S. v. Trans-Missouri Freight Association*[19] came before the Supreme Court, it was the language of the statute, not an interpretation of common law, that was

[17] Since our main interest is in the period after 1890, the common law prior to that is being treated only briefly. For greater detail, see among others: Taft's opinion in *U.S. v. Addyston Pipe and Steel Co.*, 85 F. 271; John C. Peppin, "Price-Fixing Agreements"; Milton Hander, *A Study in the Construction and Enforcement of the Federal Anti-trust Laws*, T.N.E.C. Monograph No. 38 (Washington, 1941); Myron W. Watkins, *Industrial Combinations and Public Policy* (New York, 1927); Franklin P. Jones, "Historical Development of the Law of Business Competition," *Yale Law Journal* (1926, 1927); Hans B. Thorelli, *The Federal Antitrust Policy* (Baltimore, 1955); and Donald Dewey, *Monopoly in Economics and Law* (Chicago, 1959).

[18] See comments by Senator Hoar, *Congressional Record,* XXI, 3151–3152, and Thorelli, *Federal Antitrust Policy,* p. 228.

[19] 166 U.S. 290 (1897).

controlling. Both of the lower courts had held the agreement to be reasonable. Justice Peckham, writing for a majority in the five-to-four decision, held that:

> The language of the act includes *every* contract, combination . . . , or conspiracy, in restraint of trade . . . We see no escape from the conclusion that if any agreement . . . does restrain it, the agreement is condemned by this act.[20]

The court flatly refused to allow the competitive conditions of the industry to influence it:

> It may be that the policy evidenced by the passage of the act itself will, if carried out, result in disaster to the roads . . . These considerations are, however, not for us.[21]

In the dissent, Justice White took a different attack and considered the pricing problems of the carriers:

> The contract between the railway companies . . . substantially embodies only an agreement . . . by which a uniform classification of freight is obtained, by which the secret under-cutting of rates is sought to be avoided . . . [It is conceded by the majority that] the particular contract here under consideration is reasonable . . . I think a brief consideration of the history and development of the law . . . will not only establish the inaccuracy of [the proposition that the act means every restraint is illegal], but also demonstrate that the words 'restraint of trade' embrace only contracts which unreasonably restrain trade, and, therefore, that reasonable contracts, although they, in some measure, 'restrain trade,' are not within the meaning of the words.[22]

The court was asked and refused to reconsider its *Trans-Missouri* holding in *U.S. v. Joint-Traffic Association.*[23] Justice Peckham again wrote the decision and again refused to con-

[20] *Ibid.,* p. 312. Yet in *Hopkins v. U.S.,* 171 U.S. 578, 600 (1898), "The act of Congress must have a reasonable construction or else there would scarcely be an agreement or contract among businessmen that could not be said to have, indirectly or remotely, some bearing on interstate commerce, and possibly to restrain it."

[21] *Ibid.,* p. 340.

[22] *Ibid.,* pp. 343, 344, 346.

[23] 171 U.S. 505 (1898).

sider that the purpose of the agreement was to avoid ruinous competition. In one digression, noted in Chapter III, he indicated that he felt ruinous competition would not exist in the absence of the contracts:

It is not only possible but probable that good sense and integrity of purpose would prevail among the managers, and while making no agreement and entering into no combination . . . , the managers of each road might yet make such reasonable charges for the business done by it as the facts might justify.[24]

It should be noted — though it is not asserted that the *Trans-Missouri* and *Joint-Traffic Association* cases were the only cause — that a rapid merger movement occurred in the industry shortly after these decisions.[25]

The next case before the Supreme Court was *Addyston Pipe and Steel.* A general affirmation of Taft's opinion was written, quoting the portions which showed that both the agreement and the prices fixed were unreasonable. Details of the case were presented in a preceding chapter. It is interesting that the Court did not rely on either Peckham's interpretation of "every" restraint being illegal or on Taft's analysis of the common law. It seems rather that Taft's opinion was affirmed because the contract was an unreasonable restraint of trade. A per se rule was not used.[26]

In *E. Bement and Sons v. National Harrow Company,*[27]

[24] *Ibid.,* p. 577. Peckham seems somewhat less sure of his interpretation of "every" restraint in this case as compared with *Trans-Missouri.* He notes that, "An agreement entered into for the purpose of promoting the legitimate business of an individual or corporation, with no purpose to thereby . . . restrain interstate commerce, and which does not directly restrain such commerce, is not, we think, covered by the act, although the agreement may indirectly and remotely affect that commerce." *Ibid.,* p. 568.

[25] See D. P. Locklin, *Economics of Transportation* (Homewood, 1954), pp. 304–317. Locklin concludes that the mergers of this period "were not so much for the purpose of building up railroad systems which would be strong from an operating and a traffic standpoint as for the purpose of eliminating competition" (p. 314). This suggests that the consolidations were an alternative to the traffic associations which had been declared unlawful.

[26] Cf. Peppin, "Price-Fixing Agreements," pp. 698–700.

[27] 186 U.S. 70 (1902).

Justice Peckham wrote an opinion upholding the legality of price-fixing provisions in patent licenses. Two years later in *W. W. Montague and Co. v. Edward S. Lowry*,[28] Peckham held that an agreement among tile dealers which established list prices, restricted the manufacturers from whom tile should be purchased, and discriminated in prices of tile sold to non-members of an association was illegal since "The agreement directly affected and restrained interstate commerce." The charges in *Swift and Company v. U.S.*[29] involved price fixing but Justice Holmes' opinion did not treat them separately from the general charge of monopolizing.

Dr. Miles Medical Company v. John D. Park and Sons Company[30] related to resale price maintenance contracts. The majority opinion, written by Justice Hughes, implies that horizontal price-fixing agreements are illegal per se. The resale contracts were held illegal because their effect is the same as if the dealers had combined to fix uniform prices. Justice Holmes dissent reflects some interesting thoughts on the virtues of unrestricted price rivalry:

> I think that we greatly exaggerate the value and importance to the public of competition in the production or distribution of an article . . . as fixing a fair price . . . I see nothing to warrant my assuming that the public will not be served best by the company being allowed to carry out its plan. I cannot believe that in the long run the public will profit by this court permitting knaves to cut reasonable prices for some ulterior purpose of their own, and thus to impair, if not destroy, the production and sale of articles which it is assumed to be desirable that the public should be able to get.[31]

Justice White announced the famous "rule of reason" in his decisions in *Standard Oil Company v. U.S.*[32] and *U.S. v.*

[28] 193 U.S. 38 (1904).
[29] 196 U.S. 375 (1905).
[30] 220 U.S. 373 (1911).
[31] *Ibid.*, p. 412.
[32] 221 U.S. 1 (1911).

American Tobacco Company.[33] The language of the *Standard Oil* decision leaves little room to doubt that White would have applied the rule to all cases arising under the Sherman Act. Thus he states:

> The merely generic enumeration which the statute makes of the acts to which it refers and the absence of any definition of restraint of trade as used in the statute leaves room for but one conclusion, which is, that it was expressly designed not to unduly limit the application of the act by precise definition, but while clearly fixing a standard, . . . to leave it to be determined by the light of reason, guided by the principles of law and the duty to apply and enforce the public policy embodied in the statute, in *every* given case whether *any* particular act or *contract* was within the contemplation of the statute.[34]

White made an effort to show that the Court had always applied the standards of reasonableness and that this did not represent a break in the Court's interpretation of the law.[35] He argued that even the *Joint-Traffic Association* and *Trans-Missouri* cases had been decided on this basis. The argument, however, is unconvincing; the rule of reason in the *Standard Oil* and *Tobacco* cases sounds, not surprisingly, more in accord with White's dissent in the former cases than with the majority opinions. In any event, it seemed clear in 1911 that *every* contract in restraint of trade was no longer unlawful and that a per se rule, if it had existed prior to then, was no longer to be the approach even in price-fixing cases. The behavior, intent, and market power of the parties involved were the criteria to be used in testing reasonableness.

A year later, in *Standard Sanitary Manufacturing Company v. U.S.*,[36] price-fixing agreements among patent licensees were

[33] 221 U.S. 106 (1911).

[34] 221 U.S. 63, 64 (emphasis added).

[35] Justice Harlan wrote a strong minority opinion protesting the Court's resort to the "process of judicial legislation wholly unjustifiable." The statement that the Court had used the rule previously surprised Harlan "quite as much as would a statement that black was white or white was black," 221 U.S. 191.

[36] 226 U.S. 20 (1912).

declared a violation of the Sherman Act. The decision, written by Justice McKenna, looked to the purpose of the agreements, their effects, and whether they were necessary to protect the legitimate patent monopoly. While the case appears inconsistent with the *Bement* decision, it was not based on per se reasoning.

The *Thomsen v. Cayser* case,[37] with all its legal confusion, revolved about the question of whether the rule of reason was applicable to price-fixing agreements. A trial court applied the test of reasonableness to a price-fixing contract among steamship lines and concluded that there was no cause of action under the Sherman Act. The Circuit Court of Appeals, receiving the case in 1908 and prior to the *Standard Oil* and *Tobacco* decisions, reversed the judgment, holding that the question of reasonableness was immaterial. With these instructions the jury found a violation of the Sherman Act in retrial. When this was appealed, the *Standard Oil* and *Tobacco* decisions had been rendered and the appellate court stated that its original interpretation of the law had been in error. Reasonableness was material after all. The Supreme Court received the case on a writ of error. Justice McKenna, somewhat strangely, wrote a decision which upheld the lower court's second verdict, but he did so even while affirming that the rule of reason was applicable. His statements that "a combination is not excused because it was induced by good motives or produced good results." [38] seems somewhat in conflict with White's rule of reason, however, and, in sum, the decision adds confusion rather than clarity to the issue.

It is scarcely conceivable that the same court which approved McKenna's language in *Thomsen v. Cayser* could, a year later, approve the words of Justice Brandeis in *Board of Trade of the City of Chicago v. U.S.*[39] The purposes and

[37] 243 U.S. 66 (1917).
[38] 243 U.S. 86.
[39] 246 U.S. 231 (1918).

effects of the agreements were markedly different in the two cases, of course. But compare McKenna's statement about motives and results with Brandeis':

The case was rested upon the bald proposition, that a rule or agreement by which men occupying positions of strength in any branch of trade, fixed prices at which they would buy or sell during an important part of the business day, is an illegal restraint of trade under the Anti-Trust Law. But the legality of an agreement or regulation cannot be determined by so simple a test, as whether it restrains competition. Every agreement concerning trade, every regulation of trade, restrains. To bind, to restrain, is of their very essence. The true test of legality is whether the restraint imposed is such as merely regulates and perhaps thereby promotes competition or whether it is such as may suppress or even destroy competition. To determine that question the court must ordinarily consider the facts peculiar to the business to which the restraint is applied; its condition before and after the restraint was imposed; the nature of the restraint and its effect, actual or probable. The history of the restraint, the evil believed to exist, the reason for adopting the particular remedy, the purpose or end sought to be attained, are all relevant facts. This is not because a good intention will save an otherwise objectionable regulation or the reverse; but because knowledge of intent may help the court to interpret facts and to predict consequences.[40]

Chicago Board of Trade is consistent with even the broadest interpretation of the rule of reason. But the search for consistent application of any rule must continue. In *American Column and Lumber Company v. U.S.*[41] the Court went back to something close to per se. Speaking through Justice Clarke, and after quoting section one of the Sherman Act, the Court held:

Obviously the organization of the defendants constitutes a combination and confessedly they are engaged . . . in interstate commerce so that there remains for decision only the question whether the system of doing business adopted resulted in that direct and

[40] 246 U.S. 238.
[41] 257 U.S. 377 (1921).

undue restraint of interstate commerce which is condemned by this anti-trust statute.

It has been repeatedly held by this court that . . . any combination, . . . which in fact does cause, direct and undue restraint of competition . . . is unlawful.[42]

Clarke considered the purposes of the plan and found it to be "a concerted effort to raise prices." [43] He did not consider in any detail the conditions of trade which led to the adoption of the "Open Competition Plan" or whether the defendants had adequate market control to produce substantial effects on prices.

Justice Holmes dissented:

A combination to get and distribute . . . knowledge, not withstanding its tendency to equalize, not necessarily to raise, prices, is very far from a combination in unreasonable restraint of trade . . . A combination in unreasonable restraint of trade imports an attempt to override normal market conditions. An attempt to conform to them seems to me the most reasonable thing in the world . . . The parties to the combination are free to do as they will . . . I cannot believe that the fact, if it be assumed, that the acts have been done with a sinister purpose, justifies excluding mills in the backwoods from information, in order to enable centralized purchasers to take advantage of their ignorance of the facts.[44]

Justice Brandeis wrote another dissent in which McKenna and Holmes joined. Brandeis would have reversed Clarke since both the elements of coercion and market power were absent:

Words of advice, seemingly innocent and perhaps benevolent, may restrain, when uttered under circumstances that make advice equivalent to command. For the essence of restraint is power; and power may arise merely out of position. Wherever a dominant position has been attained, restraint necessarily arises. And when dominance is attained, or is sought, through combination — however good the motives or the manners of those participating — the

[42] *Ibid.*, pp. 399-400.
[43] *Ibid.*, p. 409.
[44] 257 U.S. 412–413. Note the suggestion contained here that the combination was for the purpose of exerting "countervailing power."

Sherman Law is violated, provided, of course, that the restraint be what is called unreasonable.

In the case before us there was clearly no coercion. There is no claim that a monopoly was sought or created. There is no claim that a division of territory was planned or secured. There is no claim that uniform prices were established or desired . . . No information . . . was kept secret from any producer, any buyer, or the public . . .

The refusal to permit a multitude of small rivals to co-operate . . . in order to protect themselves and the public from the chaos and havoc wrought in their trade by ignorance, may result in suppressing competition in the hardwood industry . . . This court held . . . that it was not unlawful to vest in a single corporation control of practically the whole shoe machinery industry. May not these hardwood lumber concerns, frustrated in their efforts to rationalize competition, be led to enter the inviting field of consolidation? And, if they do, may not another huge trust, with highly centralized control over vast resources, natural, manufacturing, and financial, become so powerful as to dominate competitors, wholesalers, retailers, consumers, employees, and, in large measure, the community? [45]

U.S. v. American Linseed Oil Company[46] conforms with the majority opinion in *American Column and Lumber*. But *Maple Flooring Manufacturers' Association v. U.S.*[47] has an opposite tone. The Court maintained through Justice Stone that:

It is not, we think, open to question that the dissemination of pertinent information concerning any trade or business tends to stabilize that trade or business and to produce uniformity of price and trade practice. Exchange of price quotations of market commodities tends to produce uniformity of prices in the markets of the world. Knowledge of the supplies of available merchandise tends to prevent overproduction and to avoid the economic disturbances produced by business crises resulting from overproduction. But the natural effect of the acquisition of wider and more

[45] 257 U.S. 414–419.
[46] 262 U.S. 371 (1923).
[47] 268 U.S. 563 (1925).

scientific knowledge of business conditions, on the minds of the individuals engaged in commerce and its consequent effect in stabilizing production and price, can hardly be deemed a restraint of commerce, or, if so, it cannot, we think, be said to be an unreasonable restraint, or in any respect unlawful . . . Persons who unite in gathering and disseminating information in trade journals and statistical reports on industry, who gather and publish statistics as to the amount of production of commodities in interstate commerce, and who report market prices, are not engaged in unlawful conspiracies in restraint of trade merely because the ultimate result of their efforts may be to stabilize prices or limit production through a better understanding of economic laws and a more general ability to conform to them, for the simple reason that the Sherman Law neither repeals economic laws nor prohibits the gathering and dissemination of information.[48]

The decision in *Cement Manufacturers' Protective Association v. U.S.,*[49] has the same general line of reasoning as the *Maple Flooring* case. It, too, was written by Stone. In one passage, Stone observes that, "Agreements or understanding among competitors for the maintenance of uniform prices are, of course, unlawful . . ." [50] This seems out of harmony with the rest of the decision and comes close to supporting a per se rule. It is difficult to see any less agreement to maintain uniform prices in the *Cement* case than in, say, *American Column and Lumber.* The distinction drawn between express agreements to set uniform prices and loose "arrangements" (i.e., implicit agreements) which have the same effect is hard to justify in terms of effects on rivalry. The distinction must have seemed valid to Stone, however, for shortly after this he wrote the decision in *U.S. v. Trenton Potteries Company.*[51]

The trial judge, Van Fleet, charged the jury that if it found

[48] 268 U.S. 582–584.

[49] 268 U.S. 588 (1925). Chief Justice Taft and Associate Justices Sanford and McReynolds dissented in both the *Maple Flooring and Cement Manufacturers* cases. The dissents are based principally on their observations that these opinions conflict with that in *American Column and Lumber,* which they thought correct.

[50] *Ibid.,* pp. 604–605.

[51] 273 U.S. 392 (1927).

an agreement "on the part of the members of a combination controlling a substantial part of an industry, upon the prices which the members are to charge for their commodity, [such agreement] is in itself an undue and unreasonable restraint of trade . . ." [52] It further instructed that "it was immaterial whether the agreements were ever actually carried out, whether the purpose of the conspiracy was accomplished in whole or in part, or whether an effort was made to carry the object of the conspiracy into effect." [53]

The Circuit Court of Appeals reversed the trial court's conviction because it felt that such instructions were in error. It believed, that is, that the instructions conflicted with the opinions in the *Standard Oil, Tobacco,* and *Chicago Board of Trade* cases. Justice Stone reversed the Circuit Court of Appeals and reinstated the verdict of the trial court. In his opinion he wrote:

That only those restraints upon interstate commerce which are unreasonable are prohibited by the Sherman Law was the rule laid down by the opinions of this Court in the *Standard Oil* and *Tobacco* Cases. But it does not follow that agreements to fix or maintain prices are reasonable restraints and therefore permitted by the statute, merely because the prices themselves are reasonable. Reasonableness is not a concept of definite and unchanging content . . . Our view of what is a reasonable restraint of commerce is controlled by the recognized purpose of the Sherman Law itself. Whether this type of restraint is reasonable or not must be judged in part at least, in the light of its effect on competition, for, whatever difference of opinion there may be among economists as to the social and economic desirability of an unrestrained competitive system, it cannot be doubted that the Sherman Law and the judicial decisions interpreting it are based upon the assumption that the public interest is best protected from the evils of monopoly and price control by the maintenance of competition.

The aim and result of every price-fixing agreement, if effective, is the elimination of one form of competition. The power to fix prices,

[52] *Ibid.,* p. 396.
[53] *Ibid.,* p. 402.

whether reasonably exercised or not, involves power to control the market and to fix arbitrary and unreasonable prices. The reasonable price fixed today may through economic and business changes become the unreasonable price of tomorrow . . . Agreements which create such potential power may well be held to be in themselves unreasonable or unlawful restraints . . .[54]

Justice Stone, it may be observed, ignored some of his own qualifications. Price information introduced in the trial court casts doubt on whether the agreement, if there were one, was effective. And the whole question of the power created by the combination is relegated by Stone to the simple assertion that the respondents manufactured or distributed 82 per cent of total United States production.

Justices Van Devanter, Sutherland and Butler dissented. Brandeis disqualified himself because his daughter had been involved in the case on behalf of the Government. In 1931, Brandeis wrote the decision in *Standard Oil Company* (*Indiana*) *v. U.S.*[55] The case involved cross-licensing and royalty sharing on "cracking" patents among four large refining companies and forty-six smaller ones, the effect of which might, it was alleged, create adequate power to fix prices. Brandeis' opinion was rather guarded, neither affirming nor in disagreement with Stone's *Trenton Potteries* decision. He did, however, resort to a rule of reason approach:

Such contracts must be scrutinized to ascertain whether the restraints imposed are regulations reasonable under the circumstances, or whether their effect is to suppress or unduly restrict competition . . . Moreover, while manufacture is not interstate commerce, agreements concerning it which tend to limit the supply or to fix the price of goods . . . are within the prohibitions of the Act . . . The rate of royalties may, of course be a decisive factor in the cost of production. If combining patent owners effectively dominate an industry, the power to fix and maintain royalties is tantamount to the power to fix prices . . . Under [the] circumstances the primary defendants could not effectively

[54] 273 U.S. 396–397.
[55] 283 U.S. 163 (1931).

control the supply or fix the price of cracked gasoline . . . unless they could control, through some means, the remainer of the total gasoline production from all sources . . . In the absence of proof that the primary defendants had such control of the entire industry as would make effective the alleged domination of a part, it is difficult to see how they could by agreeing on royalty rates control either the price or the supply of gasoline, or otherwise restrain competition . . .[56]

The famous *Appalachian Coals*[57] case was decided in 1933. Despite allegations to the contrary,[58] it is impossible to reconcile the Supreme Court's opinion here with its decision in *Trenton Potteries.* The latter, following a fairly narrow per se approach, is certainly in opposition to the extended use of the rule of reason in *Appalachian Coals.* Judge Parker, in the lower court,[59] concluded that the proposed joint selling agency in *Appalachian Coals* was illegal per se, even though it was admitted that the agency would not have monopoly control of any market. Chief Justice Hughes held to the contrary:

As a charter of freedom, the Act has a generality and adaptability comparable to that found to be desirable in constitutional provisions . . . The restrictions the act imposes are not mechanical or artificial. Its general phrases, interpreted to attain its fundamental objects, set up the essential standard of reasonableness . . . [T]hey do not seek to establish a mere delusive liberty either by making impossible the normal and fair expansion of . . . commerce or the adoption of reasonable measures to protect it from injurious and destructive practices and to promote competition upon a sound basis.

In applying this test, a close and objective scrutiny of particular conditions and purposes is necessary in each case. . . . The mere fact that the parties to an agreement eliminate competition between themselves is not enough to condemn it . . . It is therefore necessary in this instance to consider the economic conditions peculiar

[56] 283 U.S. 169, 174, 176, 177, 179.
[57] Appalachian Coals, Inc. v. U.S., 288 U.S. 344 (1933).
[58] See, for example, Douglas' reasoning in *U.S. v. Socony-Vacuum Oil Co.,* 310 U.S. 214–216 (1940).
[59] 1 F. Supp. 339 (W. D. Va. 1932).

to the coal industry, the practices which have obtained, the nature of defendant's (sic) plan of making sales, the reasons which led to its adoption, and the probable consequences of the carrying out of that plan in relation to market prices and other matters affecting the public interest . . .[60]

Hughes proceeded to review conditions in the industry and concluded:

The evidence leaves no doubt of the existence of the evils at which defendants' plan was aimed. The industry was in distress. It suffered from overexpansion and from a serious relative decline through the growing use of substitute fuels. It was afflicted by injurious practices within itself — practices which demanded correction. If evil conditions could not be entirely cured, they at least might be alleviated. The unfortunate state of the industry would not justify any attempt unduly to restrain competition or to monopolize, but the existing situation prompted defendants to make, and the statute did not preclude them from making an honest effort to remove abuses, to make competition fairer, and thus to promote the essential interests of commerce. The interests of producers and consumers are interlinked. When industry is grievously hurt, when producing concerns fail, when unemployment mounts and communities dependent upon profitable production are prostrated, the wells of commerce go dry. So far as actual purposes are concerned, the conclusion of the court below was amply supported that defendants were engaged in a fair and open endeavor to aid the industry in a measurable recovery from its plight. The inquiry then, must be whether despite this objective the inherent nature of their plan was such as to create an undue restraint upon interstate commerce . . .

The contention is, and the court below found, that while defendants could not fix market prices, the concerted action would 'affect' them, that is, that it would have a tendency to stabilize market prices and to raise them to a higher level than would otherwise obtain. But the facts found do not establish, and the evidence fails to show, that any effect will be produced which in the circumstances of this industry will be detrimental to fair competition. A co-operative enterprise, otherwise free from objection, which carries with it no monopolistic menace, is not to be condemned

[60] 288 U.S. 359, 360, 361.

as an undue restraint merely because it may effect a change in market conditions, where the change would be in mitigation of recognized evils and would not impair, but rather foster, fair competitive opportunities . . .

The question remains whether, despite the foregoing conclusions, the fact that the defendants' plan eliminates competition between themselves is alone sufficient to condemn it . . . Defendants insist that . . . no valid objection could have been interposed under the Sherman Act if the defendants had eliminated competition between themselves by a complete integration of their mining properties in a single ownership . . . We agree that there is no ground for holding defendants' plan illegal merely because they have not integrated their properties and have chosen to maintain their independent plants, seeking not to limit but rather to facilitate production . . . If the mere size of a single, embracing entity is not enough to bring a combination in corporate form within the statutory inhibition, the mere number and extent of the production of those engaged in a co-operative endeavor to remedy evils which may exist in an industry, and to improve competitive conditions, should not be regarded as producing illegality. The argument that integration may be considered a normal expansion of business, while a combination of independent producers in a common selling agency should be treated as abnormal — that one is a legitimate enterprise and the other is not — makes but an artificial distinction. The Anti-Trust Act aims at substance . . .[61]

In the last few remarks Hughes came close to discarding the whole notion of market power which must be one of the crucial elements in any test of reasonableness. Despite the strong language, however, the Court must have had reservations as to whether it was not allowing too great an accretion of monopoly power. For in the end the plan was not declared legal. The defendants were allowed to start the plan, if they wished, without legal prejudice, but the lower court retained jurisdiction and was instructed to "take further proceedings if future developments justify that course in the appropriate enforcement of the Anti-Trust Act." [62]

[61] 288 U.S. 372, 373, 374, 376, 377.
[62] *Ibid.*, p. 378.

The Court applied the doctrine of *Appalachian Coals* again in the *Sugar Institute* case.[63] The sugar refiners involved refined "practically all the imported raw sugar processed in this country" and supplied "70 to 80 per cent. of the sugar consumed." [64] The District Court had enjoined the refiners from engaging in any program "in connection with the sale, marketing, shipment, transportation, storage, distribution or delivery of refined sugar," [65] effectively prohibiting the continuance of an open price and statistical reporting system. Hughes again wrote the opinion:

> The restrictions imposed by the Sherman Anti-Trust Act . . . are not mechanical or artificial. We have repeatedly said that they set up the essential standard of reasonableness . . . Designed to frustrate unreasonable restraints, they do not prevent the adoption of reasonable means to protect interstate commerce from destructive or injurious practices and to promote competition upon a sound basis. Voluntary action to end abuses and to foster fair competitive opportunities in the public interest may be more effective than legal processes . . . Nor does the fact that the correction of abuses may tend to stabilize a business, or to produce fairer price levels, require that abuses should go uncorrected or that an effort to correct them should for that reason alone be stamped as an unreasonable restraint of trade . . .[66]

The lower court's order was modified substantially by the Supreme Court when the rule of reason was applied. Thus, nine years after *Trenton Potteries,* the per se rule seemed abandoned. Yet the next major case before the Court where price fixing or price stabilizing was the paramount issue was *Socony-Vacuum*. And in that case, as we have seen, per se was applied and defined more broadly than in any previous case.

By and large, per se had been consistently applied since

[63] Sugar Institute, Inc. v. U.S., 297 U.S. 553 (1936).
[64] *Ibid.,* p. 600.
[65] *Ibid.,* p. 602.
[66] 297 U.S. 597, 598.

Socony-Vacuum. In *U.S. v. Masonite Corporation*[67] the Court, in another opinion by Douglas, was in diametric opposition to the views which had prevailed in *Appalachian Coals* and *Sugar Institute*:

Since there was price-fixing, the fact that there were business reasons which made the arrangements desirable to the appellees, the fact that the effect of the combination may have been to increase the distribution of hardboard without increase of price to the consumer or even to promote competition between dealers, or the fact that from other points of view the arrangements might be deemed to have desirable consequences would be no more a legal justification for price-fixing than were the 'competitive evils' in the *Socony-Vacuum* case.[68]

Justice Black, in *U.S. v. Frankfort Distilleries,*[69] expressly used a per se rule.[70] Justice Reed followed similar law in *U.S. v. United States Gypsum Co.*[71] and in *U.S. v. Line Material Co.*[72] Justice Douglas applied it in *Schine Chain Theatres, Inc., v. U.S.*[73] The *Mandeville Island Farms, Inc., v. American Crystal Sugar Co.* case,[74] written by Justice Rutledge, concerns the effects of a price-fixing agreement among buyers of sugar beets and there are places where it appears that reasonableness is being considered. On the whole, however, especially since the principal precedent cited is the *Frankfort Distilleries* case, *Mandeville* falls more appropriately into the per se category.

The *Triangle Conduit* case[75] did not reach the Supreme Court and was brought under section 5 of the Federal Trade Commission Act. While *Cement Institute*[76] had been decided

[67] 316 U.S. 265 (1942).
[68] *Ibid.*, p. 276.
[69] 324 U.S. 293 (1945).
[70] *Ibid.*, p. 296.
[71] 333 U.S. 364 (1948). See p. 400 for the express use of per se.
[72] 333 U.S. 287 (1948).
[73] 334 U.S. 110 (1948).
[74] 334 U.S. 219 (1948).
[75] Triangle Conduit and Cable Co., Inc., v. Federal Trade Commission, 168 F. 2d 175 (7th Cir. 1948).
[76] Federal Trade Commission v. Cement Institute, 333 U.S. 683 (1948).

mainly on the basis of price discrimination rather than price fixing, the Circuit Court in *Triangle Conduit* relied on cases such as *Line Material, Trenton Potteries,* and *Socony-Vacuum* to show that the multiple-basing point system constituted an agreement to suppress price competition and that it was therefore unlawful.

The courts have not been uniform in their treatment of price-fixing charges when brought under the Federal Trade Commission Act, however. The *Tag Manufacturers* case[77] presented facts not unlike those of *Trenton Potteries* — uniform list prices, statistical reporting, a trade association, and a substantial volume (25 per cent) of sales at prices less than the list. The Circuit Court did not use per se, but instead applied a sweeping rule of reason. The contention that the list prices were the actual prices was rejected because "manufacturers are free to make off-list sales; and in practice . . . have freely done so." [78] "They all engaged in off-list pricing to such an extent that it would be wholly irrational to infer that the essence of their agreement was that they would all adhere to their current price lists . . ." [79] For support in setting aside the Commission's cease and desist order, the appeals court relied on *Maple Flooring* rather than on *Trenton Potteries* or *Socony-Vacuum.*

Subsequent Sherman Act cases were not influenced by the *Tag case. U.S. v. United States Alkali Export Association, Inc.*[80] applied the *Socony-Vacuum* rules. The Supreme Court expressly reaffirmed *Socony-Vacuum* in *Kiefer-Stewart Co. v. Joseph E. Seagram and Sons,*[81] even though an intracorporate conspiracy was at issue. In 1952, in *U.S. v. New Wrinkle*[82] the Court held that, "Certainly since *United States v. Trenton*

[77] Tag Manufacturers Institute v. Federal Trade Commission, 174 F. 2d 452 (1st Cir. 1949).

[78] *Ibid.*, p. 458.

[79] *Ibid.*, p. 459.

[80] 86 F. Supp. 59 (D.C. N.Y. 1949).

[81] 340 U.S. 211 (1951).

[82] 342 U.S. 371 (1952).

Potteries Co., . . . price fixing in commerce, reasonable or unreasonable, has been considered a *per se* violation of the Sherman Act." [83]

There has been at least one instance, however, in which a trial court has refused to apply the per se rule. In *U.S. v. Morgan,*[84] a Sherman Act case, Judge Medina queried:

> Has the rule of reason been abandoned to make way for a cliche or rubric to the effect that any agreement relative to price maintenance is taboo, irrespective of whether it fosters and promotes rather than restricts and restrains competition, irrespective of whether it is intended to or does or can affect general market prices, and irrespective of any and all other factors? [85]

After extensive citation and an exhaustive investigation of the nature of the securities underwriting business, he concluded:

> Despite all the general condemnation of price-fixing, I find nothing in any of these cases which can be regarded as controlling precedent here or which binds me to hold the clauses of these syndicate agreements now under attack to be illegal *per se.*[86]

[83] *Ibid.,* p. 377.
[84] 118 F. Supp. 621 (S.D.N.Y. 1954).
[85] *Ibid.,* p. 687.
[86] *Ibid.,* p. 689.

CHAPTER XI

POLICY CONCLUSIONS

INTRODUCTION

The mainstream of present day economic thought emphasizes the need of complete independence of action among sellers and among buyers for the existence of "free" competition. The translation of this emphasis on independence into antitrust policy is only partly the result of the persuasiveness of the economists' models. The development of the legal doctrine of per se was to some extent fortuitous, reflecting a tendency on the part of the judicial system to adopt legal procedures which would lessen the burden on the courts.[1] Too, the notion of independent action is harmonious with nineteenth-century liberalism, in which the political and economic destiny of society was thought to be guided to a welfare ideal by the operation of immutable natural laws.

There have always been some among the nineteenth-century variety of utilitarians and liberals who called attention to the lack of realism in the rationalistic assumptions underlying economic theory and who hesitated to leap directly from the conclusions of theory to the formation of policy. Even so, economists have for the most part advocated public policies which were directed at making the real world more like their assumptions rather than changing their assumptions to afford a better analysis of the real world. In view of the intrinsic beauty of the theoretical model, this is not difficult to understand.

[1] For an elaboration, see Donald Dewey, *Monopoly in Economics and Law* (Chicago, 1959), pp. 165–166.

There have been some, too, who have called attention to the need for interference with the free market process, especially for a limited amount of government interference to assure that the rules of conduct in the market were compatible with continued free enterprise and to exercise a policing function to see that the rules were enforced.[2] It is in this respect that the economic liberal can be distinguished from the economic anarchist.[3]

This attention to the unrealism of assumptions and the need for limited interference is different from the theory of interfirm organization developed in the previous chapters. In general, economists have not yet recognized the paradoxical and nearly self-contradictory nature of the concept of economic liberty. So long as economic liberty includes the right to associate with others in economic pursuits, it also includes the right to forego truly free, independent, individual action and to substitute group action for it. Man can be truly free only when he exists in isolation from his fellows. In a group his behavior is modified and codified whether he likes it or not, and whether he likes it or not being a member of some group is unavoidable. The fabric of every stable social structure is of necessity a complex of finely woven, overlapping, interrelated groups. Man is, indeed, a social animal. Even anarchists organize.

It is true, of course, that the operation of the pricing system requires the formation and enforcement of rules. And it is as true that at the extreme it is the responsibility of the government to make and enforce such rules. Nonetheless, only a small portion of all rule-making and policing is done by government. Most comes from very subsidiary groups which perform their functions in less obvious ways. Without this co-

[2] For an interesting discussion of the views of the English classical economists on this point, see Lionel Robbins, *The Theory of Economic Policy* (London, 1952).

[3] See Frank H. Knight, "The Role of Principles in Economics and Politics," *American Economic Review,* 41:16–17 (March 1951).

optative process in the various groups and organizations of society, the task of government would be hopelessly burdensome. Thus the whole of the social structure — composed of human beings with limited knowledge, foresight and rationality — is a complex of organizations and organizations of organizations, each governing behavior, establishing goals, and providing means of communication.

The market system is not a mechanism apart from other social phenomena. Firms and the men who direct them are thrown into contact with one another in a variety of relationships. One relationship is an essentially competitive one, but not exclusively so. Rival firms, as a group, face a changing external environment as well as internal competition. It is not unreasonable to suppose that firms are led to certain organized and co-operative activities because of their mutual problems. The exact form of their organization, the nature of its functions and its efficiency vary with circumstances outlined in the theory. But in every case, the interfirm organization restrains "free" competition in a fashion parallel to the restraints on other freedoms necessarily imposed by other types of social organizations.

If freedom and independence can never be absolute, it is both futile and unwise to insist on completely free and independent competition among firms. Rather, the appropriate policy should distinguish between organizational behavior which is compatible with the larger public interest and that which is not. The important policy question is not whether firms are independent of one another but rather whether market performance can be improved by changing the character of the interfirm organization.

THE FUNCTIONS OF THE PRICE SYSTEM

The function of the price system in a capitalistic economy is to allocate scarce resources efficiently. The measuring of the system's efficiency is most difficult, however. Theoretical welfare economics suggests some criteria, particularly the equality of price to marginal cost, but in practice the use of these criteria is severely restricted. The problems involved in measuring prices and costs are not negligible. Beyond these, however, are greater obstacles. For example, if sumptuary legislation or accepted sumptuary practices upset the price-marginal cost equality in the market for one good, the welfare connotation of maintaining the equality of prices and marginal costs for all other goods is lost.[4] Since society imposes sumptuary restrictions of many sorts and for many reasons, this alone — and for theoretical reasons alone — negates much of the worth of the theoretical welfare guides so far as policy is concerned.

Similarly, the guides of welfare economics are based on the assumption that personal preference functions are independent of one another. Whether such independence of utilities exists in fact has been questioned by numerous writers. The organizational view of society which has been expressed above ought to be sufficient to indicate an additional argument against the assumption of independent utilities.

Perhaps these are minor matters. If so, there are other reasons for not wishing to fashion policy solely on the conclusions of theoretical welfare norms. Most important, welfare theory has remained almost entirely static while the greatest fact of the market economy is its dynamic character. There have been persuasive if not conclusive arguments — especially by Schumpeter[5] and Galbraith[6] — to the effect that a degree of monopoly is essential to technological change. None of these arguments refutes the logic of the competitive models

[4] See R. G. Lipsey and R. K. Lancaster, "The General Theory of Second Best," *Review of Economic Studies,* 24:11 (1956–57). For an excellent recent survey, see E. J. Mishan, "A Survey of Welfare Economics," *Economic Journal,* 70:197 (June 1960).

[5] Joseph A. Schumpeter, *Capitalism, Socialism and Democracy,* 3rd ed. (New York, 1950).

[6] John Kenneth Galbraith, *American Capitalism* (Cambridge, Mass., 1952).

which incorporate saving and investment decisions; none denies the attractiveness which lower costs resulting from technical change would have for the theoretical entrepreneur in the theoretical competitive system. The arguments are instead based on misgivings of an institutional sort — that the real world just does not work that way. The failure of welfare economics to consider directly the welfare implications of novel products and new processes is a sufficient reason for questioning its applicability to policy questions.

The lack of strictly objective standards for judging its performance does not imply that there is no way to assess the market economy. There are several relatively specific goals — all within the more general context of efficient resource allocation — which offer some help in policy formation. First, the system should operate so that resource usage is responsive to changes in demand and to changes in supply. Second, the system should operate so as to discourage unjustifiable differences in income. Third, the system should encourage technological change, both in the processes of production and in the development of new products. And fourth, the system should not be incompatible with political and social goals of greater importance than economic goals.

This listing, of course, is not helpful without elaboration. To say that resource utilization ought to be responsive to supply and demand has a specific meaning in the context of the competitive model but is nearly meaningless outside that context, without clarification. By way of clarification, if the price mechanism is to allocate resources, the resources must flow in the direction indicated by changes in demand. In the short run, output ought to increase as demand does and vice versa. In the long run, the capacity of the industry should behave similarly, either through the expansion or contraction of existing firms or through a change in the number of firms. This appears much like the theoretical meaning but, unembellished with the theoretical refinements, it is actually quite different in two respects. Most important, the definition here does not depend on price and profit variation, either ex ante or ex post, as the sole causal nexus in the resource response. Prices and profits may be causal — even the principal cause — of changes in resource usage in response to changes in demand, but so long as the resource usage is in the direction indicated by demand, the system is performing its *main* function even with little or no change in prices. Adjustments in resource utilization to changes in demand may not be *ideal* in the absence of the price changes included in the competitive model, but reflection does indicate that, especially in the short run, the price changes described by the model are important principally for explaining *why* the resource utilization changes with demand, not because of the impact of the price changes, in and of themselves, on the public welfare.

The second distinction between the responsiveness of resource use to demand as presented here and as presented in conventional competitive theory is in the element of timing. The theoretical shift is frictionless and timeless in the calendar sense. The process of the shift, the institutional changes the shift involves, are all ignored. But the world is not frictionless and shifts in resource allocation require time. Instantaneous response to changes in demand would bring chaos. The output of the best run firms cannot be changed without forethought, planning and, often, organizational adjustments. Changes in the scale of plant and in the number of firms cannot occur overnight. In practice it requires some knowledge of an industry to judge whether the output responds well to changes in demand. Knowledge of economics, by itself, helps little.

Similar connotations apply to the meaning of responsiveness to supply conditions. There are, however, additional considerations. One of these is differences in the willingness to supply on the part of rival firms due to differences in costs. In the theoretical long-run equilibrium, rents provide a con-

of the public. Greater generalization of this point seems impractical.

Finally, it must be remembered that antitrust policy is "not necessarily actuated by economic motives alone." [8] Unfortunately, Congress has not articulated any of the goals of antitrust policy — economic, political or social — so that a specification of goals can at best be no more than impressionistic. But at least some of the reasons for wishing to maintain a market system for allocating resources stem from political and social considerations. The pricing system ought not unreasonably discourage social mutability. Neither should it interfere with the political process by making it impossible for none save a particular group of income recipients to have an effective political voice.

THE INTERFIRM ORGANIZATION AND THE PRICE SYSTEM

It has been argued that interfirm organizations develop as a consequence of the market indeterminacy and instability which accompany purely individualistic firm behavior in simple oligopolistic or complex, linked interdependent market structures. The question remains whether interfirm organizations restrain rivalry to the point that the price system must fail in its task of allocating resources. To this question there is no general answer. Sometimes the interfirm organization goes beyond the limits required to keep competition workable and resource allocation suffers. Sometimes the organization does not accomplish even the requisite restraint to keep competition within the bounds of workability and, again, resources are poorly allocated.

The theory of interfirm organization suggests the variables which might be studied to analyze the extent to which competition is restrained in particular circumstances. Of particular importance are the number of firms in the organization, the

[8] From Judge Learned Hand's opinion in *U.S. v. Aluminum Company of America,* 148 F. 2d 427 (2nd. Cir. 1945).

distribution of power and leadership among the firms, the homogeneity of the value systems and objectives of the firms and the influence of factors external to the group, especially from other organizations. But these variables and their relationship to competition and good resource allocation cannot be specified to the point that one or a few simple rules can be developed which would eliminate the need for a study of the particular market in question. It is doubtful that any theory of competition can ever be so precise as to obviate the need for economics as an "art" as contrasted with economics as a "science."

It is probably safe to assert, however, that the general tendency among both economists and lawyers is to overestimate the restraining effects of interfirm organizations. This tendency is in part due to the historically dominant emphasis on the desirability of free individualism which has already been noted. Probably of more importance is the failure to recognize the substantial amount of freedom of choice and action which remains even after a person or a firm joins an organization. Assume, for example, that several firms have agreed on prices; then consider the range of freedom to compete which remains. Each firm is still free to compete with quality and advertising. Each may vary its output or add new products. Each may alter its system of distribution. Each may voice its continued assent to the agreement or voice discontent which may lead to changes in the agreed upon price which are not radically different from those which would occur in the absence of the agreement. Most important, each is legally free to violate the agreement at will, a point which causes the ambitious cartel manager no little worry. In addition to the freedom remaining within the group, there may also be the freedom of others to enter the market and competition from substitute products. None of these is necessarily a perfect substitute for internal group competition, but the danger of simple price fixing is often exaggerated.

Most interfirm organizations do not, and private organizations, it will be concluded, should not fix actual market prices. But all such organizations influence actual market prices if they have any effect at all. Their very raison d'etre, it will be recalled, is to eliminate market indeterminacy and instability through the adoption and enforcement of behavioral rules.

PER SE AND THE INTERFIRM ORGANIZATION

It is appropriate to re-examine the per se rule on price fixing. Generally speaking, the present legal approach in both overt price-fixing and conscious parallelism cases is to determine first whether the conduct of the defendants constitutes an agreement to fix prices. This is in fact a twofold determination, with inquiry into whether an agreement exists and inquiry into whether the agreement is for the purpose of fixing prices. If the court finds agreement, either from direct evidence or from inferences drawn from parallel conduct, and if the agreement is to fix prices, the guilt of defendants is then unreasonable per se. If price fixing is not found, but the conduct of the defendants influences prices, then a rule of reason which inquires whether competition is unduely restrained is employed.[9]

Considered outside the context of cases, this approach seems warranted. In a case context, however, it becomes apparent that in the law the greatest emphasis is placed on the question of whether there is agreement, and much less attention is given the question of whether prices are really fixed. Further, the law has extended the concept of price fixing to the point that influencing prices may constitute legal, if not economic, price fixing.

In the *Socony-Vacuum* decision it was not found that competition in price was eliminated or that prices were fixed in

[9] See *Report of the Attorney General's National Committee to Study the Antitrust Laws* (Washington, 1955), pp. 12–14.

the sense of being uniform and inflexible.[10] The conviction was based instead on the fact that there was an agreement (conspiracy) with the purpose of raising the general level of prices and that the conduct of the defendants contributed to a price rise. No matter how great were the competitive evils faced by the industry, no matter how ruinous the competition, the Court could find no excuse for any kind of co-optative behavior which might improve the industry. The defendants' could jointly do nothing which tampered with the price structure without running afoul of the antitrust laws. Even if the interfirm organization were in "no position to control the market," joint action in an effort to stabilize conditions would be illegal because it "would be directly interfering with the *free* play of market forces." The Sherman Act, it was said, "protects . . . against any degree of interference." Any prices are fixed if they are agreed upon and any group effort to stabilize the market is an agreement to manipulate or fix prices.

Taken literally, the *Socony-Vacuum* decision, on which all subsequent Sherman Act price-fixing cases rely, virtually outlaws the socially useful as well as the socially harmful functions of interfirm organizations. The decision's frequent references to "free competition" is ample testimony to the individualistic and naturalistic view of the social structure used in interpreting competition and the purposes of the Sherman Act. The decision and those subsequent to it pay no attention to the alternatives forced on the market system when the operation of the interfirm organization is denied. This lack of attention is, of course, a consequence of the failure to recognize that the competitive system does require rationalization of some sort and that the market is not self-regulating in the absence of accepted rules of conduct for buyers and sellers. Given this lack of attention to the alternative means of estab-

[10] 310 U.S. 220, 222.

lishing and enforcing market rules, there is some danger that the policy of per se prohibiting the functioning of formal or informal interfirm organizations which admittedly influence the pricing structure will compound the tendencies toward more concentrated markets (where the interfirm organization is less obvious but just as effective) and toward more government market regulation.[11]

It can easily be argued that the danger of per se is being exaggerated. Perhaps it is, for in the usual circumstances a case does not come to the attention of enforcement authorities unless the restraints are unreasonable. Certainly, at least, there are many interfirm organizations operating openly whose activities are not being challenged. This is not much of an excuse, however, for a policy based on an imperfect understanding of the competitive process. It would have been better to have declared guilt in *Socony-Vacuum* on the basis of the unreasonableness of the conduct than to have stretched the meaning of price fixing so that a per se rule could be applied.[12] As it now stands, price fixing seems to be defined legally as conduct that is unreasonable, and whether prices are fixed is barely considered.

There are, too, more than semantic reasons for suggesting that the present per se approach be abandoned. Cases do come up which are exceptions to the general principle that

[11] The contrast on this very point between Justice Douglas' opinion in *Socony-Vacuum* and his dissent in *Standard Oil Co. of California v. U.S.*, 337 U.S. 293 (1949) is startling. The latter case dealt with exclusive dealing contracts and the majority of the Court had ruled the contracts unlawful in terms which approached a per se rule. Douglas dissented, arguing that the Court should make its choice "on the basis not of abstractions but of the realities of modern industrial life." He saw an end to small independent businessmen and vertical integration of the majors as a result of the majority rule and the failure of the Court to consider the alternatives the industry would take.

[12] See 310 U.S. 214–216. The stretching of meaning was really extreme, for in the same opinion it was noted with approval that the *Appalachian Coals* decision found no price fixing of bituminous coal.

enforcement authorities bring only the unreasonable cases. The *Tag Manufacturers Institute* case,[13] for example, charged "an understanding, agreement, combination, and conspiracy to restrict, restrain, suppress and eliminate price competition" and could have been brought under the Sherman Act. Had this occurred, there is a good chance that the defendants would have been found guilty under the per se rule. As it turned out, however, the court could distinguish between an agreement to use uniform price lists and an agreement to fix market prices. Only 25 per cent of sales were off list, yet the court concluded that in this particular industry there was a vital distinction between issuing a price list and charging a price.

At the same time the court was not deluded about the price lists and whether they influenced prices. They were "more than an object of academic historical interest and . . . designed for a practical business purpose." [14] Still, "it would be wholly irrational to infer that the essence of their agreement was that they would all adhere to their current price lists . . ." [15] In this particular industry, uniform price lists and an open reporting system did not, it was concluded, unreasonably restrain competition. Economically it is impossible to reconcile *Tag Manufacturers* with, say, *Trenton Potteries*. The two cases are quite similar in many respects — thirty-one manufacturers of tags with 95 per cent of national output; twenty-three manufacturers of vitreous sanitary ware with 82 per cent of national output; there was a large variety of products in both cases which favored the use of price lists; both used an open price system. In some respects, more restraint on competition is obvious in the *Tag* case. The tag industry was somewhat more concentrated, there was a history of definite written agreements with penalties for not reporting and there were

[13] Tag Manufacturers Institute v. Federal Trade Commission, 174 F. 2d 452 (1st Cir. 1949).

[14] *Ibid.*, p. 458.

[15] *Ibid.*, p. 459.

fewer sales off list. The difference in the decisions is a difference in rules. One used a rule of reason and the other a per se rule. There was certainly as much influence on prices in the operation of the tag interfirm organization as in that of the vitreous sanitary ware industry.

The per se legalities of the exempting statutes present somewhat the reverse dangers. Even while a policy of moderating rivalry may be consistent with a total policy directed toward good market performance, absolute exemption from the antitrust laws and government aid in establishing formal organizations have in some instances gone too far. Excess rivalry has been replaced by too little rivalry. The retention of small, inefficient production units — as in the milk industry and in retail drug stores — has been encouraged and prices have failed to respond to long-run market conditions. Many of the exemptions statutes do, however, treat specific industries, all of which tend to have similar characteristics. Their inflexibility may, therefore, be partially justifiable and of less consequence than the inflexibility of the general antitrust laws which must be applied to diverse structural-performance-behavioral conditions. Still, if there is the possibility that too little rivalry may exist, it would appear preferable to have all markets subject to public policy directed toward increasing rivalry.

A PROPOSED RULE OF REASON

The appropriate antitrust policy toward interfirm organizations and their impact of rivalry would substitute a rule of reason for both per se legalities and per se illegalities. The need for this substitution is clearly not because of a conclusion that the rigid fixing of actual market prices is beneficial. Neither is it because of a conclusion that unrestrained rivalry promotes good performance. It is rather because of a more complex relationship between rivalry and performance than can be adequately coped with by simple rules. If it were true that performance improves monotonically with increases in rivalry, and that rivalry itself varies monotonically with a set of structural and behavioral variables, there would be a place for inflexible, per se rules in competitive policy. Under these circumstances, efforts to maximize (or minimize, if that is the nature of the function) any one or all of the independent variables in the function determining rivalry would improve performance.

The abandoning of per se rules is suggested not because of prejudice in favor of the use of discretion rather than rules but because of the complicated relationships between structure, behavior and performance. The immunity statutes appear less inconsistent with achieving desirable market performance when analyzed with the theory of interfirm organization than with traditional value theory only because of the view that performance is not monotonically related to rivalry. To a point, increases in rivalry improve performance. The point, however, is not uniquely defined by any one of the variables which determine rivalry. Per se rules which establish either absolute legality or absolute illegality depending on a condition of but one of the variables may improve or may worsen market performance.

Actually, the change in policy which is advocated is not great. One suggestion is the elimination of complete immunities from the Sherman Act — a change which the Supreme Court has now read into at least one immunity statute[16] — and the substitution of a rule of reason. Without the latter, the elimination of per se legalities appears quite impossible. The immunity of labor unions, for example, could hardly be abrogated if the alternative were to subject them to the per se illegality doctrine currently used for section 1 enforcement.

The other suggestion — really but the reverse of the first — is that the per se illegality doctrine be dropped. As noted in

[16] Maryland and Virginia Milk Producers' Ass'n. v. U.S., 362 U.S. 458 (1960).

Chapter III, recent decisions suggest that market analyses are made in fact in conscious parallelism cases. The courts tend to find agreement only if the parallelism is complex, predatory or otherwise unreasonable. Thus, group behavior which has no adverse effects on performance is ignored and only that which is unreasonable is labelled agreement. Conscious parallelism can be brought into consistency with the rule of reason approach simply by giving explicit recognition to the implicit test of reasonableness which is currently conducted. And if the test were explicit, there would be greater likelihood of its being well-conducted rather than hidden in the sham of "alternative hypotheses." Rather than leading to nonenforcement, the substitute rule of reason should foster enforcement in parallelism cases since the crucial test would involve an analysis of performance, not the inference of agreement.

The same rule would, of course, allow some formal agreements now per se illegal, but this would occur only when other variables tend to create a high degree of rivalry and when alternatives to formal organization — mergers and exemptions and government regulation — pose as serious threats to market performance as do the formal agreements. The implications of the theory of interfirm organization do not constitute an apology for monopoly. When compared with current policies, the suggested policy changes favor more competition in every case save those in which extreme rivalry is present.

The rule of reason must look beyond the question of agreement, for tacit or express agreement among the members of a group is a fact of organized social and economic life. The rule of reason must look beyond the factual circumstance of an agreement which relates to or influences prices, for the effect on rivalry of a particular type of agreement varies with other characteristics of the market. An agreement which has the effect of practically eliminating rivalry in one market might, if imposed in another, serve to improve its functioning.

The use of reason in price-fixing cases should not mean that the "reasonableness" of the prices themselves would be the primary concern. Justice Stone's position on this point in the *Trenton Potteries* case, while not very relevant to the facts there, was certainly correct. Rather, the primary concern should be to ascertain as clearly as possible the degree of rivalry and to judge whether increases in rivalry would improve market performance. Rivalry in price cannot be neatly categorized into two compartments, "fixed prices" and "free prices"; price rivalry appears in various degrees. Actual price behavior — the reasonableness of prices — is important only to the extent that it is indicative of the degree of rivalry. Thus, one need not "quail at turning the courts into price administrators, working ex post facto with the certainty that today's decision as to what was a reasonable price is already obsolete and no assurance that the approved price will be reasonable tomorrow." [17]

Reasonableness in price-fixing cases concerns the question of whether so much power is lodged in an interfirm organization that the organization, qua organization, can effectively override or eliminate forces tending to change price, tending to bring new firms in or to cause old firms to leave the market, or tending to cause output to respond to changes in demand. The restraint is clearly unreasonable if neither the individual firms *within* the restraining group nor individual firms or organizations *external* to the restraining group can influence prices, regardless of the level of the price set. If competitive evils are so great that such extraordinary power must be lodged in an organization to assure good performance, government regulation should supplement or government ownership replace private enterprise.

The recent conspiracies among manufacturers of electrical equipment perhaps provide an illustration of clear-cut unrea-

[17] Quoted from a letter from a friend who disagrees emphatically.

sonableness.[18] The prices charged may have been reasonable by any criterion, there was occasional "cheating" by some of the firms, and in some instances prices seem even to have responded to general business conditions. Nonetheless, prices were almost universally determined explicitly by the respective groups, independent pricing decisions were almost totally absent, customers were allocated in advance, etc. The agreements would have been unreasonable even if the goods were given away free! Group behavior had subordinated individual behavior to near oblivion.

It may be argued with more justification that the adoption of a rule of reason would lead to nonenforcement of the antitrust laws. The rule of reason *and* some of its advocates seem to favor lax enforcement. The rule of reason, it is said, would lead to the expensive and protracted "big case," with the result that fewer cases could be brought. At the extreme, "each case would be a field day for defense counsel, and the length of the trial would be limited only by counsel's ingenuity in adducing evidence purporting to show that his client's interfirm organization was not 'too efficient.' "[19] Lawyers would, in addition, be unable to give wise counsel to their clients because of the vagueness inherent in the rule of reason approach.

Lawyers are in a better position than economists to argue the comparative legal problems of enforcing per se rules and enforcing a rule of reason. It should be pointed out, however, that as with most alternatives, the choice between them is not dictated by one or the other having all the advantages. The principal advantage of per se is that it "is a relatively cheap and quick method of enforcing the law."[20] The value placed

[18] Reference is to a series of cases brought against General Electric Co., Westinghouse Electric Corp. and several others (E. D. Penna. 1960).

[19] Quoted from another letter from another dissenting friend.

[20] Edward S. Mason, "Market Power and Business Conduct: Some Comments on the Report of the Attorney General's Committee on Antitrust

on this advantage over the admittedly less cheap and more time consuming rule of reason should not be very great, however. While administrative ease is a factor to consider in adopting a rule, it surely is of less importance than the objectives which the rule is intended to accomplish. The per se rule is better than no rule at all. Still it tends to work some mischief in the competitive system which could be avoided with a rule of reason. The question should revolve around the issue of whether the enforcement difficulties presented by a rule of reason are so great that, despite the weaknesses of the purely economic rationale of per se, the latter accomplishes more in practice.[21]

The administrative ease of enforcing the per se rule compared with enforcing the rule of reason has probably been exaggerated. In the absence of express agreements — now quite rare in price-fixing litigation — the promise of a short trial may be quite false; "grave difficulty may arise as to whether a given transaction does or does not fit the label." [22] The trial in the *Socony-Vacuum* case, it may be recalled, was conducted with the use of the per se rule, yet the trial record ran to more than 12,000 pages, in addition to over 1,000 exhibits. Nearly forty pages were used by Justice Douglas to summarize the background and nature of the price-fixing agreement in his affirmation of the trial court's conviction. The case was a full scale investigation of the markets which the per se approach failed to stop.

When facts exist which are as complicated as those in *Socony-Vacuum,* it probably is impossible to bring suit under the Sherman Act without full investigation and a long trial.

Policy," *American Economic Review,* vol. 46, no. 2 (May 1956), reprinted in *Economic Concentration and the Monopoly Problem* (Cambridge, 1957), p. 393.

[21] See Dewey, *Monopoly in Law and Economics* (Chicago, 1959), p. 166.

[22] James A. Rahl, "Per Se Rules and Boycotts Under the Sherman Act: Some Reflections on the Klor's Case," *Virginia Law Review,* 45:1173 (November 1959).

And with such complicated facts, the end result is very likely determined by an unstated test of reasonableness whether or not a per se rule is invoked. In less complicated cases, however, "[n]either *per se* nor the rule of reason calls, in fact, for such an investigation. The justification of any kind of effective antitrust policy depends upon the possibility of valid inferences from relatively simple statements of fact. At most the rule of reason requires a somewhat more detailed elaboration of the market situation and course of business conduct . . . from which inferences are drawn." [23] Limited to this approach, the rule of reason need not result in nonenforcement.

The suggestion by Professor Oppenheim that a prima facie case of illegality should be used in place of the per se rule in restraint of trade cases bears on the enforcement problem.[24] Placing the burden of proof on the defendants to show that an *overt* agreement is reasonable rather than on the enforcement agency to demonstrate unreasonableness might make enforcement in this restricted area significantly less difficult. The presumption that all agreements which restrain trade are illegal, however — especially if the meaning of agreement is extended to include adherence to implicitly agreed upon organizational norms — is inconsistent with the view of the economic process provided by the theory of interfirm organization. A prima facie illegality doctrine applied to the "agreements" entailed in conscious parallelism appears incorrect from an economic point of view and could, therefore, complicate rather than simplify realistic antitrust enforcement. Agreements, whether tacit or express, should not by statute be presumptively legal or illegal. Rather, the judicial procedure should put particular agreements in their market contexts so that valid inferences concerning their competitive effects can be judged by reasonable men.

[23] Mason, "Market Power and Business Conduct," p. 398. Mason, it should be noted, maintains a preference for per se.

[24] S. Chesterfield Oppenheim, "Federal Antitrust Legislation: Guideposts to a Revised National Antitrust Policy," *Michigan Law Review,* 50:1158 (1951–52).

The rule of reason will not work perfectly — judges, juries, lawyers and economists will employ differing standards of reasonableness. But the rule will at least allow of interpretation which meets the facts of the modern, capitalistic economy. "The search for a shortcut to wisdom sealed in a Latin capsule ought to give way to the hunt for better understanding of the competition we revere and of the free economic system which the Sherman Act symbolizes." [25] "American antitrust policy will never come to grips with the inescapable task inherent in the administration and enforcement of the federal antitrust laws so long as either government or business hides its head in the sand to shut out the constantly changing and varied conditions in American industries and markets as they actually exist in structure, behavior, and accomplishments." [26]

[25] Rahl, "Per Se Rules and Boycotts under the Sherman Act," p. 1174. The context of the quoted phrase in the article cited is not identical to the context here.

[26] Oppenheim, "Federal Antitrust Legislation," p. 1161.

TABLE OF CASES

INDEX

TABLE OF CASES

Alcoa, *see* U.S. v. Aluminum Company of America.

American Column and Lumber Company v. U.S., 257 U.S. 377 (1921), 8, 50, 51, 138, 140, 141, 144, 145, 146, 147, 148, 149, 150, 151, 152, 154, 156, 157, 158, 159, 160, 161, 208, 209, 210, 211.

American Tobacco Company v. U.S., 328 U.S. 781 (1946), 55, 56.

Apex Hosiery Company v. Leader, 310 U.S. 469 (1940), 19.

Appalachian Coals, Inc. v. U.S., 288 U.S. 344 (1933), 19, 122, 125, 129, 130, 131, 134, 214, 215, 216, 217, 218, 233.

Berry v. Brown, 188 Mass. 353 (1905), 96.

Board of Trade of the City of Chicago v. U.S., 246 U.S. 231 (1918), 129, 169, 170, 207, 208, 212.

Cement Manufacturers' Protective Association v. U.S., 268 U.S. 588 (1925), 211.

Chicago Board of Trade, *see* Board of Trade of the City of Chicago.

C-O-Two Fire Equipment Company v. U.S., 197 F. 2d 489 (9th Cir. 1952), certiorari denied 344 U.S. 892, 64, 65, 70, 71, 72.

Dr. Miles Medical Company v. John D. Park and Sons Company, 220 U.S. 373 (1911), 205.

Duplex Printing Press Company v. Deering, 254 U.S. 443 (1921), 94.

Eastern States Retail Lumber Dealers' Association v. U.S., 234 U.S. 600 (1914), 48.

E. Bement and Sons v. National Harrow Company, 186 U.S. 70 (1902), 204, 207.

Federal Trade Commission v. Cement Institute, 333 U.S. 683 (1948), 58, 60, 61, 66, 157, 218.

General Electric Company, Westinghouse Electric Corporation and several others (E. D. Penna. 1960), 239.
Gompers v. Bucks Stove and Range Company, 221 U.S. 418 (1911), 93.

Hopkins v. U.S., 171 U.S. 578 (1898), 203.

Interstate Circuit, Inc. v. U.S., 306 U.S. 208 (1939), 51, 52, 53, 58.

Kiefer-Stewart Company v. Joseph E. Seagram and Sons, 340 U.S. 211 (1951), 219.

Loewe v. Lawlor, 208 U.S. 274 (1908), 93.

Mandeville Island Farms, Inc. v. American Crystal Sugar Company, 334 U.S. 219 (1948), 218.
Maple Flooring Manufacturers' Association v. U.S., 268 U.S. 563 (1925), 8, 138, 141, 153, 154, 155, 156, 157, 159, 160, 161, 210, 211, 219.
Maryland and Virginia Milk Producers' Association v. U.S., 362 U.S. 458 (1960), 236.
Milgram v. Loews, Inc., 192 F. 2d 579 (3rd Cir. 1951), certiorari denied 343 U.S. 929, 63, 64.
Morton Salt Company v. U.S., 235 F. 2d 573 (10th Cir. 1956), 66, 67, 70, 71, 72.

Pevely Dairy Company v. U.S., 178 F. 2d 363 (8th Cir. 1949), certiorari denied 339 U.S. 942, 61, 62, 63, 64, 65.
Pittsburgh Plate Glass Company v. U.S., 260 F.2d 397 (4th Cir. 1958), 360 U.S. 395 (1959), 73, 177.
Plant v. Woods, 176 Mass. 492 (1900), 96.

Rigid Steel Conduit, *see* Triangle Conduit and Cable Company.

Schine Chain Theatres, Inc. v. U.S., 334 U.S. 110 (1948), 60, 218.
Socony-Vacuum Oil Company v. U.S., 105 F. 2d 809 (7th Cir. 1939), 200.

Standard Oil Company v. U.S., 221 U.S. 1 (1911), 170, 205, 206, 207, 212.
Standard Oil Company (Indiana) v. U.S., 283 U.S. 163 (1931), 213, 214.
Standard Oil Company of California v. U.S., 337 U.S. 293 (1949), 233.
Standard Sanitary Manufacturing Company v. U.S., 226 U.S. 20 (1912), 206.
Sugar Institute, Inc. v. U.S., 297 U.S. 553 (1936), 128, 217, 218.
Swift and Company v. U.S., 196 U.S. 375 (1905), 205.

Tag Manufacturers Institute v. Federal Trade Commission, 174 F. 2d 452 (1st Cir. 1949), 169, 174, 219, 234.
Theatre Enterprises, Inc. v. Paramount Film Distributing Corporation, 346 U.S. 537 (1954), 65, 66.
Thomsen v. Cayser, 243 U.S. 66 (1917), 207.
Trenton Potteries Company v. U.S., 300 F. 550 (2nd Cir. 1924), 170.
Triangle Conduit and Cable Company v. Federal Trade Commission, 168 F. 2d 175 (7th Cir. 1948), 60, 61, 218, 219.

U.S. v. Addyston Pipe and Steel Company, 78 F. 712 (E.D. Tenn. 1897), 113.
U.S. v. Addyston Pipe and Steel Company, 171 U.S. 614 (1899), 85 F. 271 (6th Cir. 1898), 7, 99, 104, 107, 108, 110, 111, 113, 114, 116, 118, 127, 192, 199, 200, 202, 204.
U.S. v. Aluminum Company of America, 148 F. 2d 416 (2nd Cir. 1945), 5, 126, 229.
U.S. v. American Column and Lumber Company, et al., 263 F. 147 (W.D. Tenn. 1920), 147, 149, 150, 152.
U.S. v. American Linseed Oil Company, 262 U.S. 371 (1923), 156, 157, 210.
U.S. v. American Tobacco Company, 221 U.S. 106 (1911), 170, 206, 207, 212.
U.S. v. Appalachian Coals, Inc., I F. Supp. 339 (W.D. Va. 1932), 126, 127, 129, 214.
U.S. v. Eastern Retail Lumber Dealers' Association, 201 F. 581 (S.D.N.Y. 1913), 143.
U.S. v. E. C. Knight, 156 U.S. 1 (1895), 113.
U.S. v. Eli Lilly & Company, Crim. no. 173–58, D.N.J. (1959), 68, 69, 70, 71, 72.

U.S. v. Frankfort Distilleries, 324 U.S. 293 (1945), 218.
U.S. v. Griffith, 334 U.S. 100 (1948), 59, 60.
U.S. v. International Harvester Company, 274 U.S. 693 (1927), 50, 51.
U.S. v. Joint-Traffic Association, 171 U.S. 505 (1898), 48, 203, 204, 206.
U.S. v. Line Material Company, 333 U.S. 287 (1948), 218, 219.
U.S. v. Masonite Corporation, 316 U.S. 265 (1942), 218
U.S. v. Morgan, 118 F. Supp. 621 (S.D.N.Y. 1954), 220.
U.S. v. New Wrinkle, 342 U.S. 371 (1952), 219, 220.
U.S. v. Paramount Pictures, Inc., 334 U.S. 131 (1948), 56, 57, 58.
U.S. v. Pittsburgh Plate Glass Company, Carolina Mirror Corporation, Galax Mirror Company, Inc., Mount Airy Mirror Company, Stroupe Mirror Company, Virginia Mirror Company, Inc., Weaver Mirror Company, Inc., and three individuals, Crim. Action no. 5790 (W.D.Va. 1957), 177, 188, 193, 195.
U.S. v. Socony-Vacuum Oil Company, 310 U.S. 150 (1940), 19, 52, 54, 199, 200, 201, 214, 217, 218, 219, 231, 232, 233, 240.
U.S. v. Trans-Missouri Freight Association, 166 U.S. 290 (1897), 202, 203, 204, 206.
U.S. v. Trenton Potteries Company, 273 U.S. 392 (1927), 8, 19, 52, 126, 127, 129, 161, 162, 168, 169, 172, 173, 175, 177, 188, 193, 195, 200, 211, 212, 213, 214, 217, 219, 220, 234, 238.
U.S. v. United States Alkali Export Association, Inc., 86 F. Supp. 59 (D.C.N.Y. 1949), 219.
U.S. v. United States Gypsum Company, 333 U.S. 364 (1948), 68 S. Ct. 525, 57, 218.
U.S. v. U.S. Steel, 251 U.S. 417 (1920), 5, 49, 50.

W.W. Montague and Company v. Edward S. Lowry, 193 U.S. 38 (1904), 205.

INDEX

Ackoff, R. L., 27n, 28
Agreements: various views on, 10, 11, 17, 19–20, 22; implicit, 29, 117; in oligopoly, 48–73 *passim;* and rivalry, 39; in conscious parallelism cases, 47–73 *passim,* 237; agricultural marketing, 75, 85; in *Addyston* case, 105–109, 113, 117, 118; in *Appalachian Coals* case, 125–126, 129; tendency to breakdown, 127–128, 173; reasonableness of, 130; in Hardwood cases, 141–153 *passim;* in *Trenton Potteries* case, 162–173 *passim;* in Mirror case, 183–192 *passim;* conditions conducive to, 195; legal approach to finding, 231, 233; and proposed rule of reason, 237–241.
Agricultural Marketing Agreement Act, 85
Agriculture, Department of, 82n, 86
Agriculture, Secretary of, 75
Agriculture Adjustment Acts, 85
American Federation of Labor, 94
Antitrust laws. *See* Clayton Act; Sherman Act; Robinson-Patman Act; Miller-Tydings Act; McGuire Act; Exemptions, from antitrust laws; Competition, public policy toward
Associations: Smith on, 10, 13; competition among, 15; producers', in milk industry, 81, 83, 84, 90, 92. *See also* Combinations; Conspiracy; Co-operatives; Trade Associations; Traffic Associations
Bain, J., 21
Bakke, E. W., 94n, 96n, 97n
Barnard, C. I., 31n, 94n
Basing point pricing system, 58, 219
Baumol, W., 21
Behavioral sciences: and theory of interfirm organization, 5, 22–23, 27
Berle, A. A., Jr., 9
Bertrand, J., 5
Bituminous Coal Act of 1937, 133
Bituminous Coal Conservation Act of 1935, 133
Black, Justice, 218
Boulding, K. E., 21
Bowron, J., 100n, 105n
Brandeis, Justice, 151n, 156, 207, 208, 209, 213
Bressler, R. G., Jr., 89n
Brown, H. F., 96n
Brown, N. C., 140n
Bryant, R. C., 139n, 141n, 142, 143n, 144, 145n, 146n, 153, 154n, 156n, 158, 159n
Buchan, R., 184, 185, 186, 187
Burns, A. F., 142
Burns, A. R., 9
Burton, Justice, 55, 56
Butler, Justice, 156n, 213

Capacity: of firms in *Addyston* case, 101, 105; role in 1894 *Addyston* agreements, 107; and profits of *Addyston* firms, 112; of U.S. Cast Iron Pipe and Foundry Co., 115; responsiveness to demand, 225. *See also* Excess capacity

Capper-Volstead Act, 85
Cartwright, D., 31n
Cast-iron pipe industry, 99–118, 119, 128
Cement industry, 58
Chiseling, 41, 160
Chamberlin, E. H., 5, 9, 21, 39n
Civil Aeronautics Board, 75
Clark, D. F., 27n, 28
Clark, J. B., 9
Clark, J. M., 3, 9, 16, 18
Clarke, Justice, 156n, 208, 209
Clayton Act, 58, 85, 93, 94, 116
Closed Shop, 96, 97
Coal Commission, U.S., 120n, 123
Coal industry: example of complex, large-number interdependence, 25; exemption from antitrust laws, 75; discussion of, 119-137; excess capacity in, 120–122 *passim,* 131–135 *passim;* number of firms in, 121; concentration in, 121, 136n; difficulty of mergers in, 128, 135–136; unionization of, 134
Collective bargaining: Taussig on, 17; analogy of in milk industry, 92; difficulty in attaining, 93–94; industry-wide, 97
Collusion: tendency to breakdown with large number of sellers, 14n, 77, 162; J. M. Clark on, 17; in pottery industry, 172, 173, 195; in mirror industry, 192, 195. *See also* Agreements; Combinations; Conscious parallelism; Price fixing; Restraint of trade
Combination Acts. 14
Combinations: Smith on, 10, 12–13; of workers, 14, 91; in U.S., 15, 16; Taussig on, 17–18; Jaffe and Tobriner on, 19; in conscious parallelism cases, 47–60 *passim,* 69; in *Addyston* case, 109, 113, 116; Judge Parker on, in *Appalachian Coals* case, 126–127; "loose combination" compared with merger, 126–128; in lumber industry, 143, 152; in *Potteries* case, 164, 173; in Mirror case, 183, 188; and per se rule, 199–220 *passim;* in *Tag* case, 234. *See also* Agreements; Associations; Collusion; Conspiracy; Price fixing; Restraint of trade
Commerce and Labor, Department of, 143
Common law on restraint of trade: Judge Taft on, 113–114, 116, 199, 200; summary of, 201–202; references on, 202n
Communication: developments in, and competition, 15, 39; in oligopoly, 26–27, 28, 73; nonverbal, 26, 30, 56; in definition of organization, 27; and number of firms, 29–30; and "satisficing," 30, 31n; function of interfirm organization in, 30; and value systems of firms, 33; and profit maximization, 41; in game theory, 44n; in *Morton Salt* case, 67; in *Potteries* case, 173; and conspiracy, 195; and social organizations, 223
Competition: pure, 3, 6, 16, 23, 37, 136; workable or realistic, 3, 16, 17, 18, 36, 51, 192; public policy toward, 4, 6, 8, 9, 10, 71–73, 74, 95–97, 116–117, 138, 199–242; theory of, 4, 6, 120, 125, 175; rationalization of, 7, 99, 128, 140, 177, 193, 210, 232; illusion of, 9; decline of, 9, 15; Smith's views on, 9–14; atomistic, 10, 12; perfect, 12, 99, 136; cutthroat, ruinous or excessive, 14n, 18, 37–41, 104, 116, 129, 149, 200, 232; Eddy's views on, 17; Clark's views on, 18; Schumpeter's views on, 18–19; monopolistic, 23; free, 221, 222; intra-group, 230. *See also* Conflict; Rivalry
Compton, W., 139n, 141, 142
Conflict: intra-group, 27, 28, 42; among groups, 34
Conscious parallelism, 47–73, 231, 237
Conspiracy: overt, 12, 77, 192; implied or inferred, 47–73 *passim,* 201; of laborers, 91. *See also* Agreements; Collusion; Combina-

tions; Competition, public policy toward; Price fixing; Restraint of trade
Cooperation, 18, 148, 152, 159
Co-operatives, agricultural, 75, 78, 81–90 *passim*
Costs: differences in, and rivalry, 28–29, 193–194; ratio of fixed to variable, 92, 105, 116; in *Addyston* case, 105, 107, 108, 111–112; joint, 122; in Mirror case, 193–194
Countervailing power, 40, 92, 209n
Cournot, A., 5
Cyert, R. M., 5n, 21

Day, Justice, 48, 156n
Delivered pricing system, 155, 160
Demand: elasticity of, and rivalry, 28–29; cross-elasticity of, and leadership, 32; elasticity considered in *Morton Salt* case, 67; for milk, 82, 84, 92; derived, 84; for labor, 91; in *Addyston* case, 101, 102, 103, 110, 116; for coal, 120, 125, 135; for furniture, 181; for plate glass, 182; in Mirror case, 182, 189; responsiveness of resource use to changes in, 225, 226, 228
de Roover, R., 12n, 13n
Dewey, D., 114
Disequilibrium, 43
Douglas, Justice, 52, 57, 59, 199, 200, 201, 214n, 218, 233n, 240
Drug industry, 68–71

Eddy, A. J., 17
Edgeworth, F. V., 5
Edwards, C. D., 16
Effectiveness: of organization, 94; defined, 94n
Efficiency: of interfirm organization, 36, 94; social interest in economic, 38, 39. *See also* Demand, responsiveness of resource use to changes in
Entry: mentioned, 8; Smith's views on, 12–13; preventative behavior, 21, 33–34, 77; and value systems, 33; and relation to rivalry, 33, 38, 78; by existing firms, 34, 35; into milk marketing areas, 87, 88; in *Addyston* case, 99, 102, 103, 104, 105, 118; in coal industry, 121, 131, 136; and price system, 227; and intra-group agreements, 230
Equilibrium: and interdependence, 6, 37; of group, in relation to individual firms in group, 28, 42; and interfirm organization, 37, 43
Excess capacity: and rivalry, 38; in *Addyston* case, 103; in coal industry, 120–135 *passim*. *See also* Capacity
Exclusion, of competitors, 55, 56
Exemption, from antitrust laws: and number of firms, 7, 74, 76, 78, 91; public policy toward, 8, 235; scope of, 74–76; and formal interfirm organizations, 74–98 *passim;* and Capper-Volstead Act, 85; and Clayton Act, 85, 93–94

Fair trade laws, 75–77
Federal Communications Commission, 75
Federal Maritime Board, 75
Federal Trade Commission, 9, 58n, 60, 61, 62
Federal Trade Commission Act, 58, 60, 218, 219
Feldman, G. J., 17n
Fellner, W., 21, 22, 27
Festinger, L., 33n
Fetter, F. A., 9
Firms: as members of a group, 7, 22, 28, 192; scale of, 37, 38, 78, 226, 227
Fisher, W. E., 124n, 125n, 132n, 133n
Forman, Judge, 70n
Furniture industry, 177, 178, 181

Gadd, F. R., 147, 148, 149, 150, 151, 160
Galbraith, J. K., 39n, 40, 224, 228
Galenson, W., 97n
Games, theory of, 6, 21, 43–44
Gardner, E. F., 186, 187
Goals: economic, 225–229; noneco-

nomic, 225, 229. *See also* Objectives, of firms, of market group; Profits, maximization of; Subgoals, of members of group
Gordon, E. B., 154n
Gordon, W. A., 184, 185, 187
Government: regulation or ownership by, alternative to private power, 8, 41, 238; effect on group behavior, 35; sets rules of game, 44, 222; regulation of milk industry, 61, 85–90; establishing or encouraging interfirm organizations, 74, 76, 85; role of state and local, 75, 123; regulation of coal industry, 123, 132–133, 134; regulation and concentration, 137
Group behavior: of oligopolists, 25–27, 36, 57; of juvenile gangs, 26; cohesiveness of, 40. *See also* Interfirm organization; Leadership; Objectives, of market group; Oligopoly
Group decision-making, 22, 53, 72

Hall, G. R., 68n, 139n
Hamilton, W., 37n, 119n, 120n, 123n, 124, 131, 134n, 195
Hand, Judge, 126, 229
Handler, M., 20n, 202n
Haney, L., 18
Hare, A. P., 31n
Harlan, Justice, 113, 206n
Harris, H., 94n
Harvesting machinery industry, 50–51
Health, Education and Welfare, Department of, 68, 71
Hearn, K., 183, 184, 185
Heflebower, R. B., 32n
Henderson, A., 22, 23, 24, 27
Henderson, J. M., 134n, 136n
Hennipman, P., 39n
Herbst, P. G., 27n
Hillman, J. S., 86n
Hoar, Senator, 202n
Hobby, O. C., Secretary of Health, Education and Welfare, 71
Holmes, Justice, 96n, 156, 205, 209
Homeostatic behavior, 21
Homestead strike, 93
Hughes, Justice, 129, 130, 205, 214, 215, 216, 217

Immunity, from antitrust laws. *See* Exemption, from antitrust laws
Interdependence: and optimization, 6; ubiquity of, 23–25; complex, with large number of firms, 23–25, 36, 74, 76; and nonmonotonic relation between rivalry and performance, 37. *See also* Oligopoly
Interfirm organization: theory of, 5, 21–44, 138, 229, 241; nature and functions of, 27–29; and communication among firms, 30; effectiveness or efficiency of, 36, 46, 71, 73; and market stability, 37; and mitigation of rivalry, 42; and oligopoly, 46–73 *passim;* alternative to change in market structure or government regulation, 118, 137, 232–233, 237; restraints imposed by, 230; and per se rule, 231–235. *See also* Market organization
Interstate Commerce Commission, 75, 123
Israelson, V. L., 86n

Jaffe, L. L., 19
James, C. M., 124n, 125n, 132n, 133n
Joint cost conditions, 122
Jonas, A. G., 184, 185, 186, 187, 192
Jones, F. P., 202n

Kaplan, A. D. H., 39n
Kerr, C., 94n, 96n, 97n
Knauth, O. W., 17n
Knight, F. H., 222n

Labor: organizations of, 14, 29, 34, 35, 39, 90–98; market for, 17, 39, 76, 77, 90–98; movement, theories of, 92–93; public policy toward, 93–98; market power of, 95, 97–98; and closed shop, 96–97; and industry-wide bargaining, 97; and rule of reason, 236

Lancaster, R. K., 224n
Leadership: mentioned, 8; spontaneous recognition of, 26; relation to rivalry, 31–32, 40; in oligopoly, 50, 51, 54, 56; in *Addyston* case, 99, 118; in *Potteries* case, 162, 174, 175; in Mirror case, 193. *See also* Market power
Lester, R. A., 97, 97n
Levine, A., 17n
Licensing, occupational, 76
Lilienthal, D., 39n
Lippett, R., 31n
Lipset, S. M., 97n
Lipsey, R. G., 224n
Locklin, D. P., 204n
Lumber industry, 24, 48, 50, 51, 136, 138–160
Lurton, Judge, 113

Macgregor, D. H., 13, 14n
Magruder, Judge, 174
March, J. G., 5n, 21, 31n, 33n
Marginal analysis. *See* Profits, maximization of
Market, stability of, 26, 28, 32n
Market organization (or group): firms as members of, 6, 7, 25–29; Taussig on need of, 18; and mitigation of rivalry, 28–29; in conscious parallelism, 46, 51, 53, 54, 56, 58, 60, 64, 71, 73; in exempted industries, 78, 79; in milk industry, 81, 90; in labor markets, 18, 91, 93, 94; in *Addyston* case, 118; of coal industry, 119, 123–126, 129, 134, 135; in lumber industry, 138, 139–143, 148, 153–156; in *Potteries* case, 8, 163–164; lack of, in Mirror case, 193. *See also* Firms, as members of a group; Interfirm organization
Market performance: relation to market structure and organization, 6–7, 8, 36–41; and rule of reason, 20, 238; and interdependence, 23–24; relation to rivalry, 36–38, 235–236, 238; and excess rivalry, 40; in *Addyston* case, 99, 103–105, 117, 118; of coal industry, 119, 129, 133, 134, 135, 136; of lumber industry, 141; in Mirror case, 192; criteria for judging, 225–229
Market power: sources of, 31–32; and leadership, 31; unequal distribution of, 31, 36; of buyers or suppliers, 34, 35, 36, 74, 78, 79, 83, 90, 91, 93, 94, 194; in oligopoly, 51, 71; in exempted industries, 77, 78, 81, 90, 91; of unions, 91, 94, 96, 97; of employers, 94, 95; in *Potteries* case, 172, 174, 175; and test of reasonableness, 216, 238
Market structure: relation to market organization and performance, 6–7, 23, 36–41, 117; in exempted industries, 76; in *Addyston* case, 100–103, 115, 117; in coal industry, 119, 126, 129, 135; in lumber industry, 139; in *Potteries* case, 162–163, 175, 176; in Mirror case, 177–179, 192
Marshall, A., 84
Mason, E. S., 9, 97n, 239n, 241n
McCall, Judge, 151
McGuire Act, 75
McKenna, Justice, 156, 157n, 207, 208, 209
McReynolds, Justice, 156, 157, 211n
Means, G. C., 9
Medina, Judge, 220
Mercantilism, 11
Mergers: and illusion of competition, 9; and transportation growth, 16n; and excess rivalry, 39; in exempted industries, 78; in coal industry, 128, 135–136; in *Addyston* case, 114–115, 116, 117, 118, 128; in *Potteries* case, 176; in railroad industry, 204
Messer, J., Sr., 183, 184, 185, 186, 187, 189, 192
Milk industry, 61–63, 79, 80–90, 91
Miller-Tydings Act, 75
Mirror industry, 177–195
Mishan, E. J., 224n
Mitchel, W. C., 110n, 142
Modigliani, F., 21n
Moldenke, R., 100n, 102n, 104

Monopoly: and policies toward competition, 4, 8; and illusion of competition, 9; Smith's views on, 10–13; power, 13, 14, 16, 19. *See also* Market power
Moody, J., 9
Moore, W. D., 100n, 104
Motion picture industry: conscious parallelism cases involving, 51–54, 56–58, 59–60, 63–64, 65–66

National Bituminous Coal Commission, 133, 135
National Foundation for Infantile Paralysis, 68
National Industrial Recovery Act, 75, 133
National Recovery Administration, 133, 135
Nelson, R. L., 16n
Newman, W. H., 31n
Nonprice competition, 26
Numbers of firms: mentioned, 7–8; Smith's views on, 12, 13, 14n; and interdependence, 23–25; and rivalry, 29–30, 36, 74, 77, 90, 160; and improvements in transportation and communication, 39; and excess rivalry, 40; in exempted industries, 74, 76, 91; in cast-iron pipe industry, 99, 100, 101, 118; in coal industry, 121; in Hardwood cases, 138, 139, 154, 158, 159, 160; in Mirror case, 177, 189

Objectives: of firms, 5, 22, 174; of market group, 22, 27, 28, 36, 94n, 175. *See also* Goals; Profits, maximization of; Subgoals, of members of group
Oligopoly: problem of, 5; in Smith's time, 13; and workable competition, 18; and new theory of, 22; complex form of, 23–24; and interdependence, 24–25, 41; and informal interfirm organization, 29, 36, 41, 47–73; and market performance, 36; individual decision-making in, 66, 69, 70, 72, 73; and *Addyston* case, 102. *See also* Interdependence; Group Behavior
Olmstead, M. S., 26n
Open price systems, 18, 145–146, 147–149, 152, 164–165, 234
Open shop, 96n
Oppenheim, S. C., 20, 241, 242n
Organization: theory, 23; definition of, 27. *See also* Interfirm Organization; Market Organization
Organized exchanges, 25n, 129–130, 175, 193

Parallel behavior. *See* Conscious parallelism
Parker, Judge, 126, 127, 214
Peckham, Justice, 48, 115, 203, 204, 205
Peppin, J. C., 20n, 114, 201n, 202n, 204n
Performance. *See* Market performance
Perlman, S., 92
Per se legalities, 199, 235. *See also* Exemption, from antitrust laws
Per se rule: mentioned, 8; Oppenheim on, 20; in conscious parallelism cases, 52, 55, 57; and Taft's decision in *Addyston* case, 113, 114, 116; and *Appalachian Coals* case, 129; and *Potteries* case, 161; and Mirror case, 188; development of, 199–200, 221; and interfirm organization, 231–235; ease of enforcement, 239–241. *See also* Price fixing
Petroleum industry, 54–55, 75
Phillips, A., 39n, 68n
Pitney, Justice, 156n
Polansky, N., 31n
Polio Assistance Act, 68
Pottery industry, 161–176
Price cutting: in coal industry, 134; in *Potteries* case, 174; in Mirror case, 181, 186. *See also* Chiseling; Competition, cutthroat, ruinous or excessive; Rivalry, excessive
Price fixing: Edward's views on, 16; Jaffe and Tobriner on, 19; Peppin on, 19–20; Justice Douglas on, 57, 199, 200–201, 218; in *Morton Salt* case, 67; in *Addyston* case, 103,

105–109, 113, 114, 116; in *Appalachian Coals* case, 127, 130, 131; in lumber industry, 140, 141, 152, 154; in *Potteries* case, 161, 164, 166, 170, 171–172; in Mirror case, 183–188; per se rule on, 199–220, 231–242; and proposed rule of reason, 235–242. *See also* Agreements; Collusion; Conscious parallelism; Combinations; Conspiracy; Per se rule; Restraint of trade
Price leadership. *See* Leadership; Market power
Price system, functions of, 223–229
Price uniformity. *See* Conscious parallelism
Prices: stability or rigidity of, 19, 49; responsiveness to changes in cost, supply or demand, 38, 56, 226–227; administered, 56, 137; behavior of, in Hardwood cases, 141–157 *passim;* fixed, reasonableness of, 161, 169, 170, 171, 172, 188, 202, 212–213, 238; announced contrasted with actual, 166–168, 169, 171, 172, 180, 181, 182, 188–189, 219, 234; behavior of, in *Potteries* case, 166–168, 174; behavior of, in Mirror case, 180, 181, 182, 183–189, 191
Pritchard, S. J., 187
Production (or output) control: coal industry, 131–136 *passim;* lumber industry, 141, 151, 153, 160
Profits: maximization of, 5, 6, 21–22, 28, 41–42, 99, 103, 110; in coal industry, 121, 122, 125; in *Potteries* case, 161, 173; in Mirror case, 184, 189; incentive to play economic game, 227; and technological change, 228. *See also* Objectives, of firms; Subgoals, of members of group
Pullen, A. M., and Co., 182
Pullman strike, 93

Quasi-agreements, 22, 27
Quasi-rents, 108

Rahl, J. A., 240n, 242n
Recalcitrants, punishment of, 41, 58, 175
Redl, F., 31n
Reed, Justice, 218
Refusals to deal, 143, 164, 168
Restraint of trade: Schumpeter on, 18–79; at common law, 113–114, 115–116, 199, 200, 201–202. *See also* Agreements; Combinations; Collusion; Conscious parallelism; Conspiracy; Market organization; Monopoly; Per se rule; Price fixing
Retaliation, 29, 35
Rivalry: and interdependence, 23–25; distinguished from competition, 25; determinants of, 25–35; and formality of interfirm organization, 25–29; and intra-group conflict, 28, 116, 161; and number of firms, 29–30, 41; and leadership, 31–32; and value systems, 32–34; and external factors, 34–35, 36, 40, 107, 108; relation to performance, 36–41, 236; excessive or cutthroat, 37–41, 116, 117, 137; and entry, 38; historical changes in, 38–41; among groups of firms, 54, 99, 100, 107, 108, 110, 111, 112, 131; mitigation or elimination of, 75, 90, 105, 192. *See also* Competition; Interdependence; Interfirm organization; Oligopoly
Robbins, L., 222n
Robie, E. A., 97n
Robinson, J., 9, 21
Robinson-Patman Act, 79
Robinson, R., 43n
Roosevelt, T., President, 17
Rosen, S., 31n
Rowell, J. D., 86n
Rule of reason: proposed for restraint of trade cases, 8, 235–242; Oppenheim on, 20; Dewey on, 114; Judge Parker on, 126; in Hardwood cases, 158n, 210–211; and *Potteries* case, 170, 171, 172n, 212; Justice White on, 203, 205–

206; in *Thompsen v. Cayser,* 207; Justice Brandeis on, 208, 209–210, 213–214; Justice Hughes on, in *Appalachian Coals* case, 214–216; in *Sugar Institute* case, 217; in *Tag* case, 219; in *U.S. v. Morgan,* 220; and enforcement problems, 238–242
Rutledge, Justice, 218

Salk, J., 68
Sanford, Justice, 156, 157, 211n
Satisficing, 21, 30, 31n, 42
Schelling, T. C., 44n
Schlesinger, J. R., 90n, 95n
Schmookler, J., 39n
Schumpeter, J. A., 18, 39n, 224
Sharfman, J. L., 157
Sherman Act: and policy inconsistencies, 4, 5; Jaffe and Tobriner on, 19; Peppin on, 20; and labor organizations, 40, and conscious parallelism cases, 48–73 *passim;* exemptions from, 75–80, 93, 235–236; in *Addyston* case, 100, 113–114, 116; in *Appalachian Coals* case, 119, 126–127, 214–216; in Hardwood cases, 138, 143, 152, 157, 208–210, 211; in *Potteries* case, 162, 171, 212–213; in Mirror case, 188; and development of per se rule, 199–220, 232, 234; proposed rule of reason for, 235–242
Shields, B. F., 15n
Simon, H. A., 21, 31n, 33n
Slichter, S., 18
Smith, A., 4, 9–14, 16, 160
Stackelberg, H. von, 5
Steel industry, 49–50, 78, 118
Stigler, G. J., 13n
Stone, Justice, 52, 53, 156, 157, 161, 171, 172, 210, 211, 212, 213, 238
Stroupe, G., 185, 186, 187
Stroupe, R., 183, 184
Subgoals: of members of group, 27, 28, 41–42, 192; optimization of, 29, 30; and communications, 30. *See also* Goals; Objectives, of firms; Profits, maximixation of
Supply: and demand, law of, 42–43, 156; responsiveness of resource use to change in, 225, 226–228
Sutherland, Justice, 156n, 213
Sylos, P. L., 21

Taft, Justice, 111, 113, 114, 115, 116, 127, 156, 157, 199, 200, 201, 202, 204, 211n
Taft-Hartley Act, 96
Tannenbaum, F., 92
Taussig, F. W., 17–18, 91
Temporary National Economic Committee, 9, 20n, 37n
Technocracy, 123n
Technological change: and competition, 15, 16, 38, 39n, responsiveness of price to, 19; and excess rivalry, 38; in milk industry, 81–82, 92; and union movement, 94; in coal industry, 120; in pottery industry, 162, 175–176; and functions of price system, 224–228 *passim*
Thorelli, H. B., 202n
Thorp, W. F., 110n
Thrasher, F. M., 26n, 31n
Till, 37n, 195n
Tobriner, M. O., 19
Tosdal, H. R., 146n
Trade Associations: export, 75; in coal industry, 121; in lumber industry, 138–159 *passim;* in *Potteries* case, 161, 163–164; in Mirror case, 179, 180, 183, 192
Traffic associations, railroad, 48
Transportation: and competition, 15, 16n; and effective number of firms, 39; and milk industry, 80, 82, 86; and lumber industry, 139; and cast-iron pipe industry, 101–116 *passim*

Union shop, 96n
Unionization, effect of, in coal industry, 134
Unions, labor, 39, 61, 75, 78, 90–98
United Mine Workers of America, 123, 124

Value systems: homogeneity of, and rivalry, 8, 32–33, 36, 39, 40, 62, 74, 79, 90, 91, 93; factors included in, 32; in game theory, 44n; and oligopoly, 54, 56, 58, 62; and sizes of firms, 63, 79–80; effect of unionization on, 134; in Hardwood cases, 138, 159, 160; in *Potteries* case, 162; in Mirror case, 192
Van Devanter, Justice, 213
Van Fleet, Judge, 170, 211
Van Sickle, J. V., 97n
Villard, H. H., 39n

Wagner Act, 96
Watkins, M. H., 157, 158n, 202n
Watson, Senator, 124
Weaver, R., 191
Webb, B., 92n, 93
Webb, S., 92n, 93
Webb-Pomerene Export Trade Act, 75
Welfare economics, 224–225
White, Justice, 203, 205, 206
Whitney, S. N., 112n, 116n, 118n, 128n
Whyte, W. F., 32n
Wilcox, C., 23, 134n
Wilson-Gorman Tariff Act, 105
Wright, H. R., 119n, 120n, 123n, 124, 131, 134n

Zander, A., 31n